Madagascar
A NATURAL HISTORY

Madagascar
A NATURAL HISTORY

Ken Preston-Mafham
Foreword by Sir David Attenborough

Facts On File
Oxford • New York

Facts On File Limited   or
Collins Street
Oxford OX4 1XJ
UK

Facts On File, Inc.
460 Park Avenue South
New York NY10016

A British CIP catalogue record for this book is available from the British Library.

A United States of America CIP catalogue record for this book is available from the Library of Congress.

ISBN 0-8160-2403-0

Facts On File books are available at special discounts when purchased in bulk quantities for businesses, associations, institutions or sales promotions. Please contact the Special Sales Department of our Oxford office on 0865 728399 or our New York office on 212/683-2244 (dial 800/322-8755 except in NY, Ak or HI).

Edited, designed, and produced by Curtis Garratt Limited, The Old Vicarage, Horton cum Studley, Oxford OX9 1BT.

Index by Jean Preston-Mafham

Printed in Spain

10 9 8 7 6 5 4 3 2 1

This book is printed on acid-free paper.

Acknowledgements

On my two trips to Madagascar, I was fortunate enough to come across a number of people who were generous with their expert advice and with their friendship. Without their unselfish help, the photographs in this book would have been of a far less comprehensive nature. My first trip, from September to December 1988, would have been an almost complete failure were it not for the assistance and ingenuity of Patrick Daniels, at that time in charge of the Duke University Ranomafana Forest Project. Patrick it was who jerry-rigged the means to charge the batteries on my most vital flash unit when the mains charger had melted after being set to the incorrect voltage (a mistake caused by inaccurate information in a well-known guidebook — beware). If Patrick hadn't spent hours patiently fiddling in semi-darkness with bits of wire, I should have ended the first trip with very little to show for it. The open-hearted way in which the rest of the Duke team welcomed me into their humble forest camp is also a warm and lingering memory. Particular thanks are due to Michael Todd, Claire Kremen, the 'two Robs', Judy Rosenthal and, most especially, to Deborah Overdorff who also kindly supplied me with unpublished observations on red-fronted and red-bellied lemurs. Warren Steiner Jr of the Smithsonian Institution was also part of the project and has helped in a number of ways.

My thanks go to the officers of La Corporation Suisse, who so generously allowed me to stay in their camp in the Kirindy Forest near Morondava, and who arranged for transport in both directions. Members of the Oxford University 'Votsotsa 88' expedition, studying the giant jumping rat at Kirindy, also gave freely of their time and experience. I am particularly indebted to their leader Dr James Cook who supplied me with the preliminary report of their work.

On Nosy Mangabe I owe much to Eleanor Sterling for making available her extensive knowledge of aye-ayes, and for determinedly acting as a guide even when in distress after a nasty fall in the forest at night — one of the attendant hazards of observing the lives of animals, and one to which we seldom give much thought. Don Read at the Ampijeroa Forest Reserve gave freely of his advice and his friendship, and made my two weeks stay there both enjoyable and rewarding. Thanks also to Dr Bob Sussman at Beza-Mahafaly for welcoming me so wholeheartedly into the research life of that reserve. Dr David Stone of WWF Switzerland helped in a number of ways with information after my return from Madagascar.

Several people here at home have helped with identifications. I owe particular gratitude to Simon Tonge of the Jersey Wildlife Preservation Trust for dealing so quickly and expertly with the reptiles and amphibians; and to Chris O'Toole of Oxford University for identifying the wasps and for assistance with the research for this book. Various specialists at the Natural History Museum dealt with other groups of insects.

Previous spread: **Chamaeleo lateralis *is one of the most widespread and abundant chameleons in Madagascar.***

Overleaf: **The beautiful water lily Nymphaea stellata *is widespread in still waters throughout the island.***

Contents

Foreword

Browsing through an atlas, you might get the impression that Madagascar is a mere chip of the eastern flank of Africa, a small island of no particular significance with a fauna that is little more than an impoverished version of that of its big neighbour. You would be greatly mistaken. To start with, the island is not small but gigantic, nearly a thousand miles long from north to south. Secondly, its animals and plants are as different from Africa's as they are from Asia's. They are unique.

The most obviously dramatic are the lemurs — furry mammals like monkeys with foxy faces, many vividly patterned, and varying in size from mice to chimpanzees. They are the most famous, but the continental splitting and drifting in the ancient geological past that bequeathed the island its lemurs also gave it other populations that are equally extraordinary and distinctive. Two-thirds of all species of chameleons in the world live here. Indeed, it could be that the island was the place where they first evolved. There are frogs and spiders, orchids and tortoises that are equally strange and characteristic — but far less known.

The world at large has only recently become aware of this naturalist's treasure chest. When I first went there, in 1960, it was a wildlife film-maker's paradise. Wherever we looked, we found animals that had never been filmed before. Inadequate though our film may have been, it made a great impression simply because no one had ever seen such creatures on their television screens. Since then, lemurs have been filmed many times. But there are still spectacular discoveries to be made by photographers and there are few more inquisitive, thorough and discerning than the author of this book.

Ken Preston-Mafham does not restrict his attention to the big and the famous. He examines every category of creature with the same undimmed enthusiasm. Had he lived in the nineteenth century, he would have been one of those intrepid solitary naturalists who came back from the unexplored jungles of Borneo or the remote headwaters of the Amazon with a vast collection of insects and birds, reptiles and mammals, all beautifully preserved, packed and labelled which then enriched our museums and revealed the reality of the natural world to the astonished eyes of the public. Today, he uses, not a net and a killing jar, but a macro-lens and sophisticated electronic flash, and his haul comes back on 35 mm transparencies.

In this book, he methodically surveys Madagascar's inhabitants group by group. Had he done this for some other part of the world, you might think that the result would be predictable, even routine. But, because his subject is Madagascar, this book is just the reverse. It is full of surprises where you least expect them and studded with pictures of animals whose portraits have never before appeared in print. Few territories could have produced so many new riches. Few photographers and writers could have portrayed them with such brilliance.

Sir David Attenborough
Richmond, 1991

Introduction

Madagascar is like nowhere else on Earth. I first went there in 1988 after years of experience of travelling in Central and South America, Africa and the Far East. For the first few weeks in 'the great red island', I felt strangely disoriented; neither the landscape nor the people of Madagascar quite fitted in with any of my previous impressions of tropical lands. In some ways, there was a sense that Madagascar was a mixture of South America, Africa and Asia but with no close similarities to any of these. After my second trip, in 1990, I finally came to terms with the fact that trying to compare Madagascar with anywhere else is fruitless — there is only one Madagascar and it is unique in so many different ways.

To begin with, there is the scenery, the first thing the visitor notices as the aircraft descends towards Antananarivo Airport. For the wildlife enthusiast, this first glimpse of Madagascar's vast expanse of bare uplands can be disheartening in the extreme because the vista which unfolds below is totally artificial, a seemingly endless sea of barren grasslands forming the desiccated skin of the island, pock marked with the livid scars of erosion gullies, the open bleeding veins of a moribund landscape. The depressing uniformity is relieved only by the occasional emerald chess boards of the rice fields nestling between the hills and the odd line of trees strung out precariously along the unburnt valley bottoms. It seems impossible to imagine that such a land could be renowned for the richness of its wildlife and, of course, this desolate central plateau, which forms the island's backbone, has long ago lost its once-diverse fauna and flora. But extensive areas of tropical forest, wet in the east and dry in the west, still remain — far away out of sight, just waiting quietly for the visitor to discover their natural wonders.

The first view of the 'spiny desert' in the south, the bizarre limestone pinnacles of Ankarana, the breathtaking forest of giant baobabs near Morondava or the ring-tailed lemurs strutting down a path at Berenty soon softens the memories of the interminable steppes of the Hauts Plateaux. So, after that initial feeling of shock and disappointment, it is only a matter of time before one realizes that, although much has already been lost, a great deal still remains to delight the palate of even the most jaded of globe-trotting wildlife photographers, let alone the first-time visitor to the tropics.

Then there are the people. Whatever the drawbacks of the landscape as first encountered, the Malagasies are among the friendliest and most charming people I have ever met. One only needs to look at the orderly lines of people queuing for buses in Antananarivo, or waiting to check in at the airports, to realize that good manners come naturally here and it is refreshing to be among people who behave politely and wait their turn. The Malagasy islanders also enjoy talking to foreigners and finding out what they think of Madagascar so that, to satisfy their curiosity and to enjoy your visit to the full, it helps to speak French.

The origins of the people are complex. It seems likely that humans first arrived on the island between 1500 and 2500 years ago after leaving a Malaysian-Indonesian homeland and setting out across the empty

The island of Madagascar is situated in the Indian Ocean off the east coast of the African continent. By the 1987 census, the human population is 10,568,000.

oceans for reasons which we shall probably never know. These first colonists settled in the highlands and began the process of clearing and burning which eventually led to the degraded landscapes which we see today over much of the island. Later influxes from Africa and further arrivals from the east boosted the colonization of the lowland areas and the west and south. Despite these disparate origins, a single language (although with many dialects) finally evolved and this played a vital role in uniting the people into one nation. Eighteen different 'tribes' now exist in Madagascar, based mainly on former kingdoms rather than on distinct ethnic groupings, which are stronger in some tribes than others, and never very obvious to the visitor from abroad.

Madagascar has long been famed for its unique wildlife which has evolved in isolation as the island gradually drifted away from the African continent like some giant ark. The most interesting of the animals (and also the cuddliest), the lemurs, have become well known around the world through television. Indeed, my first experience of these charming creatures was of the strange, unearthly wailing of an indri blaring forth from an ancient black-and-white television set as Sir

David (or plain David as he then was) Attenborough's superb *Zoo Quest to Madagascar* introduced a spellbound audience to the mysterious world of Madagascar's wildlife in the 1960s. Oddly, the Malagasies themselves are often puzzled about why we should come so far to admire small, 'ordinary' animals, such as lemurs, when the teeming 'big game' of Africa is perceived as a far greater lure for the camera-toting tourist. It is difficult to explain how 'big is not always best', and that Madagascar's natural menagerie of lemurs, its spiny tenrecs, its plethora of colourful chameleons and its dazzling day-geckoes have a very special charm which is not to be found elsewhere.

Madagascar has so much to offer, and a long stay is not strictly necessary, for making close acquaintance with many of the lemurs is delightfully quick and easy because there are many groups that are used to close human contact. The visitor is in the fortunate position of being able to watch a genuinely wild animal in its natural surroundings from the kind of distance normally possible only in a zoo — or closer.

Visiting Madagascar is not prohibitively expensive; it would make a memorable once-in-a-lifetime adventure for anyone wishing to discover some of the wildlife illustrated in the following pages. Controlled tourism is one of the best ways of ensuring that something of Madagascar's wealth of fauna and flora will remain. The government of Madagascar is committed to wildlife conservation but, in a country as poor as Madagascar, it is not easy to fulfil such a commitment. Tourists bring with them much-needed foreign exchange and, by visiting the nature reserves to see animals in their natural environment, they help preserve such vital habitats as the heavily depleted eastern rainforests.

Several international conservation organizations, most especially the World Wide Fund for Nature, are now helping the Madagascan government to survey and to protect the richest areas. Let us hope that the considerable effort now underway to put in place an integrated development programme involving the people and the wildlife is a success.

A brief note about the photographs in the later chapters might be in order. Madagascar is an excellent place in which to take good wildlife pictures. Following the philosophy which has consistently dominated my photography, all the pictures in this book were taken of animals wild and free in their natural environment. As far as possible, they are also depicted 'as found' and behaving in a normal way. The only partial exception concerns some of the chameleons, notably camera-shy animals which usually start trotting off in the opposite direction as soon as they spot an intruder. For this reason it can be very difficult to photograph one of these lizards just sitting peacefully in a tree, and many of the illustrations depict them setting off at a vigorous walk as they do their best to make themselves scarce.

A Coquerel's sifaka **Propithecus verreauxi coquereli** *chews a tiny red berry which it has just picked with its right hand.*

Chapter 1
The Physical Background

Madagascar is the fourth largest island in the world, after Greenland, New Guinea and Borneo. With a total land area of 226,739 square miles (587,000 sq km) it is 994 miles (1600 km) long and 360 miles (580 km) broad at its widest point. Although much of the island consists of an upland plateau, there are no really high mountains, and no peaks exceed 9840 feet (3000 m), a height easily surpassed by the Piton des Neiges on the tiny island of Réunion. Madagascar is separated from Africa by the Mozambique channel, a tract of water only 186 miles (300 km) broad at its narrowest point, yet of fundamental importance in having shaped the evolutionary destiny of Madagascar's plants and animals by allowing them to evolve in isolation.

At one time, Madagascar was connected to Africa and to India in the supercontinent of Gondwanaland which also included South America, Antarctica and Australia, although these were not directly connected to Madagascar (*see* map). There is some argument as to the exact point of connection with Africa; some authorities place it to the north near Tanzania, others further south not far from its present position. Either way, some time in the late Cretaceous Period (more than 65 million years ago) Madagascar broke free and headed eastwards, separated from Africa by the gradually widening Mozambique channel, irrevocably embarked on its journey of separate development. As this eastward drift began at an early point in the evolutionary history of plants and animals, only a few of the current members of the fauna and flora are thought to have developed directly from the original castaways. The bulk has probably arrived in dribs and drabs as immigrants from outside, probably island-hopping across specks of land or continuous ridges exposed during times of lowered sea levels, such as during glacial periods.

The smooth granite domes or 'inselbergs' near Ambalavao are reminiscent of the scenery near Rio de Janeiro in Brazil. These exposed rock outcrops provide the sole habitat for an interesting collection of endemic succulents.

Geology

Two-thirds of the island consists of a Precambrian crystalline basement covering an area of 154,500 square miles (400,000 sq km) and extensively metamorphosed over the intervening period. On its eastern side, this basement ends abruptly at an almost perfectly straight fault line which accounts for the amazingly unindented aspect of the coast from Fort Dauphin to Tamatave, a distance of 404 miles (650 km). A narrow coastal plain lies behind this seaboard, soon interrupted by a steep escarpment which rises abruptly from the warm lowlands to form a plateau varying in height from 2600 to 4900 feet (800 to 1500 m); but in many places the main plateau is reached only after the occurrence of a second escarpment. This upland region, usually called the Hauts Plateaux or central plateau, forms a vast area which gradually dips downwards towards the northern and southern extremities. On its western edge there is no impressive escarpment, but rather a gradual sloping down towards the western lowlands, broken only by occasional cliffs. The Hauts Plateaux is not a flat area, but consists of a complex blend of hills and valleys brought about by extensive reworking of the crystalline basement, by geological forces and by eons of erosion. This has given rise to numerous outcropping peaks made up of rocks such as quartz and granite, which are more resistant to weathering; hence the upthrust of the granite peaks of Andringitra and the quartz of the Itremo.

The best region for observing the spectacular results of differential weathering lies between Fianarantsoa and Ambalavao. Here, isolated monoliths of smooth, rounded granite, known as inselbergs, dominate the grassy plains and scattered rice fields, their well-drained rocky summits providing refuge for numerous fascinating succulent plants, most of which are found nowhere else. These rocky islands protrude from a vast blanket of red lateritic clay which covers the chief part of the Precambrian basement rocks, varying in depth from 33 feet (10 m) to as much as 260 feet (80 m). This forms the characteristic red soils of Madagascar, source of the often-used epithet 'great red island', and responsible for the 'rivers of blood' when the torrential rains sweep the easily eroded lateritic soils into the nearest rivers, turning them red as the land bleeds. Most of area of the Hauts Plateaux is now covered with grassland which is burned off annually. Stripped of its protective mantle of forest and laid bare by the constant burning, the land is at the mercy of the elements. The hillsides become scarred by fan-shaped erosion gullies called 'lavaka' which creep inexorably outwards, taking an ever-growing share of the grassy slopes like some giant cancer devouring the land.

Many of the major massifs jutting out from the Hauts Plateaux are not derived directly from the original basement rocks, however, but are the results of more recent (but still very ancient) volcanic events. The northern massif of Tsaratanana, the highest on the island, was formed in this way, as were the massifs of Itasy and Ankaratra in the Hauts Plateaux near

The gneiss outcrop of Windsor Castle north-west of Diégo Suarez is home to the rare succulent **Pachypodium baroni windsori** *along with less local species such as* **Euphorbia viguieri**, *a cream-flowered form of* **E. millii** *and* **Aloe suarezensis**. *Despite the poor access road, the* **Pachypodium** *has been illegally collected on a large scale at this location. The crowned lemur* **Lemur coronatus** *still occurs in the fragments of dry forest in this area.*

This attractive small **Begonia** *species produces its flowers in the leafless state on the rocks of Windsor Castle during the dry season in June.*

Above: **Typical lavaka erosion gullies eating into a denuded hillside on the Hauts Plateaux north of Antsirabe. The resulting silt ends up in the rivers, turning them red, hence the oft-used term 'rivers of blood'.**

Above right: **The spectacular wilderness of limestone karst or 'tsingy' in Ankarana Special Reserve is one of the most amazing landscapes on the island. The open 'tsingy' provides the habitat of a number of rare succulent plants, while the accompanying areas of dry forest hold high populations of Sanford's lemurs Lemur fulvus sanfordi and crowned lemurs Lemur coronatus.**

Below: **The sandstones of the Isalo mountains in the Isalo National Park provide some of the most breathtaking scenery in Madagascar. Although mammals are relatively scarce, the endemic Benson's rockthrush Monticola bensoni is confined to this desolate habitat, which is also the home of several rare succulents, such as Pachypodium rosulatum gracilius, Aloe contigua and the endemic A. isaloensis. The picture was taken during the dry season in mid-June.**

Antananarivo. The Ankaratra covers an area of 1545 square miles (4000 sq km) featuring a line of extinct volcanoes forming summits over 7875 feet (2400 m) accompanied by huge flows of basalt and scattered crater lakes. Much of this activity took place in the Pliocene (27-26 million years ago), although some is more recent. In the south, the Androy massif consists of heavily eroded rocks formed during massive volcanic events in the Cretaceous Period.

The western third of the island is generally of much lower relief, consisting of sedimentary deposits 19-124 miles (30-200 km) wide which exhibit a limited amount of folding. Ancient Permian deposits (280-225 million years old) are overlain by sediments from the Jurassic (190-136 million years ago) and Cretaceous Periods, the latter being mainly of marine origin. Much of this region is overlain by more recent superficial deposits. Weathering of the sedimentary rocks has produced some of the most spectacular scenery in Madagascar. In the Isalo mountains in the south-west, the sandstones have been intensely eroded into a magnificent   landscape of winding canyons set among a chaos of weirdly shaped rocks. The 'tsingy' massifs of Bemaraha, Namoroka and Ankarana are, if anything, even more impressive, for their limestones have submitted to long periods of karst processes, giving rise to a crazy jigsaw of knife-edged pinnacles (dangerous to walk on) overlying extensive cave systems. Karst formations are thought to cover around 12,750 square miles (33,000 sq km) in the west and also include the Kelifely plateau; Mahafaly; Mahajanga; Sitampiky and the Narinda peninsula.

Numerous rivers rise in the Hauts Plateaux and meander towards the coast, often reaching the lowlands via a series of spectacular waterfalls and foaming rapids. The impressive rapids of the 'red river', the Betsiboka, near Maevatanana lie below the bridge carrying the main road to Mahajanga, so their beauty can be readily appreciated. The much clearer waters of the Namorona river tumble down a series of falls between forested hillsides west of Ranomafana, where the proximity of the main road also permits an intimate appreciation of the power of the waters. In the south, even the major rivers are mostly highly seasonal so that, during the dry season, a bare sandy bed is all that remains. The local people know that, despite this outwardly barren appearance, a subterranean flow can be relied on throughout the year, although it is only accessible by digging deep pits in the river bed.

Climate

Madagascar lies primarily within the tropical zone, the Tropic of Capricorn cutting across the southern half of the island just south of Tulear. The prevailing influence on temperature and rainfall is the presence of the great north-south mountain ranges, which interrupt the moisture-bearing winds coming off the Indian Ocean and dictate to a large extent where their moisture is precipitated. Temperature varies according to altitude and latitude. Thus, in the lowland town of Diégo Suarez in the north, the annual mean temperature is 81 °F (27 °C), dropping to 73 °F (23 °C) in Fort Dauphin in the far south-east. On the Hauts Plateaux, the mean annual temperature is much lower, varying between 61 °F (16 °C) and 66 °F (19 °C); even summer nights can feel very cool in Antananarivo at 4530 feet (1381 m). Above 4900 feet (1500 m) frost

may occur in midwinter, although lying snow is very rare and has only been recorded at sporadic intervals on the Andringitra massif.

Rainfall shows a much greater range of variation. The wettest areas are in the east and north-west (Montagne d'Ambre), and the amount of rain and the number of months in which it falls decrease as one moves west and south. Whereas the east coast is drenched with rain more or less throughout the year, the extreme south-west has a characteristic semidesert regime, with a prolonged dry season broken by sparse and unpredictable rains, which may miss out completely in some years. Fortunately, the dry season occurs during the southern winter (June to October), so pleasantly warm, cloudless days are the norm, and there is none of the chilling effect which would result from winter downpours.

The interplay of temperature and rainfall has such a major effect on the fauna and flora that several 'bioclimatic' regions can be identified in Madagascar.

1 **The east coast** (including the first escarpment) with rainfall of 59-118 inches (1500-3000 mm) annually, distributed more or less throughout the year in a regime of continuous high temperatures.

2 **The interior escarpment and eastern plateau region** which still receives more than 59 inches (1500 mm) of rainfall per year but has a definite dry season of one to four months; temperature varies according to altitude, but is generally much cooler than in the previous region.

3 **The western plateau region** where there is a prolonged dry season of five or six months and rainfall is 37-59 inches (950-1500 mm) annually. The mean annual temperature is 62.6-68 °F (17-20 °C). Summer days can be very hot and the nights sweltering and humid. The forestry station at Ampijeroa south of Mahajanga and the Ankarana massif near Diégo Suarez lie in this region.

4 **The western plains** where the dry season may last up to seven months and rainfall reaches only 20-59 inches (500-1500 mm) per year, decreasing southwards. The mean annual temperature lies in the range 77-79 °F (25-26 °C), but very high temperatures of 104 °F (40 °C) and above are frequent. The fascinating Kirindy forest north of Morondava lies in this region; large areas of 'spiny desert' in the south are also subject to this climatic regime.

5 **The extreme south-west** which has a semidesert climate. Rainfall averages 14 inches (350 mm) annually, but is so unpredictable that no rain may fall for a year or more. The mean annual temperature is 79 °F (26 °C) but, in summer, the days are hot and temperatures frequently reach 104 °F (40 °C). This region comprises only a narrow coastal strip perhaps 19 miles (30 km) wide, running from Morombe to Cap Sainte Marie, much of it

The River Namorona above Ranomafana spills off the central plateau in a series of waterfalls and rapids. Even in times of heavy rain, the water is relatively clear, never turning red from a burden of lateritic silt as so many rivers in Madagascar do as the country bleeds into the sea. Only the presence of forest along much of its course prevents the Namorona, too, from becoming another 'red river'.

characterized by a forest of *Didierea madagascariensis* and coralliform types of *Euphorbia*.

Vegetation — the primary formations

For broad descriptive purposes the vegetation of Madagascar can be split into two regions — eastern and western. The first of these encompasses the Hauts Plateaux and the land to the east down to the coast. Similar climate and vegetation are also found in the Sambirano domain in the north-west which forms an isolated outpost. Further brief descriptions of the vegetation in certain areas of outstanding interest are given in the section on reserves in the final chapter.

1   **The eastern lowland evergreen rainforests**
This formation is the richest of all, but has suffered considerable attrition from humankind, and now most of the forest on the low, flat coastal plain has been destroyed. This formation formerly extended virtually the length of the east coast, from sea level to around 2600 feet (800 m), forming a continuous blanket of green in which 90 per cent of the constituent plants were endemic to the island. The diversity of species in this type of forest is extraordinary, and it may be rare to find two individuals of the same species in close proximity to one another. This is particularly true of the trees, which abound in a plethora of species, each of which is present mainly as widely scattered individuals. As a result, no single species dominates in the way which seems so normal to people from the northern temperate regions, long familiar with almost pure stands of oak, beech, aspen or birch.

The canopy is not particularly high, averaging only 100 feet (30 m), and the frequent large emergent trees typical of the rainforests of Africa or South America are absent. Certain families are particularly well represented, however, especially the palms (Palmae) which are far more numerous in numbers and in species than in any equivalent African forest. Bamboos are also abundant. The trunks and branches of the trees provide an aerial foothold for huge, bright-green epiphytic ferns, especially the bird's-nest fern *Asplenium nidus*. Orchids are also abundant, far more so than in any African forest.

Features in common with rainforests in other continents are the relative frequency of trees with stilt-like or buttress roots and the common habit of flowering and fruiting directly from the branch or main trunk, known as caulifory. One of the characteristic genera of trees inhabiting these rainforests, *Tambourissa*, exhibits this habit. The most accessible examples of this type of forest are near Mananara and on Nosy Mangabe.

2   **The eastern montane rainforest** occurs mainly at 2600-4265 feet (800-1300 m). The canopy is lower [65-80 feet (20-25 m)] than in the previous type and many of the trees branch freely from near the ground, so there are fewer straight trunks reaching impressively upwards towards the light. Tree ferns are often abundant, and there is usually a rich growth of mosses and lichens festooning the trees. The leaves of the trees are smaller and tougher. The herb layer is

richer, with many species of ferns, *Impatiens* and members of the family Labiatae. Accessible examples of this forest type occur at Périnet, Ranomafana and on the Montagne d'Ambre.

3   **High-altitude montane forest** generally occurs at 4265-7545 feet (1300-2300 m). It is characterized by a still lower canopy, generally at 33-43 feet (10-13 m), but is often difficult to distinguish because the trees branch prolifically from near the base and are not easy to separate from shrubby growth. The leaves of the trees are even smaller, a response to the greater daily and seasonal variations in temperature and humidity, compounded by the drying effects of the winds which force them to restrict water loss by becoming smaller and more leathery. This is typical 'moss forest' in which mosses clothe the ground in a soft carpet and hang in sombre garlands from the trees, along with interlacing tassels of grey lichens, especially the old man's beard lichens (*Usnea*, also familiar in temperate forests). The hummocky carpet of mosses consists mainly of pleurocarpous species (so-called 'feather-mosses' having mainly creeping stems which often resemble miniature ferns) providing anchorage for large numbers of plants, such as orchids, ferns and tiny species of *Peperomia*, which, at lower altitudes, would be epiphytic. Ericaceous plants are typical members of the understorey.

Opposite top: **A** Lycopodium *clubmoss is accompanied by the leaves of ferns and flowering plants densely clothing the base of a tree in lowland tropical rainforest on Nosy Mangabe.*

Opposite bottom: **Ferns are often abundant in the damp environment alongside streams in the lowland rainforests. The spore bodies are visible as dark spots on the underside of this** Phymatodes scolopendria

Above: **The flowers of the wild ginger** Afromomum angustifolium **(Zingiberaceae) appear at the base of the plant. This species often forms dense stands in lowland tropical rainforest.**

Below: **Trees of the genus** Tambourissa **are one of the most characteristic elements of the lowland rainforests. As in many tropical trees, the fruits arise directly from the trunk. When ripe, these strange-looking fruits split open to reveal brilliant orange seeds.**

Tropical rainforest above Ranomafana clothes the steep slopes above the gorge of the Namorona river as it tumbles off the central plateau in a series of waterfalls and rapids. This forest is home to 12 different kinds of lemurs, including the two rarest, the golden bamboo lemur Hapalemur aureus *and greater bamboo lemur* H. simus. *The river itself provides one of the few known habitats for the rare aquatic tenrec* Limnogale mergulus.

4   **Eastern tapia forest** is named after the tapia tree *Uapaca bojeri* which forms the main constituent of the canopy at 33-39 feet (10-12 m). This forest grows at 2625-5250 feet (800-1600 m) on the western slopes of the Hauts Plateaux, where it closely resembles forests of the Mediterranean cork oak *Quercus suber.* As it lies in the rain shadow of the eastern mountains, this formation is much drier than the other types, so epiphytes and a ground layer of mosses are correspondingly rare or absent. This forest is particularly susceptible to fire, and few examples remain in their natural state, mostly being replaced by secondary formations in which the fire-resistant tapia is the dominant species.

5   **Eastern montane bushland and thicket** This occurs above 6500 feet (2000 m). It is characterized by only a single stratum of woody plants up to 19 feet (6 m) high, typically richly branched and layered with small, tough, evergreen leaves. Species diversity is low, although there are interesting trees belonging to the daisy family (Compositae). Bryophytes are quite abundant, though not as luxuriant as in montane forest. It is important to note that the specialized plant communities typical of many African mountain tops, with their giant species of *Lobelia* and *Senecio*, are absent from the mountains of Madagascar.

6   **Rupicolous shrubland** Rocky outcrops and isolated inselbergs throughout the Hauts Plateaux are colonized by a characteristic vegetation. This is relatively poor in species but of particular interest because it includes many of Madagascar's most

sought-after and ornamental succulent plants, such as species of *Aloe, Kalanchoe* and *Euphorbia.* These often grow among mats of *Fimbristylis* sedges, constituting a community of plants adapted to the drought conditions ruling on these well-drained habitats, as well as lying cruelly exposed to sun and wind. In addition to leaf and stem succulence, some species have underground storage tubers, while certain pteridophytes adopt the 'resurrection plant' type of strategy, shrivelling when dry but rapidly becoming green and plump as soon as rain arrives. One aspect of this floral community is the regular presence of species or subspecies endemic to just one particular outcrop.

7   **Western dry deciduous forest** This formation is constantly mentioned in later chapters, particularly when dealing with animals resident in the forests of Ankarafantsika, Ankarana and Kirindy, which are of this type. These forests lie in the rain shadow cast by the eastern mountains, so there is a prolonged dry season of seven or eight months, during which most of the trees forming the main canopy shed their leaves, although a few delay this until the onset of the rains and the production of fresh young leaves. The flora is broad and varied but generally less rich than in the eastern forests. The canopy is generally lower, from 40-50 feet (12-15 m), and prominent large emergent trees are rare, attaining heights of only

The orange bells of Ipomoea carnea *(Convolvulaceae) add a welcome splash of colour to the western dry forests in the April dry season.*

80 feet (25 m) or so. Lianas are abundant but epiphytes of all kinds are rare, while ferns and palms are absent. The herb-layer is depauperate, leaving the ground bare save for a carpet of dead leaves. Along rivers, gallery forest develops, usually dominated by large tamarind trees *Tamarindus indica*. Deciduous forests are mainly situated on sandy or clayey soils but also occur on lime-rich plateaus. On the latter substrate the canopy is considerably lower and there is a predominance of trees, such as baobabs *Adansonia* spp, with swollen water-storing stems (pachycauly). Near Morondava there are superb examples of this formation on sandy soils dominated by thousands of huge examples of the baobab *Adansonia grandidieri*. Unfortunately, the majority of these dry forests have already been destroyed by people and replaced with vast tracts of depressingly sterile savannas.

8 **Western deciduous thicket (the 'spiny desert')** For the first-time visitor this forms one of the most bizarre landscapes in the island. Although it bears a superficial similarity to certain parts of the south-western United States or Mexico, where candelabra cacti dominate the scene, the 'spiny desert' formation is unique to Madagascar, for the dominant thorny, cactus-like plants belong to an endemic family, the Didiereaceae. This formation is characteristic of the dry south, where rainfall is 12-20 inches (300-500 mm) per year, falling mostly in

December and January in the form of powerful thunderstorms bringing torrential short-lived downpours. This rainfall is unreliable, however, so the vegetation has to be capable of resisting a reign of drought and high temperatures for as long as 18 months. In addition to members of the Didiereaceae, there are numerous tree-like species of *Euphorbia* with woody trunks and slim, succulent, green, leafless stems which carry out the process of photosynthesis. Other succulents include species of *Kalanchoe* and *Aloe* as well as trees with bottle-like distended trunks, such as *Adansonia* (baobabs), *Moringa* and *Pachypodium*.

9 **Mangrove** The mangrove communities have probably suffered least from the destructive results of human activities, and there is still about 815,000 acres (330,000 ha) of this vegetation type, the largest remaining example in the western Indian Ocean. Well over 90 per cent is on the west coast, where seven tracts exceed 50,000 acres (20,000 ha) in extent.

Around the Bay of Bombetoka, mangrove communities are estimated to cover about 114,000 acres (46,000 ha). The trees concerned are all typical of the Indian Ocean mangrove systems, comprising nine species in three families, none of which is endemic. *Avicennia marina* (Avicenniaceae) often forms low, thick forests around shallow bays. Each tree is surrounded by dense stands of its long, slim, upward-pointing rootlets (pneumatophores) which function as the roots' 'lungs' in the oxygen-poor, salt-laden mud.

The darker-leaved *Sonneratia alba* (Sonneratiaceae) also has pneumatophores, but they are shorter and have blunt tips. The three members of the Rhizophoraceae do not have pneumatophores, but are renowned for their viviparous fruits which develop a long green root even while still attached to the tree. When this fruit eventually falls, its pointed tip pierces

East of Ambovombe there are large areas of 'spiny desert' dominated by the octopus tree Alluaudia procera, *a member of the endemic Didiereaceae family.*

the mud. Rapidly growing rootlets soon anchor the seedling in position, even pulling it upright if it should fail to land in a vertical position.

The effects of people

Most of the formations described above have been severely depleted by humans. In some instances, only small patches remain, remnants of once-vast tracts which are now lost forever, along with their never-to-be-known plant and animal life. It has been estimated that around 75 per cent of the original forests (of all types) have been destroyed in the remarkably short period of 2500 years since people first arrived in Madagascar. In the eastern region, destruction of the original 27.7 million acres (11.2 million ha) of rainforest has proceeded over many years, mainly in the form of small-scale clearance for subsistence farming, commonly known as 'slash-and-burn' although, in Madagascar, it goes under the name of 'tavy'. In this form of shifting agriculture the original plot is cultivated for a year or two, until the nutrients in the soil derived from the ash of the burnt trees are exhausted. The farmer then moves on to clear another plot, leaving the original one to revert to forest before it is again cleared. Ideally, this should be at least 15 to

An example of shifting agriculture or 'tavy' in the eastern rainforests. Bananas are planted in the foreground, while the secondary forest on the slope behind has recently been cleared, burned and planted with a crop of cassava. Within a year or two the temporary bonus of nutrients derived from the ash of the felled trees will be exhausted and the area will be left to revert to secondary forest before the cycle is repeated.

20 years later, but intensifying population pressure, in Madagascar and elsewhere in the tropics, is increasingly dictating a return to the original plot before the forest has had time to replenish the nutrient supply. In Madagascar, fresh demands on the land beneath the regrowing forest are made after only ten years. And here, however, the situation is worsened by the fact that, on many of the poorer soils, the abandonment of the cleared area seldom leads to the establishment of proper secondary forest (known locally as 'savoka') and the eventual return of something like the original formation. This is because Madagascar lacks any vigorous colonizing trees capable of providing quickly a woody cover for cleared ground, in the manner so capably performed by certain African trees or by the highly efficient South American *Cecropia*.

All too often, cleared hillsides left to regenerate are quickly smothered with an alien vegetation, such as sprawling masses of the Asian raspberry *Rubus moluccanus* and the South American trees *Psidium cattleyanum* and *P. guajava*. Large tracts of *P. cattleyanum* can easily be seen monopolizing secondary forest at Ranomafana. The dense growth of this tree inhibits the establishment of seedlings of native tree species. The most typical native tree of secondary forest is the travellers' tree *Ravenala madagascariensis*, a member of the banana family Musaceae. This elegant tree often covers denuded hillsides, although further burning eliminates even this and finally leads to permanent grassland. Large sweeps of open hillsides dominated by thousands of travellers' trees can be seen from the Tamatave-Antananarivo railway line where the train begins its climb out of the flat coastal plain.

In some areas, the bamboo *Ochlandra capitata* is the colonizing species and may form dense thickets. When the soils are reasonably good and large reservoirs of original forest remain nearby, however, some kind of seminatural forest will eventually re-establish itself. Unfortunately, the original composition of the fauna and flora seems to be lost permanently, and anyway, in Madagascar, repeated burnings usually interrupt the cycle of renewal at a premature stage. Repeated clearance for tavy eventually leads to a less and less vigorous regrowth, even by normally rampant alien trees, and the eventual spiral downwards to a virtually useless, hopelessly degraded landscape dominated by coarse grasses and bracken. The process of degradation is accelerated when steep slopes are utilized (as they all too often are where local populations are high) when rapid run-off during heavy rains quickly erodes the bare soils. Under these extremes even the first cycle of regeneration may fail to become established.

By 1985 only 9.4 million acres (3.8 million ha) of the original rainforest were left, victim of an accelerating rate of destruction which accounted for a 50 per cent reduction in the short period of 35 years between 1950 and 1985. With its phenomenal rate of population growth, one wonders for how much longer Madagascar can retain any rainforest at all, and what

The Betsileo people of the south-central Hauts Plateaux are experts in the cultivation of rice on hillside terraces, a method which gives intensive utilization of the land with reduced erosion. This typical scene near Ambalavao was photographed during the mid-winter fallow period.

the fate of the people will be if it all disappears. This is particularly pertinent, because the majority of the remaining forests have avoided the axe either because they are on slopes too steep to cultivate easily, or because they protect watersheds vital to the survival of large human settlements lower down. Desperate people resort to desperate measures, and a pressing need for land must eventually force an empty-bellied farmer to torch the forest, even when he knows it to be unwise practice, with all the negative and possibly disastrous consequences of erosion, crop inundation and loss of reliable year-round water supplies.

That most blatant and disheartening example of the end result of repeated burning — the unending vistas of barren grasslands comprising the Hauts Plateaux — is starkly laid out beneath the shocked gaze of any visitor arriving by air. Journeying across these vast 'pseudosteppes' by road is even more depressing, as the true extent of the tragedy becomes evident at close range. It is difficult to imagine the sprawling forest which once clothed these barren uplands, now reduced to just a few tiny scattered remnants. All the rest, together with its priceless reservoir of plant and animal species, has been replaced by one of the most impoverished forms of vegetation on the planet, sterile grasslands characterized by just a meagre handful of plants capable of surviving in this recent and unnatural environment.

Perhaps it is the sheer scale of the destruction which is most puzzling, for anyone driving through these sweeping grasslands is constantly faced with the same enigma; why has so much been destroyed by so few for so little? Madagascar has always had a relatively low population density — until recent times very low. Even now it is possible to drive across huge areas of the Hauts Plateaux without seeing a village or any sign of human presence. Yet this devastated landscape was apparently created by agricultural practices aimed at providing food for people. This started with the initial clearances of the original forest for repeated cycles of tavy; then, when the forest finally failed to return, the grasslands produced grazing for the introduced zebu cattle. These rapidly gained importance as ceremonial animals which bestowed status on their owners. As a result, every year and for hundreds of years past, Madagascar has burned from end to end as the farmers set fire to the grasslands. This is designed to stimulate a fresh growth of tender shoots with the coming of the rains, the so-called 'green bite'. Yet every passing year sees any advantage gained by this process sadly lost in the increasing soil erosion and unremitting depletion of what few nutrients still remain in the soils.

The Hauts Plateaux have been described as a grassy desert, and with some reason, yet only 2500

Top left: **The Corporation Suisses's forest utilization project in their huge concession in the Kirindy forest near Morondava is intended to provide a viable long-term economic alternative to the destruction of this valuable example of tropical dry forest for farming. Bands 220 metres (722 ft) long are cut at regular intervals into the forest and the timber extracted. These are then replanted with native species of trees raised in their nursery. As these are slow-growing species, the avoidance of clear-felling over even a limited area ensures that the young trees always enjoy the protection of mature forest close on either side.**

Top centre: **One of the most valuable trees in the Kirindy forest is** Commiphora guillaumini *with its characteristic peeling bark.*

Top right: **Corporation Suisse's tree nursery at Morondava with seedlings of** Neobeguea mahafalensis. **Practice in germinating the seeds of tropical trees and the after-care of the seedlings to replant with native species has been a relatively neglected area of forestry in the tropics. It is to be hoped that this example will be followed by others, especially in relation to tropical rainforest trees.**

Left above: **Timber is extracted from the Kirindy forest by mechanical means and transported to the sawmill at Morondava by road.**

Left: **Neat stacks of sawn timber at the Corporation Suisse's sawmill in Morondava. Being put to such a practical final use is surely a far more sensible way for a tropical tree to end its days than as a pile of ash in a landscape devastated by fire, especially when replanting with saplings of the same species ensures the long-term future of the forest.**

Below: **In an effort to ensure that nothing is wasted, the Corporation Suisse has been experimenting to find the most economical method for the production of charcoal from scraps of timber. Creosote is an additional saleable by-product of this process.**

years ago this was all covered in upland rainforest, a dense tangle of trees festooned with mosses and lichens. Or was it really all like that? We know that there always were gaps in the canopy formed by rock outcrops with their attendant flora of specialized succulents; it is possible that these openings were more extensive than was once thought. The widespread occurrence of slow-growing, sun-loving, endemic succulents, such as *Euphorbia primulifolia*, rooted in lateritic soils on the grasslands of the Hauts Plateaux (even near Antananarivo) could indicate that such open habitats might have existed on a fairly wide scale. Perhaps people and their fires only accelerated a process of change to a drier climate which was already inexorably under way.

Forests are now making a comeback on parts of this open landscape, but they are very different from the original cover. These are artificial plantations of Australian *Eucalyptus* and several kinds of alien pines, planted for use in construction and for firewood. The claim that these plantations are also valuable in preventing erosion is, however, somewhat dubious because the tree species grown are notorious for suppressing any kind of herbaceous growth beneath. Clear felling immediately leads to particularly rapid and damaging erosion, as the ground is denied even the basic protection afforded by grasses. More widely spaced plantings are the answer. There are also exciting suggestions to replant an area of the Hauts Plateaux with a mixture of native trees, thus recreating an area of seminatural forest. This would gradually become more and more like the original formation as plants and animals are slowly recruited from nearby remnant patches of natural forest.

The western forests have generally suffered the same destructive inroads, so that vast areas of an open, featureless, savanna-like habitat now greet the traveller over more than 80 per cent of the region. This grassland is taller than in the east but even more impoverished, for the majority of its associated flora consists of non-native weeds, a sure sign of its recent origin. As in the east and the Hauts Plateaux, the grassland is burnt off every year, although this has not yet succeeded in erasing every last vestige of arboreal presence as comprehensively as in the east. This is because some western trees are able to survive coppicing by the flames, and it is the frequent occurrence of bushes and small copses which gives rise to the savanna-like appearance. Unfortunately, the remaining areas of forest are inexorably nibbled away by the fires each year, as the trees around their perimeters gradually retreat before the flames. This annual burning, combined with grazing by the estimated 10 million head of zebu cattle on the island, prevents any attempts by the western forest at natural regeneration. But, even in the absence of any such hindrance, the soils over vast areas have reached a state of such sterility that any form of unassisted comeback is no longer possible. In fact, the western dry forest seems scarcely capable of naturally recolonizing cleared land, unlike in the east where several cycles of tavy are often possible before natural

regeneration is completely halted. Current estimates place the remaining area of western forests at 7,768,000 acres (3,145,000 ha), but much of this exists in a semi-degraded state, although this has not always passed the point at which regeneration back to something near the original type could easily take place. Even forests theoretically protected in reserves suffer damage through lack of adequate management, and there is a pressing need for far stricter enforcement of the ban on burning and logging. These forests are also extensively utilized for the production of charcoal which is the main fuel used for cooking on the island.

The southern forests are presently estimated to cover an area of 7,163,000 acres (2,900,000 ha). In general, these formations have suffered less damage and are the least disturbed of the island's climax habitats. This is partly because much of this forest lies on the shallow, well-drained Mahafaly plateau, an area inherently hostile to attempts at farming because of the poor soils and the long periods of drought. The lack of flammable material, mainly thanks to the succulent nature of much of the vegetation, means that fire cannot rage unchecked through this forest as it can in many of the other types. Where the soils are more favourable, however, large tracts of the 'spiny desert' formation have been cleared for commercial production of sisal *Agave sisalana*, and for subsistence crops such as sorghum and maize. The people of the south are often conspicuously poor so, with the usual rise in population, there will be an inevitable increase in pressure on this fragile habitat, especially for the production of charcoal, which already makes major inroads into the southern forests. The *Alluaudia* trees are also felled to provide timber for homes, so an increase in the human population will also raise the level of this form of exploitation.

The production of charcoal is generally one of the greatest threats to the dry forests of the south and west. Here a charcoal seller near Andranavory loads his wares into a cart. Rising levels of human population will increase such pressure

Chapter 2
The Flora

There are several widely differing estimates of the total numbers of species of vascular plants in Madagascar, and, no matter which of these we choose to accept, there is no question that Madagascar has one of the richest floras in the world. In common with most of the fauna dealt with in later chapters, the majority of this floral wealth consists of species endemic to the island. In marked contrast to most of the animal groups, however, which often show a relatively poor variety at the specific and family levels, the diversity of the flora at all levels is far higher than in the neighbouring continental landmass. Our knowledge of

the flora, particularly from many of the more inaccessible parts of the eastern rainforests, is inadequate which is why we can not be sure of the exact number of species. Even when dealing with well-worked and popular 'hobbyist' plants such as *Aloe*, however, which live in reasonably accessible areas, a great deal undoubtedly still remains to be discovered. Hence the description of two new species of *Aloe* by Professor Werner Rauh (the accepted authority on Madagascan succulents) in late 1990: *A. delphinensis* from granite rocks near Fort Dauphin; and *A. alfredii* from Mount Ibity near Antsirabe. The floras of these areas have been quite well explored, especially for their succulent plants, so who knows how many more species await discovery and description from the eastern rainforests, and some of the more remote mountains?

The lowest estimate currently suggests a total of around 7300 species, while 12,000 is quoted at the upper end, which would elevate Madagascar to the world's number one floral hot-spot for an area of its size. The true number probably lies somewhere between, although such is the high degree of local endemism in Madagascar, that even the upper limit may well prove to be on the low side, assuming that there is any natural vegetation left to study in future years. Narrow endemism is particularly strong on some of the higher mountain tops. Take, for example, the Andringitra massif which has over 150 species of endemic vascular plants; this is despite the destruction of large areas of the original vegetation, probably taking with it yet more endemics which we shall now never know. The inclusion of the Andringitra in so many specific names is enough to give us some immediate idea of its uniqueness. Thus, there is *Geranium andringitrense, Alchemilla andringitrensis, Osbeckia andringitrensis, Coniza andringitrana, Senecio andringitrensis, Disa andringitrana, Liparis andringitrana, Bulbophyllum andringitranum, Aloe andringitrensis, Mariscus andringitrensis, Scleria andringitrensis, Carex andringitrensis* and *Dichanthium andringitrense*. These, and the host of other endemics, which includes 25 species of orchids and the enigmatic *Pelargonium madagascariensis*, with no obvious close relatives, are mostly sun lovers, growing in the open on rocks in full sun.

The Tsaratanana massif has a similarly high rate of endemism, with a probable total of around 200 species

The beautiful water lily Nymphaea stellata *is widespread in still waters throughout the island.*

The pitcher plants (Nepenthaceae) are found mainly in the Malayan region, especially on the island of Borneo, with a few species scattered to the east and west of this core area; two species get as far west as Madagascar. This is **Nepenthes madagascariensis** *which grows abundantly in swamps near Fort Dauphin.*

Geosiridaceae (one species); Humbertiaceae (one species); Sphaerosepalaceae (14 species in two genera); and Sarcolaenaceae, also often called the Chlaenaceae (10 genera containing 35 species). Narrowing the focus somewhat, around 238, or 20 per cent, of Madagascar's 1289 genera are endemic. The number of endemic species is uncertain, because it depends on the total species estimate, but it is probably around 6400 or 81 per cent of the total vascular flora. In common with other tropical areas, rates of endemism are highest in the rainforests (89 per cent), followed by the mainly drought-tolerant flora of rocky outcrops (82 per cent, but will probably prove to be much higher). These figures fall sharply to 56 per cent for marshes, where the visitor from Europe would encounter such familiar plants as slender reedmace *Typha angustifolia* and common reed *Phragmites communis*, both every bit as natural a feature of wetlands in Madagascar as in Britain or Africa. The figure for the seashore is even lower at 21 per cent, and reflects the almost cosmopolitan distribution of many tropical coastal plants such as *Ipomoea pes-caprae* and *Canavalia obtusifolia*. Rates of endemism based on biological types is 94 per cent for trees, 94 per cent for shrubs and 85 per cent for perennial grasses. The figure for trees probably includes certain arboreal woody succulent species of *Euphorbia*. But, if succulents are taken as a discrete group, then the figure probably exceeds 99 per cent. Such a high figure would not be surprising, because succulent plants from any part of the world are renowned for their high rates of local endemism, such that individual species are often confined to a single mountainside, let alone a single country.

The affinities of the flora are mixed, with obvious relationships to the African and Oriental floras, but also including a small but significant South American element. In fact, there are around 26 genera which are present in Madagascar and South America, but not necessarily also found in Africa. Some genera show an extraordinarily disjointed distribution. *Ravenala* (Musaceae) is represented by a single species in Madagascar and just one other in Brazil and Guiana. Although this may seem rather puzzling at first, it is readily explained by the theory of continental drift. As already mentioned, Madagascar was once part of the supercontinent of Gondwanaland, which also included Africa and South America. The ancestors of such plants as *Ravenala* survived in Madagascar and South America after Gondwanaland split apart, but have presumably been rendered extinct in Africa, probably because of a gradual tendency towards increasing dryness over the southern part of that continent.

There are some major differences between the Madagascan and African floras. Madagascar has 130 species of palms (Palmae) in 19 genera, far more than can be found in the whole of Africa. Of these 19 genera, only seven are not endemic, and each of these contains only a single species, all with African affinities. The rest are endemic, but their closest relatives are in Asia, rather than in nearby Africa. The same applies to the *Pandanus* pandan palms

found nowhere else. Unlike on the Andringitra, however, most of these grow in the shade of dwarf woodland. It is likely that the endemic flora of the Ankaratra was also once similarly rich, but fire has now destroyed for ever most of the botanical treasures which had evolved over millions of years in their isolated but dreadfully vulnerable outpost; such is the power of humankind to destroy. As on the Tsaratanana, most of the endemics on Ankaratra grew in the shade of woodland and what little remains is still threatened by fire. Only a few species can cope with the drastically changed conditions; these include the red-hot poker *Kniphophia ankaratrensis* and a few kinds of terrestrial orchids which do well in the impoverished grasslands that have replaced the original forests. Although the endemism on these mountains is extraordinarily high at a specific level, it is noticeable that they all belong to widespread genera.

The total number of families in Madagascar is 191. Eight of these are endemic: Asteropeiaceae (five to six species in a single genus); Didiereaceae (four genera with 11 species forming the dominant vegetation in parts of the south); Didymelaceae (one genus, two species); Diegodendraceae (one species);

Above: **There are 19 species of** Chrysalidocarpus *palms in* **Madagascar. The beautiful** C. isaloensis *grows along streamsides in the arid Isalo mountains.*

Above right: **The handsome palm** Ravenea glauca *grows alongside rivers in the south.*

Right: *Although most of the pandan palms (Pandanaceae) are characteristic elements of the eastern rainforests, a few are found in damp habitats in the dry south. This is* **Pandanus pulcher** *growing beside a stream in the arid eroded landscape of the Isalo mountains.*

(Pandanaceae) with 70 species in Madagascar, most of them in the east. There they are a characteristic feature of the rainforests, their water-filled leaf axils providing lodgings for a variety of frogs. Most of the true palms are also found in the eastern rainforests where they exhibit an extraordinary diversity in size and habit. Some, such as *Dypsis hildebrandii* and *D. louvelii*, are delicate-fronded miniatures which do not reach more than 3 feet (1 m) or so in height. Others, such as species of *Ravenea*, are imposing trees with long straight trunks and impressive crowns of stately fronds 10 feet (3 m) or more long. One of the commonest species at 650-5900 feet (200-1800 m) is *Phloga polystachya* with its elegantly slim, straight trunk 10 feet (3 m) or so high surmounted by a topknot of attractive curly fronds. Many other species are extremely ornamental, especially various *Chrysalidocarpus* and the dwarf kinds of *Neophloga*, the largest genus in the island with 35 species. Most of these are dependent on the forest for their survival,

and, when the axe and the flames make their mark, most of the palms disappear for good. There are a few exceptions, such as *Chrysalidocarpus decipiens*, a robust plant with well-built fronds and a trunk which is inflated towards the middle; it is well able to survive on the burned grasslands which succeed the forest.

Madagascar's total of more than 1000 species of orchids also greatly exceeds the number found throughout the whole vast continent of Africa. The most celebrated is undoubtedly the comet orchid *Angraecum sesquipedale* with its large, creamy white flowers. In 1862 Charles Darwin came across this orchid and, from observations of its incredibly long, 14-inch (35-cm) spur, he predicted that somewhere in the island there existed a giant hawkmoth with an equally long proboscis capable of taking advantage of the nectar in the lower third of the spur. Forty-one years later, a hawkmoth with a proboscis almost 9 inches (22 cm) long was discovered and named *Xanthopan morgani praedicta*. This nocturnal giant lives at quite low densities in the eastern rainforests, so the orchid flowers remain in a fresh condition over a long period, steadily distilling their sweet perfume into the night air in the hope that eventually their unpredictable pollinator will show up. Unfortunately, this seems to be rather an uncommon event, because it is rare to find seed pods on this orchid in the wild. Some more recent studies into a related species, *A. arachnites*, have brought to light an interesting variation on this theme. Its flowers are similar in appearance to others in the genus — white with a long spur — but differ in their emission not of a sweet, heady scent, but a faint nitrogenous odour which serves to attract just one pollinator, a common rainforest hawkmoth *Panogena lingens*. Although

there is a host of long-tongued hawkmoths on the island, it seems that the nectar at the base of the long, twisted *A. arachnites* spur is accessible only to this single species of moth — and not even to every individual! This is because *P. lingens* exists in two different forms — one having a proboscis around $2^{3}/_{4}$ inches (7 cm) long and the other with a $4^{3}/_{4}$-inch (12-cm) long proboscis, which is also more tapered. Only the latter pollinates *A. arachnites*, and why two forms should occur at all is a complete mystery.

The succulent plants

Succulence is generally defined as the possession of water-storing tissues, usually as fattened stems or leaves, which function as a reservoir to tide the plant

through a long dry period. Succulents grow either in areas of low rainfall and high temperatures or, if they occur in zones of relatively high rainfall, they are rooted in cracks on well-drained rocks. Here, with little soil to hold any water and fully exposed to the drying effects of sun and wind, drought may prevail even when rainfall is quite high.

The best-known examples of succulent plants are the cacti, all of which belong to a single family, the Cactaceae. This family is widely distributed in the Americas, where it evolved, and few examples are found outside this area. Madagascar is home to some of these strays, in three species of slim-stemmed, mostly spineless, very 'un-cactus-like' *Rhipsalis* which live on rocks, particularly by the shore, and epiphytically on trees. The candelabra-stemmed spiny monsters which most people think of as 'typical' cacti are not found in Madagascar. Similar-looking plants are found widely in Africa, but these are species of *Euphorbia*, members of the widespread family Euphorbiaceae. Giant multibranched *Euphorbia* trees, with green, highly succulent stems, such as *E. ingens*, *E. cooperi* and *E. candelabrum*, are very much a part of the African landscape. Superficially similar plants which form forests in southern Madagascar are, however, members of a completely different family, the Didiereaceae, one of the island's most fascinating endemic families.

Madagascar is blessed with a rich and fascinating succulent flora, which does include numerous species of *Euphorbia*. The Madagascan representatives are perhaps better classified as woody succulent, however, rather than truly succulent, because only a few of the smaller species exhibit the thick, green, water-storing stems found in the bulk of the African species. Madagascar also possesses extremely interesting, mostly endemic succulent members of the Apocynaceae, Liliaceae, Crassulaceae, Cucurbitaceae, Passifloraceae, Vitaceae and Asclepiadaceae. A surprising feature is the absence from this list of the family Aizoaceae which, in southern Africa, contains a huge number of succulent representatives. The level of interest in succulent plants (and in recent times in specifically Madagascan succulents) is so high, and some of the species so conspicuous and easily recognized, that it is worth looking at a selection of the succulent members of each of these families in considerable detail.

FAMILY APOCYNACEAE

The succulent representatives all belong to the single genus *Pachypodium*, with nine species in Madagascar and only five in the dry southern regions of Africa, none of which shows any close affinities to their Madagascan relatives. These all have a number of points in common: stems exhibiting varying degrees of succulence, from only slightly thickened to virtually globose; strong, rather thick thorns grouped in twos and threes; flowers borne on the branch-apex, usually set at the tip of a long stalk; and deciduous leaves, which sprout at the beginning of the rains as spirally arranged tufts, which wither and drop off at the onset

Pachypodium rutenbergianum in flower in June near Diégo Suarez. The green foliage belongs to a tree through which the Pachypodium *is growing — a common habit.*

of the dry season. Within Madagascar these plants can be divided into three groups based on flower colour; *Leucopodium* with white flowers; *Chrysopodium* with yellow flowers; and *Porphyropodium* with red flowers. They also fall conveniently into three groups on the basis of their mode of growth, which is immediately obvious even when the plants are not flowering:

1   **The tree-like species** characterized by a reasonably normal-looking, if rather plump, woody trunk surmounted by a multibranched crown.

2   **The caudiciform species** having an inflated stem varying from somewhat bulbous to extremely fattened at the base, and bearing a much ramified topknot of usually thorny branches.

3   **The compressed species** which looks like a lump of smooth concrete completely innocent of extraneous branches, for much of the year bearing scant likeness to any kind of living organism.

Group 1 is represented by three species which resemble short fat trees. *Pachypodium rutenbergianum* is the most widespread member of the genus and the least succulent. It has a silvery barked trunk up to 20 feet (6 m) high, only slightly thickened along its length, topped by a crown of rather slim branches which all tend to point more-or-less upwards, and are furnished with paired thorns. It is a characteristic plant of the dry, deciduous forests of the north-west. It also grows on rocky outcrops in full sun, when the trunks are often wedged into narrow, well-drained cracks in the rocks. The large, brilliant-white flowers are borne profusely during the dry season (June-September), when they are particularly conspicuous for, at this time, the plant is leafless. The var. *meridionale* (= *P. meridionale*) is a considerably larger plant, up to 26 feet (8 m) high with attractive pink or pinkish-white flowers. It inhabits the deciduous forests in south-west Madagascar, particularly to the south and south-east of Morondava. The var. *sofiense* (= *P. sofiense*) has much broader leaves and is found in a number of scattered localities in dry forests in the west-centre and north-west. The nominate subspecies occurs from north of Diégo Suarez in scattered localities down to just north of Tulear.

Pachypodium geayi has a rather fatter trunk, and is one of the typical components of the landscape of the dry south-west, where it occurs on rocky, well-drained slopes and on flatter alluvial areas which may become a quagmire for long periods during the rainy season. The amount of water available to plants growing in such diverse habitats is very different, and it is surprising that specimens which have their roots enveloped in saturated mud for several weeks of the year do not either rot off from the base, or suffer split stems caused by over-swelling with water. Young plants up to about 6 feet (2 m) high have a strong armament of spines, arranged in groups of three, so that they densely cover the trunk. As the plant grows, the trunk becomes almost spineless and of an almost smooth grey texture. During the wet season, the stems are topped with tufts of long, narrow, greyish-silver leaves although the large, showy white flowers do not put in an appearance until the depths of the dry season. *P. lamerei* is almost indistinguishable when leafless during the dry season, but is easily separated when it bears its rather broader bright green leaves. The trunk is browner than in *P. geayi* because it lacks the greyish felty covering seen in that species. Full-grown plants have fat, bottle-shaped, grey trunks up to 20 feet (6 m) high, crowned by rather short, stubby branches which bear garlands of white flowers. It, too, is found in the south and west, but extends much further north than *P. geayi*.

Group 2 contains four species covering each of the groups based on flower colour. The white-flowered example is *P. decaryi*, an elusive plant which can be seen only in its very localized habitat, on the tsingy limestones of the north-west, by expending a considerable amount of time, effort, sweat and, if you are unlucky and take a fall on the treacherous knife-edged limestone, blood and tears as well. All this dedication is required just to admire a rather odd-looking plant with a smooth, silvery trunk resembling a large inverted turnip, fat at the base and tapering upwards. This is surmounted by an untidy mop of long, thin, straggly, virtually thornless branches. The large white flowers are borne during the dry season from June to September. This outlandish plant seems to prefer the edges of the tsingy, and may be quite common over a limited area. The free-draining nature

of the substrate with its limited capacity to trap humus, coupled with the long dry season and high temperatures on the exposed heat-reflecting limestone, seem to limit the number of seedlings which become established. The plants are often all of a more-or-less uniform age, a common phenomenon in populations of large succulent plants, as germination and subsequent survival of seedlings may occur only at long intervals in especially favourable years. Fortunately, the most important habitat for this rare species lies within the Ankarana Special Reserve, from which regular burning, the greatest enemy of Madagascar's succulent flora, is excluded.

The most widespread member of the yellow-flowered group is *Pachypodium rosulatum* which is divided into three distinct varieties. The largest of these, var. *rosulatum* (= *P. drakei*) grows in north-west Madagascar on well-drained, sandy soils. It often crops up on remarkably localized 'sand-reefs', forming isolated oases for succulents in extensive areas of unsuitable forested habitat. At first sight var. *rosulatum* does not seem to be particularly succulent, merely resembling a small whitish-barked bush, but a closer examination reveals the swollen stem bases which form a water-storing caudex. The plants reach about 5 feet (1.5 m) in height, and are not particularly hazardous because the thorns are present only briefly on younger growth, and soon drop off. The large, canary-yellow flowers start to appear at the beginning

The large white flowers of **Pachypodium decaryi** *appear in June. This strange plant grows mainly on the open 'tsingy' limestones of the north-west, as here in the Ankarana Special Reserve.*

The weird, bulbous, flask-like Pachypodium rosulatum *var.* gracilius *is a typical plant of the rocky Isalo mountains. The bright-yellow flowers start to appear at the end of June.*

of the dry season in May, when most of the leaves have already been shed. The var. *borombense* occurs on the flat Horombe plateau south of Ihosy and most notably in the dry country near Bereketa further to the south-east, where it grows in dense clumps on the smooth grey sheets of gneiss rock. The altitude here is about 4600 feet (1400 m) and the landscape bleak and windswept, with cool winter nights and high summer temperatures. This variety is superficially similar to var. *rosulatum*, although generally rather smaller and more compact. The yellow flowers are the biggest in the group, and their deeply furrowed corolla tubes are the best distinguishing feature from var. *rosulatum* which has smooth corolla tubes.

The most attractive, as well as the smallest and most obviously succulent form, is var. *gracilius* which is also the easiest to recognize in habitat. The plants grow to less than 18 inches (50 cm) high and strikingly resemble smooth, grey, globular, earthenware pots. These sprout an untidy crop of rather short, wavy branches which, in the wet season, are tipped with bunches of short green leaves. The canary-yellow flowers arise at the ends of exceptionally long, slender stems. They slowly start to appear in late June, and continue to arrive sporadically over the next few months, as the dry season tightens its grip on the landscape. This variety has a remarkably scattered distribution, from near Tulear in the south to a number of localities in the north-west. Var. *gracilius* is, without

doubt, most usually associated with the spectacularly eroded Isalo mountains in south-west Madagascar. In this inhospitable terrain, thousands of these squat grey blobs find themselves very much at home, wedged into crevices on the lichen-spattered cliffs, or huddling together atop some smooth, hump-backed slab of rock, looking for all the world like further products of the erosive processes which have moulded the landscape itself. By midsummer, the temperatures on these exposed surfaces are fit to fry an egg, yet the hardy *P. r. gracilius* are apparently immune to such oven-like conditions. By the end of the dry season, the spongy tissue within the inflated caudex has become severely depleted of its store of water but, within days of even a single shower of rain, these expand and become replete with water. The local guides who take visitors to see the natural wonders of the Isalo National Park refer to this plant as '*petit baobab*'. This is botanically misleading, because the baobabs belong to a quite unrelated family, the Bombacaceae.

The second member of the yellow-flowered group, *P. densiflorum,* is one of the most characteristic plants of the monolithic granite inselbergs which are such a commanding feature of the landscape in the south-central part of the island, as between Antsirabe and Fianarantsoa, and near Zazafotsy. Here the species grows with one or more species of *Aloe* and various terrestrial orchids. In general habit, it rather resembles

Pachypodium rosulatum var. rosulatum growing on an open 'sand reef' among the dry forests in the Ampijeroa Forest Reserve. The large yellow flowers start to appear in May just as the leaves have finished dropping at the onset of the dry season.

a smaller and stouter *P. rosulatum horombense*, but the flowers are a giveaway, being quite different. They are of a much darker yellow, considerably smaller than in any variety of *P. rosulatum*, and the anthers protrude from the centre of the flower (in *P. rosulatum* they are sunk within the flower tube). *P. densiflorum* var. *brevicalyx* differs from the type in having even longer slimmer flower stalks and tiny flowers. It grows in an area cut off from the main centre of distribution. The long-term survival of *P. densiflorum* and, indeed, of all the island's fascinating and priceless array of endemic succulents, is greatly threatened by the incessant bush fires which ravage the length and breadth of central Madagascar during the dry season. Within hours, hillsides which had been decorated with colourful rock gardens of rare succulents are converted into graveyards of charred embers. Only when the plants are fortunate enough to grow on wide slabs of rock, lacking enough dry vegetation to feed the flames, do they have a chance to survive. But not always, for such is their enthusiasm for fire that the farmers will often climb across the open rock slabs, deliberately torching the sparse vegetation rooted in the crevices.

The only red-flowered member of the genus, *Pachypodium baroni*, is found at the other end of the island near Diégo Suarez. With its football-sized tuber, it looks rather like a spiny cross between *P. rosulatum gracilius* and *P. decaryi*, but any confusion would be immediately dispelled by the appearance of the

Pachypodium densiflorum *in flower on granite rocks near Zazafotsy in the wintertime dry season in late June.*

beautiful carmine flowers. It grows in crevices on hot dry limestone rocks, exposed for most of the day to the full glare of the sun. The var. *windsori* is a smaller version, almost confined to the sheer cliffs of an acidic gneiss outcrop called Windsor Castle, situated north-west of Diégo Suarez and some 185 miles (300 km) from the locality of the type. Despite the inaccessible nature of its habitat, *P. b. windsori* has been subject to extensive illegal collecting by selfish and unscrupulous succulent rustlers. It has been exported in such numbers to Europe, North America and Japan that its population is now sadly depleted. Unlike all the other *Pachypodium* species, its showy red flowers appear during the summer wet season, rather than in the height of the winter drought.

The weirdest *Pachypodium*, and one of the most grotesque succulent plants in the world, *Pachypodium brevicaule*, is the sole member of Group 3. This bizarre plant has been likened to a heap of potatoes tipped on a hillside. Its lumpy appearance results from the way in which the new branches fail to elongate as they develop, but remain short and become positively obese. The plants seldom exceed 20 inches (50 cm) in height, but may form smooth, grey-skinned domes 3 feet (1 m) or more across, as if hewn from the quartz in which they invariably grow. Development is very slow, and such venerable behemoths must be many hundreds of years old. The bright yellow flowers appear on very short stalks at the end of the dry season, when the rock-like dormant plants suddenly reveal their true nature, as members of the plant kingdom. This incredible plant enjoys a local distribution dictated by its peculiar ecology, for it lives only on quartz outcrops, such as Mount Ibity and Mount Itremo in central Madagascar. Thousands of specimens have been illegally torn from the slopes of these mountains to satisfy the unthinking greed of foreign collectors, who prize this calloused oddity above almost any other member of the world's vast succulent flora. Yet this is all such a tragic waste because such wild-grown plants are difficult to establish so far from their natural habitat.

FAMILY DIDIEREACEAE
This is one of the most interesting plant families in Madagascar, and has no obvious close affinities outside the island. It does have distant connections with the similar-looking cacti in the Cactaceae, however. Plants from both these families can be intergrafted — a clear indication of biochemical affinities. The two families also share the nitrogenous purple pigment betalain, and there are further similarities in serology and pollen structure. They have the production of spines in clusters on specialized areoles in common, too, but here the similarities probably end. The flowers, in particular, are quite different and, in the Didiereaceae, male and female blooms are always borne on separate plants. There is some dispute about whether any members of this family can be called truly succulent, because spongy water-storing tissue is found only sparingly within the stems of certain species. Thickening of the stems to

increase the water-storage capacity, a characteristic of most true succulents, is also minimal or virtually absent. Nevertheless, these plants are all eminently capable of resisting extended drought, and are among the primary members of the 'spiny desert' in the south. They all bear small deciduous leaves which fall during the dry season, and most species are well protected by long, sharp thorns.

The largest species is *Alluaudia ascendens* which reaches a height of almost 50 feet (15 m). The woody trunk is solitary, surmounted by a tuft of long, slim, upwardly pointing branches. The young plants are unbranched. In the adult state, *A. procera* is very similar, if slightly smaller, but, in this species, the juvenile plants are quite different and are extremely thorny, multistemmed bushes. These bear an extraordinary resemblance to the ocotillo *Fouquieria splendens* (Fouquieriaceae) from the deserts of the United States and Mexico, even down to the possession of deciduous leaves on the long, slim, spiny stems and terminal inflorescences — an interesting example of convergence. The tiny white flowers of *A. procera* are borne near the tips of the branches on tufted cymes. The small rounded leaves sprout prolifically along the stems, turning them green for the duration of the wet season, before shrivelling and falling at the onset of the winter dry period, leaving the plants bare and gaunt. There are numerous examples of cacti that look very similar, but these almost always have much more succulent green stems, which carry out all the necessary photosynthesis and only one or two tree-like genera develop leaves for this purpose. *A. procera* dominates the landscape in dense stands over large areas of the south where its wood is often used for house-building and charcoal production.

Left: **The tiny leaves of** Alluaudia procera **(Didiereaceae) densely clothe the spiny stems during the summer wet season. They fall at the onset of the winter drought, leaving the stems bare and gaunt. The Didiereaceae is Madagascar's most interesting endemic plant family.**

Below left: **The stems of** Alluaudia procera **are so heavily spined that it is a mystery how the lemurs which inhabit the 'spiny desert' manage to leap from one plant to another without apparently pricking their feet.**

Below: **In its juvenile stage** Alluaudia procera **is a very spiny, much-branched plant; by contrast, the related A. ascendens has a single-stemmed juvenile state.**

Alluaudia montagnacii is another extraordinary example of convergence. With its tall, often solitary tapering stems, leaning over towards the apex, and numerous small deciduous leaves and a terminal tuft of flowers, it closely parallels the boojum *Fouquieria columnaris* of Baja California. *A. montagnacii* is of very restricted distribution and grows only in dry bush near Itampalo. It has been suggested that this plant, with characters of the stem of *A. ascendens* and the inflorescences of *A. procera*, may actually be a natural hybrid between the two.

Alluaudia dumosa is perhaps the strangest member of the genus. It forms large trees with a rather normal-looking woody trunk, topped by a dense brush of greyish-brown branches which are virtually spineless and produce only tiny slim ephemeral leaves. It is the branches themselves which carry out photosynthesis and transpiration in a cactus-like way. The white flowers, with their red stigmas, are more attractive than in the other species, and develop directly on the branches. This plant prefers siliceous soils and grows between Ampanihy and Fort Dauphin.

At first glance, particularly from a passing car, *Alluaudia comosa* resembles a rather squat ordinary tree of noticeably sombre aspect, having a very dense, dark, flat-topped crown of slim, well-thorned branches formed into a characteristic anvil shape. This makes it easy to recognize, even at a distance. It is a typical plant of the dry limestone soils of the Mahafaly plateau, and is particularly easy to see alongside the road leading from Tulear to Andranavory.

Decaryia madagascariensis, the sole representative of its genus, is a remarkable plant with its complex cat's-cradle of interlocking, zig-zag, thorny branches (hence the name of 'zig-zag plant' or 'carbon molecule plant' given to plants in cultivation). The small white flowers appear profusely on multibranched cymes. It grows in the large area of 'spiny desert' between Ampanihy and Ambovombe.

The two species of *Alluaudiopsis* are bushy rather than tree-like, growing to a height of only about 6 feet (2 m). *A. fiherenensis* has long, slim, succulent leaves and yellowish-white flowers. It prefers calcareous soils and is restricted to the Fiherenana river valley north of Tulear. *A. marnieriana* has brilliant carmine-red flowers; it grows only on red sandy soils near the coast to the north of Tulear.

The red coastal sands from the region of Morondava southwards to Tulear and beyond also constitute the typical habitat for the 'octopus tree' *Didierea madagascariensis*, perhaps the most attractive member of the family. The adult plants resemble a rather small *Alluaudia procera*, but with much longer and thinner leaves of a paler, more glaucous green. These are arranged in dense rosettes of from six to ten, thickly clothing the stems. This is by far the most effectively protected member of the family, for the spines are long, needle-sharp and very numerous, being particularly crowded on juvenile plants which form a single upright stem. *D. trollii* differs by having a much-branched juvenile state with curved stems which creep over the earth like a

The octopus tree Didierea madagascariensis *is the most attractive member of the Didiereaceae, growing mainly on the coastal red sands to the north and south of Tulear. In this locality, on the edge of the town, the trees are being cut down for firewood.*

grounded octopus (similar to the cactus *Stenocereus eruca* — another example of convergence). These eventually die back when the mature trunk begins to develop, resulting in an adult plant which is similar to *D. madagascariensis*. *D. trollii* occurs to the south of its relative, from Lake Tsimanampetsotsa to the Mandrare river.

FAMILY EUPHORBIACEAE

In Madagascar, the succulent members of this family all belong to the widespread genus *Euphorbia*. All are endemic, save the tree-like *Euphorbia tirucalli* which was introduced from Africa. Many of the Madagascan species, especially the large bushy or tree-like forms which are such a prominent element of the southern 'spiny desert' (more correctly called the *Euphorbia*-Didiereaceae bush), are not truly succulent but rather woody succulent. Smaller species, with genuinely succulent stems reminiscent of many African examples, are found further north, usually growing on limestone outcrops. In the central region, there are several species in which succulence is present as an underground caudex or tuber.

The southern dry bush is often composed largely of so-called 'coralliform' types of *Euphorbia*. In age these develop a woody trunk, topped by a brush of smooth green branches which appear to be leafless. A closer

Top: **The 'sausage bush' Euphorbia oncoclada** *is a typical consituent of the southern dry bush.*

Above: **Euphorbia alluaudii** *in flower in the summer wet season. This is one of the most abundant woody succulent species in the southern dry bush.*

inspection, however, reveals numerous brown scales on the stems; these scales are actually much-reduced leaves. The most attractive and intriguing member of this group is the 'sausage bush' *E. oncoclada* which is a conspicuous feature of the dry bush on the plateau to the north-east of Tulear. It forms a bush or dwarf tree up to 13 feet (4 m) high in which the finger-like, matt pale-green, wax-veneered stems are pinched-in at irregular intervals so that the whole assembly resembles a string of small sausages. The stem constrictions represent annual growth while the numerous scattered brown dots across the surface are the scars left by shedding of the minute, scale-like leaves.

E. alluaudii (= *E. leucodendron*) is a closely related plant with no constrictions in the multibranched stems which are a much shinier, brighter shade of green. It is also larger, up to 16 feet (5 m) high, and is a widespread component of the southern dry bush. *E. plagiantha*, from the region around Tulear, has a dense brush of greyish-green, leafless stems crowning a trunk which, with its peeling, greyish-brown bark, could easily be taken for a birch tree (*Betula*). The thick blackish bark on the robust trunk of *E. enterophora* is similarly misleading, and could readily be identified as a European stone pine *Pinus pinea*. It is the dense bushy crown of slender, dark-green, leafless branches which gives away its true nature. Yet, from a distance, the resemblance to a stone pine is again compelling, both in the umbrella-like shape of the crown and in the size, for this is the largest of the coral-like euphorbias, reaching a height of 66 feet (20 m). The subspecies (ssp) *E. e. enterophora* is a typical member of the southern dry forest, in which it is often the principal element. The subspecies *E. e. crassa* is restricted to an area in far-away central Madagascar, south of Fianarantsoa, where it grows on granite inselbergs. It is smaller, seldom forming a proper trunk, and the young growth is covered in a gingery pubescence which is soon shed.

These plants all form a non-spiny element in the 'spiny desert', leaving it to Didiereaceae to provide the hostile component. Not all the Madagascan euphorbias are so poorly armed, and pushing through a dense stand of *E. stenoclada* would be far from pleasant. This species forms a low, noticeably flat-topped bush or small branching tree with blackish bark. The slim branches and the much-reduced leaves have been converted into hard sharp thorns. It always seems to grow on calcareous soils, usually near the sea, and can easily be seen by anyone catching a flight at Tulear airport, where it grows abundantly on the coastal sands. By contrast, on granite rocks near Tulear, a form of this species which is thornless has been discovered. Much further north, near Ambatofinandrahana, to the north-west of Fianarantsoa, in a very isolated locality, grows *E. s. ambatofinandrahana*, restricted to outcrops of cipolin limestone surrounded by the desolate grasslands of the Hauts Plateaux. This most interesting plant, with its very disjointed habitat, is virtually spineless.

With its slim, arching, leaf-covered stems, branching strongly from the base, *Euphorbia didierioides* is another fascinating plant of the Hauts Plateaux. In its general aspect it bears an uncanny resemblance to the American ocotillo *Fouquieria splendens*, giving us yet another impressive example of convergence. The stems of *E. didierioides* reach a height of around 13 feet (4 m), sticking up prominently from gneiss rocks in the grassy landscape between Ambalavao and Ihosy. The branches themselves have a strange, rather untidy appearance because they are covered with short branchlets. These also bristle with long spines, making the whole branch extremely prickly and unpleasant to handle. The small, pale-green leaves which clothe the stems in the wet season drop off during the long dry winter, leaving the branches bare, save for the dense armament of spines defiantly resisting the onslaughts of the zebu. Unfortunately spines provide scant protection against a far worse enemy, the inevitable fires which rage across this area every year to supply green shoots for these same cattle, threatening the long-term survival of this unique plant.

Euphorbia guillauminiana is a lower-growing plant which is closer in appearance to some of the African euphorbias than anything mentioned so far. It grows only on rock-strewn fields of basalt in the north-west near Analalava, in open, savanna-like patches between pockets of dry forest. The short spiny stems branch

The 'crown of thorns' Euphorbia milii *is the most variable member of the genus in Madagascar. This form with small cream flowers forms low dense mats on sun-baked gneiss rocks on top of Windsor Castle near Diégo Suarez.*

profusely to form squat bushes up to 28 inches (70 cm) high and 3 feet (1 m) across. During the dry season, these are leafless, and the hoary stems gleam starkly in the uninterrupted winter sunshine. At the onset of the rains, bright-green tufts of leaves sprout from the tips of each stem, completely transforming the whole plant into an unrecognizable, leafy hummock.

Madagascar's most widespread species *E. milii* (= *E. splendens*) the 'crown of thorns' exhibits a similar growth form. With a distribution extending over much of the highlands, from north of Diégo Suarez down to near the southern tip of the island, it is not surprising that this plant has evolved a confusing complex of subspecies, each confined to its own rocky outpost. Regardless of its other variations, it always has long sharp thorns, formed by modification of the stipules of the deciduous leaves. The leaves themselves are produced mainly at the tips of the shoots, rendering the plants most attractive during the rainy season, although the flowers usually arise during the leafless dry period. The blooms are often produced en masse, covering the plant in a carpet of red, yellow or white, depending on the subspecies. A robust-stemmed, red-flowered form is widely planted along the streets in Madagascan towns, and in gardens. In the wild, *E. milii* usually forms low mats up to 3 feet (1 m) or more across of crowded twig-like stems. The chosen habitat is normally on exposed rocks, such as the granite inselbergs of central Madagascar, or the limestone outcrop of Windsor Castle in the far north. There are currently 13 named subspecies, as well as

With its attractively marked stems and long shaggy spines,
Euphorbia viguieri *is one of the most attractive members of the genus
in Madagascar. The bright scarlet flowers are produced during the
dry season in June and July. This form is quite common in rocky
places, often in woodland, in the region around Diégo Suarez.*

one mode at a time. The var. *viguieri* is abundant on
Windsor Castle, where it flowers in June; it also grows
on the mountains nearer to Diégo Suarez, often in
shady woodland. Three other varieties have been
named, each differing in a number of small details.
The var. *vilanandrensis* from Reserve Naturelle No. 8;
var. *ankarafantsiensis* from Ankarafantsika; var.
cupuroniana from Ankara de Diégo; and var.
tsimbazazae from an unknown locality, described
from a plant in the zoological gardens in
Antananarivo.

Just 25 miles (40 km) to the south-west of Diégo
Suarez lies the fascinating limestone massif of
Ankarana, with its spectacular wilderness of limestone
pinnacles or 'tsingy'. This is a superb area for
succulents. The prize here is *E. pachypodioides*,
endemic to these mountains and, for many years one
of the prime targets for collectors of succulent plants.
Unfortunately, this demand has hitherto been satisfied
by ripping plants out of their protected (theoretically)
habitat. Thankfully, however, in recent years,
thousands of seed-raised plants have been brought on
to the market by European nurseries, so pressures on
the wild populations should now be reduced, or even
eliminated. The plants are rooted in tiny pockets of
humus trapped on the inimical sun-baked rock chaos
of the open tsingy. They are common enough within
this localized habitat, with plenty of evidence of
natural regeneration through seedlings. The erect
green stems form a narrow cylinder, tapering towards
the apex, 2 inches (5 cm) broad at the base and
reaching a height of 20 inches (50 cm) or more; large
plants often curve and lean with age. The apex is
covered with short thorns, and also sprouts during the

several plants, such as *E. fianarantsoae* and *E.
duranii,* which undoubtedly belong to this group, and
merely require demotion to the status of subspecies.

Anyone wishing to make close acquaintance with
some of the most truly succulent, dwarf, non-woody
members of the genus must make a pilgrimage to the
north. Perhaps the most attractive of all, and the most
'typical' example of a truly succulent *Euphorbia* in
Madagascar, is the very ornamental *E. viguieri*. The
thickened stems are green and firm-fleshed rather than
woody, and carry out the majority of the plant's
photosynthesis and transpiration in true succulent
style, aided only in the wet season by a tuft of broad
green leaves which graces the apex of the stem. As
they wither and die each year, these leaves bequeath
to the stem a series of prominent pale scars neatly
composed in five vertical rows, giving a most
elaborate variegated appearance. The long, whitish
thorns are divided so that they sprout a number of
smaller thorns, the whole very decorative effect being
further enhanced by the showy scarlet flowers, which
are produced on long peduncles during the leafless
dry-season state. The flowers can be male, female or
hermaphrodite, individual plants often exhibiting only

An ancient specimen of **Euphorbia pachypodioides** *growing
on the 'tsingy' limestones of Ankarana Special Reserve. In its
dry-season state the plant is leafless.*

The strange **Euphorbia ankarensis** *produces its rather attractive flowers during the leafless dry-season state. This plant is found on limestone in the north, particularly in the Ankarana massif.*

drenched cliffs of the Montagne des Français and Windsor Castle. The stems always have a spiral tendency (also occasionally found in the type), but the leaves are smaller and the inflorescence is a dull yellowish green.

At the opposite end of the island, among the sand dunes and *Alluaudia* forests of the extreme south, grows a group of euphorbias quite unlike anything mentioned so far. At first glance, they may not even be obviously succulent, as the water-storing tuber is wholly or partly concealed beneath the ground. Large numbers of erect or creeping, woody, twig-like shoots sprout from this, bearing at their tips a rosette of thick, semi-succulent leaves. In *E. cap-santemariensis* from the windswept limestone plateau of Cap Ste Marie, the dark green leaves have attractively crenellated margins. Unfortunately, this species has been the subject of a craze among western collectors, resulting in the extraction from habitat of large numbers of plants just to satisfy the seemingly insatiable demand for rare wild succulents. *E. tulearensis* was originally described as a variety of this species, but has now been promoted to specific status because of the unique nature of its leaves, which are covered in tiny wax-enveloped papillae. These occur in such density as to lend the leaf a peculiar greyish-green, almost frosted sheen, which is rendered very decorative by the silvery undulate leaf margin. This plant was originally described from the foot of Table Mountain, *La Table*, near Tulear, growing on limestone beneath bushes. It seems to have been swiftly collected-out here, suffering the all-too-frequent fate following

Madagascan succulents are growing in popularity among enthusiasts in Europe and America. This has led to considerable pressure on wild populations to satisfy the demand for rare field-collected plants, such as this **Euphorbia cap-santemariensis**

wet season a number of quite large, dark-green leaves with dull red undersides. The inflorescence is borne at the tip of a long stalk, and is small and far less attractive than in *E. viguieri*.

Where *E. pachypodioides* seems always to grow right out on the hot open tsingy, *E. ankarensis* prefers shadier conditions beneath small trees and bushes, usually where some reasonable depth of soil has accumulated over the bare limestone. During the dry season, it looks like nothing more than a rather twisted stick, the absence of leaves reducing it to a bare spineless stem, covered in greyish-brown, rather corky bark bearing the numerous scars of previous years' leaves. A tuft of these long-stalked, rather downy, dull-green leaves decorates the apex of the plant during the rainy season. The quite attractive, short-stalked, pinkish-green inflorescences appear during the dry season in May and June, after the leaves have been shed. This offbeat plant is very common in the open dwarf forest on the tsingy, but also occurs outside Ankarana. On the Montagne des Français near Diégo Suarez it is much smaller, protruding like a small broken stick from a carpet of humus in deep woodland shade.

A third species found on Ankarana's tsingy is the handsome *E. neohumbertii* var. *neohumbertii*. It, too, prefers the shadier nooks, but chooses barer, less humus-laden rocks than *E. ankarensis*. The finger-thick, sparingly branched stems are usually five-sided and reach a height of 20 inches (50 cm). They are highly decorative, for each year's deciduous foliage leaves behind a neat set of scars, appearing as regular white imprints up the stem. The large terminal leaves appear during the wet season, although the brilliant red inflorescences are borne towards the end of the winter drought. The var. *aureo-viridiflora* is a more prolifically branching plant which clings to the sun-

publication of a precise locality for any new species of succulent, whatever the country of origin. Luckily *E. tulearensis* has since been found elsewhere, but it is certainly very rare and in possible danger, because any publicized populations could easily meet with the same fate as the first.

The large subterranean tuber is wanting in *E. cylindrifolia* which forms small mats in the dry country to the north of Fort Dauphin. The short, erect, rounded stems, topped by almost cylindrical greyish leaves, arise from numerous creeping and rooting underground stolons. A further mat-forming species, from coastal sand dunes near Fort Dauphin, is *E. francoisii*. The root is like a small turnip and the short aerial stems exhibit a remarkable variability in leaf shape and colour, even on the same plant. *E. decaryi*, also from sand dunes at Vinanibe near Fort Dauphin, has a similar mode of growth, but the stems are curiously angled, a shape derived from the remnants of the leaf stipules, which grow in vertical rows. The var. *spirosticha* is found further inland in forests of *Alluaudia* near Ampanihy. It is smaller, but differs mainly in its rounded rather than angled stems as the leaves occur in a spiral arrangement, resulting eventually in a roundish, tuberculate stem. The related *E. parvicyathophora* was described in 1986, from plants discovered in pockets of soil in crevices on massive limestone cliffs on the south bank of the Fiherenana river, east of Tulear. This species has broader, thinner, brighter-green leaves than any of its

relatives, a noticeably bristly stem and the smallest inflorescences in the group. A unique feature is the production of tubers at random intervals along the roots, each tuber capable of giving rise to above-ground stems. Yet another allied plant from the same overall region, *E. ambovombensis* was described only in 1987. The plant produces a potato-like underground tuber, arising from which is a small number of twiggy stems, tipped by rather broad, shiny, undulate-margined, deciduous leaves. The stem is rounded and nearly smooth, in contrast to the varieties of *E. decaryi*. This new discovery appears to have a strange ecological preference, for it grows only in deep black humus in the very heavy shade of bushes and small trees near Ambovombe.

Succulence is even less obvious in the truly geophytic species, such as *E. primulifolia* and *E. quartziticola* of the Hauts Plateaux. In these species, water storage takes place in a large, tuberous root which is completely buried in the ground. During most of the dry season, its location is betrayed only by the remnants of dried leaves and flowers stuck in the soil above the tuber but, after the rains, a conspicuous rosette of leaves sprouts forth. In *E. primulifolia* the large broad leaves are pale green, and could easily be

Aloe vaombe is one of the tallest Madagascan aloes, growing to a height of 10 feet (3 m) or more. It is widely distributed in the dry country of the south, where the conspicuous red flowers provide a welcome splash of colour in the drab dry-season landscape in June and July.

mistaken for a large daisy! The whitish inflorescences appear during the dry season in July, when the leaves have shrivelled and died. This species exhibits a high degree of variability, corresponding with its wide distribution on the grasslands of the Hauts Plateaux at around 4900 feet (1500 m), where the tuber is rooted in the hard red lateritic soils so typical of the region. It even occurs in the hills immediately surrounding Antananarivo. A rather similar plant, but with narrower, darker-green leaves and less showy flowers, is the recently described *E. moratii* which grows on sheer cliffs near Antsingy. In *E. quartziticola*, the tuber is often branched, and the shiny green leaves turn red before withering. This strange plant grows only on the quartz mountains of the Itremo in central Madagascar, along with the even weirder *Pachypodium brevicaule*.

FAMILY LILIACEAE

The succulent members of this large and varied family belong to two genera, *Lomatophyllum*, with nine species, and *Aloe*. These are distinguished from one another by the possession of fleshy non-splitting fruits in the former; in *Aloe* the fruits dry and split, releasing the lightweight seeds. There are around 60 *Aloe* species in Madagascar, all endemic, and none which is at all closely related to the 300 or so African representatives of the genus. They occur in dry open habitats, from north of Diégo Suarez down to the far south of the island. Numerous attractive species are characteristic of rocky outcrops on the Hauts Plateaux, and a few, such as the widespread yet local *A. macroclada*, actually grow rooted in the grasslands themselves. The establishment of young plants is difficult in such cases because of the regular burning. The thick juicy leaves of the adult plants can withstand the regular attrition from the flames with no more than singed tips and edges, but the tender seedlings often succumb to the inferno.

Aloe includes some of the best examples of the evolution of different subspecies in isolated habitats consisting of special kinds of rock. Thus, the large tree-like *A. capitata* var. *cipolinicola* grows only on outcrops of cipolin limestone protruding through the surrounding grasslands near Ambatofinandrahana in central Madagascar. The tall stocky stems are enclosed in an untidy sheath of dead leaves. The flower spikes are branched and bear pom-poms of reddish-yellow flowers. The var. *quartziticola* is a smaller, stemless plant with grey to reddish-blue leaves, restricted to quartz on the Itremo mountains where, fortunately, it is still abundant. The var. *capitata* grows on granite outcrops near Antananarivo. It, too, is stemless, but larger than the previous variety, with darker, less attractive leaves and yellowish globular inflorescences. It is widespread in the central part of the highlands. In June, plants can be seen flowering from the Antananarivo-to-Tamatave railway, for the line passes through a zone where this species grows on the rocky railway cuttings and adjacent hillsides.

The smaller, and quite attractive *A. deltoideodonta* also varies somewhat. The nominate variety, with fairly long, narrow leaves, is widespread in rocky

places in the south. The var. *candicans* has broader, delta-shaped, rather waxy-bloomed leaves of a pale greyish green, which all curve upwards and inwards during the dry season to reduce water loss, rather like an umbrella opening and closing. The flower spike is rarely branched, appearing in April at the start of the dry season. This variety is abundant on smooth sloping gneiss rocks south of Ambalavao, particularly near Zazafotsy where it grows with several other larger kinds of *Aloe* and *Pachypodium densiflorum*. These other plants are in full flower during the height of the drought in July, when the crowded masses of *A. d.* var. *candicans* rosettes are shrivelled and tightly closed. *Aloe contigua* is a closely related but much larger plant which usually grows singly in full sun, particularly on the bare sandstone rocks of the Isalo mountains. In such an exposed situation it is an exceptionally beautiful plant, the rich terracotta leaves flushed with a hint of grey in response to the incessant bombardment by sun and wind. By the end of the dry season, they become very curled and shrivelled and much less attractive. The showy red flowers drooping from slim branching spikes appear in June and July during the winter drought.

Some of the dwarf species are very ornamental. *A. haworthioides* is named for the resemblance of its 1-3-inch (3-8-cm) wide rosettes to *Haworthia* plants

Aloe suarezensis *is common on the mountains around Diégo Suarez in the north, flowering in June.*

The handsome terracotta rosettes of Aloe contigua (= A. imalotensis, A. deltoideodonta var. contigua) *are characteristic features of the open rocky slopes of the Isalo mountains. The attractive scarlet flowers are produced during the height of the winter dry season.*

from South Africa. It grows on flat or gently sloping slabs of gneiss rocks in the central highlands, especially around Ivato. The narrowly triangular, upwardly radiating leaves bear a dense array of long, silvery white bristles, which help to camouflage the plant among carpets of *Fimbristylis* sedges. The flowers are unique in the genus, for it is the long projecting stamens which seem to advertise their attractions to pollinators, rather than the short, much-reduced petals. At Ivato, this tiny gem grows with the much larger and very striking *A. conifera* in which the bluish-red leaves form a rosette 12-16 inches (30-40 cm) across. The unbranched inflorescence is unusual in that the small yellow flowers are almost covered by the large floral bracts, giving the whole assembly a cone-like appearance. *A. bulbillifera*, from the north-west near Mahajanga, is a large plant with a tall inflorescence of scarlet flowers with yellow tips. Most of these fail to set seed, and the plant reproduces mainly from the numerous bulbils which develop from the flower stalks. Unfortunately, this interesting plant has become very rare because of the constant burning.

FAMILY CRASSULACEAE

With just a handful of exceptions, the succulent members of this family in Madagascar all belong to the genus *Kalanchoe*, with 60 species and numerous

varieties. Here it is the thickened leaves rather then fattened stems which perform the water-storing function. A few species, such as the 16-foot (5-m) high *K. arborescens* and *K. beharensis* from the dry forests of the south, resemble small trees. The majority are much smaller, and many of these are cultivated in Europe and America for their attractive leaves. One of the favourites is *K. tomentosa* in which the leaf shape exhibits a confusing degree of variability, ranging from long and narrow with a covering of relatively long silky hairs, to rather short and broad with a dense covering of felt. In the latter form, the toothed margins of the leaf apex are attractively decorated with patches of rusty brown hairs. In the wild, it forms a small bush up to 20 inches (50 cm) high and is a characteristic feature of the granite inselbergs of the Hauts Plateaux, near Fianarantsoa, for example. Small plants are often offered for sale to passengers in the long-distance taxi-brousses when they stop briefly at Antsirabe, along with the more usual produce of the area, apples and carrots. The similar-sized *K. integrifolia* has a stocky, woody trunk with numerous branches adorned with tufts of upward-pointing, very fleshy, sausage-shaped leaves which are not downy. It is a prominent feature of the bare quartzite rubble on the Itremo mountains. Another form with broader, flatter leaves grows on gneiss rocks near Ivato. As in most *Kalanchoe* species, the small, yellow flowers are not particularly showy, being borne in clusters at the tips of long stalks.

A brief search of virtually any patch of rocks in the southern part of the Hauts Plateaux is likely to yield mats of the pale-green leaves of *K. synsepala*. This species and *K. tetraphylla* are distinctive in being the only members of the genus which normally bear their inflorescences laterally from the leaf axils, rather than in a terminal position. In habitat the stems are short and stumpy, so that the broad fleshy leaves sit close against the ground. As in a number of other species (and many related *Cotyledon* spp from South Africa), the leaves are extraordinarily variable in shape. The

Species of Kalanchoe *are often grown for their attractive leaves which usually have wavy margins of some darker colour contrasting with the green of the leaf. This is* Kalanchoe synsepala *growing on granite rocks near Zazafotsy. This species is widespread in such habitats in the south-central region of the Hauts Plateaux.*

margins can be smooth or strongly toothed, or even prominently dissected (var. *dissecta*); the leaf tip rounded or pointed; the colour light green to darker greyish green; and even the leaf thickness and degree of succulence differ from one population to another. In fact, such is the bewildering extent of variation, that each population could easily be mistaken for a separate species. Within each population, however, there is noticeably little variation, because this plant employs a highly efficient method of vegetative reproduction. Long stolons appear from within the leaf axils, each bearing at its tip a miniature rosette, all primed and ready to root once it contacts the soil. Initially, the stolons are vertical, but the miniature plants at their tips steadily grow and become heavier, gradually bowing down their slender supports until they reach the ground. Once in contact with the substrate, they quickly root and take up an independent existence, upon which the stolon, its job done, withers and dies. The small white flowers are crowded into dense cymes, appearing in the dry season in May and June when a carpet of plants in bloom looks most attractive in the desiccated landscape.

K. *tetraphylla* is similar in bearing lateral inflorescences but has downy leaves and does not reproduce via stolons. It is a rare plant from gneiss rocks on the Hauts Plateaux. *K. eriophylla* is a tiny plant with hairy whitish leaves and small pink flowers. It grows only on a single rock outcrop on the Hauts Plateaux, and is regularly collected from here and sold in the markets, because it is said to bring happiness and prosperity to anyone who buys it. Not all the species are so highly succulent, however, and grow on exposed rocks in the drier areas. *K. campanulata, K. peltata* and *K. schizophylla* are thinner-leaved plants which inhabit the understorey of the eastern rainforest.

Kalanchoe (= *Bryophyllum*) *tubiflora* often merits a mention in biology text-books because it is one of the best examples of asexual, vegetative reproduction in the whole plant kingdom. Each of the long, almost cylindrical leaves bears at its tip a cluster of mini-plantlets, complete with tiny rootlets. These easily drop off and root to form miniature plants. The drooping, brilliant scarlet flowers on their tall stalks are among the most beautiful and conspicuous in the genus. During the dry season, these florid banners stick up among the sea of bleached grasses, adding a welcome splash of colour to the drab landscape. North of Ihosy the numerous flat granite slabs beside the RN7 are home to veritable rock gardens of succulents, including *Pachypodium densiflorum, Kalanchoe synsepala* and several kinds of *Aloe*. Pockets of soil overlying the smooth plates often support patches of low bush and small trees, providing the favoured habitat for one of the most beautiful of all kalanchoes, *K. orgyalis*. When posed against their bare-branched neighbours, the strongly branched bushes, which are up to 4 feet (1.2 m) high, are conspicuous by their attractive broad bronze-coloured leaves, which are up to 7 cm (3 in) long, although they are not as noticeably thickened and succulent as in many

The scarlet flowers of Kalanchoe tubiflora *contrast strongly with the browns and greys of the dry season landscape in July. This interesting plant is widespread in the south-central region of the Hauts Plateaux.*

species. Shrivelling of the leaves is very pronounced in this, as in most kalanchoes, towards the end of the dry season, and April is probably the best time to see these decorative plants in their natural habitat. They are not restricted to the southern part of the Hauts Plateaux or the southern dry bush; some kinds grow in mountain forests, others in the 'spiny desert' and several more, such as *K. suarezensis*, on the mountains in the far north around Diégo Suarez. This plant has pale-green leaves and white flowers which appear in May.

Miscellaneous succulents

Thirty succulent representatives of the enormous worldwide genus *Senecio* (Compositae) occur in Madagascar, growing on rocks or as small bushes in the southern spiny forests. As in *Kalanchoe* species, it is the leaves which are succulent, and modifications to their shape to serve the water-storing function are so similar in the two genera that the inexpert might have difficulty in assigning a non-flowering plant to its correct family. The unmistakably composite yellow flower heads in *Senecio* are absolutely diagnostic, however. The 8-12-inch (20-30-cm) tall *S. quartziticolus* is yet another member of the rich succulent flora of the quartz Itremo mountains in central Madagascar.

Succulent members of the cucumber family Cucurbitaceae are relatively few in number. Xerisicyos danguyi, with its fat coin-like leaves, is one of the most characteristic members of the southern dry bush.

The milkweed family Asclepiadaceae contains numerous rather straggling semi-succulent species in Madagascar. This is Folotsia floribundum *in flower on the Montagne des Français near Diégo Suarez.*

In the grape family, Vitaceae, stem succulence is developed to a bizarre degree in various species of *Cyphostemma*, in which the grossly bulbous bases taper off suddenly into a long, twisted, vine-like stem. Certain species could easily be confused with bottle lianas in the genus *Adenia*, rather grotesque plants which belong to the passion-flower family Passifloraceae. There are five species in Madagascar, mostly resembling nothing much more than a lump of

During the long dry season, Adenia *plants resemble lumps of rock with little hint of their vegetable nature. One of the few succulent members of the passionflower family Passifloraceae, this* Adenia neohumbertii *is growing on 'tsingy' limestone in the Ankarana massif.*

grey rock, hardly different from the boulders among which they often grow. A tuft of foliage sprouting from this inorganic-seeming carbuncle betrays its vegetable origin during the wet season, although the greenish-brown flowers are small and inconspicuous. The Asclepiadaceae or milkweed family contains many small, highly succulent species in Africa and Arabia, but the Madagascan examples in the genera *Ceropegia* (7 species), *Cynanchum* (20 spp), *Folotsia* (5 spp), *Karimbolea* (1 sp), *Sarcostemma* (3 spp) and *Stapelianthus* (8 spp) are mostly rather slim-stemmed plants straggling along the ground or scrambling over bushes. At first sight, few of them would be taken for succulents, particularly when in a shrivelled state during the dry season. In some species, notably in *Ceropegia*, the thin stems arise from a plump subterranean caudex which performs the water-storing function.

Succulent trees

A number of trees develop bloated trunks filled with pulpy tissues which hold water, the most famous of which are the baobabs in the family Bombacaceae. There are seven species in Madagascar, compared with just one, *Adansonia digitata*, in the whole of Africa. This species, with its fat grey trunk resembling a vegetable elephant, is also found in Madagascar, but only in the north near Mahajanga. Here, on the boulevard which runs along the seafront, there is a famous and very ancient specimen measuring 46 feet (14 m) around the base of the trunk. The most majestic of the island's baobabs, however, is the endemic *A. grandidieri*, a much more statuesque, neater-looking tree with its more parallel-sided, dark brownish-grey, rather glossy trunk surmounted by a surprisingly small crown of short, thick, spreading branches. For much of the year, these are bare because the leaves start to appear only in late November, and have all fallen by the beginning of April. The timber is soft and pulpy and useless for construction; but in desperately lean years, the local people cleave open the fat trunks and feed the water-filled pulp to their scrawny cattle. Not surprisingly this species is very resistant to fire, and, when the forest around Morondava is felled and burned to create farmland, the baobabs are often left standing, for it is too much trouble to cut them down, and the fires hardly touch them.

North-east of Morondava, the flat landscape of small fields and lily-covered lakes is dotted with numerous huge examples of this monumental tree, still dominating the scene long after the original forest succumbed to human ravages. Alas, because no seedlings now have any chance of long-term survival, these spectacular vistas will eventually disappear as the unyielding vegetable behemoths gradually bow to advancing years. South of the town, the forests are dominated by thousands of these monsters, so that arriving by air at Morondava airport is a memorable experience as one gazes down in awe upon this landscape ruled by giants.

A. za is a much squatter tree with an untidy crown reaching a height of 49-66 feet (15-20 m) and yellow flowers. It is restricted to the basin of the Mandrare river in the far south, where it grows together with *Alluaudia ascendens*. *A. fony* or 'little baobab' is the smallest species, reaching only 16 feet (5 m) in height and often smaller. The trunk is grossly inflated and quite bizarre, while the flowers are spectacularly flamboyant, flame coloured with a contrasting bunch of yellow stamens. It is most abundant on the red coastal sands north of Tulear where it is a characteristic constituent of the *Didierea madagascariensis* forests; but it also grows occasionally on the limestones of the Mahafaly Plateau.

A. suarezensis is a more conventional-looking tree, with the trunk only marginally inflated. It is of local distribution in the far north, but easy enough to find close to Diégo Suarez because it grows on the nearby Montagne des Français where it is seen by tourists visiting the mountain or the popular beach beyond.

With its bulbous grey trunk, the bottle tree *Moringa drouhardii* is probably taken for a baobab by most visitors to the dry southern domain. The similarity is misleading, however, for this endemic tree is a member of the Moringaceae. Within the Pedaliaceae

*The statuesque **Adansonia grandidieri** is the largest of all baobabs. It is abundant in the forests around Morondava, although the specimens seen here are isolated survivors in a sea of cultivation.*

there are nine members of the genus *Uncarina* with succulent water-storing trunks. The name *Harpagophytum*, or harpoon plant, formerly bestowed on this genus (but now replaced by *Uncarina*), aptly sums up the nature of the fruits which must be among the most hostile in the plant kingdom. They are liberally furnished with strong spines tipped by recurved hooks. The local inhabitants use piles of them surrounding some smelly bait to ensnare rodents or other small mammals; while, mounted at the tips of long poles, these lethal burrs are used as 'fishing wands' to snatch roosting flying foxes *Pteropus rufus* from cave roofs.

Economic uses of plants

Anyone who has done much travelling in the tropics will be familiar already with at least one Madagascan plant, the flamboyant tree *Delonix regia*, one of the most widely planted tropical ornamentals. It is particularly valued for the blaze of colour which envelopes the tree when the profusion of flame-coloured flowers appears. In its native home, it is quite local, growing in inaccessible areas on the dry limestones of the west, where few botanists have been fortunate enough to see it in flower in its wild surroundings.

One of the most newsworthy plants in recent years has been the Madagascar rosy periwinkle *Catharanthus roseus*, a member of the Apocynaceae. This widespread plant of the dry south contains over 75 different alkaloids, complex chemical compounds which include such familiar products as caffeine (by the coffee bush) and nicotine (by tobacco plants). Two of the alkaloids produced by the rosy periwinkle are now used in the treatment of leukaemia and other cancers in children, giving a very much higher cure rate than any previous drugs had managed.

The flamboyant tree **Delonix regia** *is one of the most widely planted ornamental trees in the tropics. Yet few people realize that it originally came from Madagascar where it is endemic to the dry limestone massifs of the north-west.*

Unfortunately, the success of this plant in treating the sick children of rich western countries has done nothing to benefit the poor people of the plant's source, Madagascar. This is because the multimillion dollar annual worldwide sales of the anti-leukaemia drug are derived from stocks of the rosy periwinkle cultivated outside Madagascar. Considerable effort is currently being directed towards the science of ethnobotany in Madagascar, cashing in on the vast fund of knowledge amassed by the local people to tell us about the medicinal values of the plants in their forests. But without the forests, these priceless resources will be lost to everyone, and it is to be hoped that at least some material benefits stemming from any future 'wonder drug' discoveries will find their way to the local people, perhaps reducing the likelihood that all the forests will one day be reduced to ashes.

Madagascar is also extremely rich in wild species of coffee *Coffea* spp, with more than 50 species, all found in the eastern rainforests, where some are now already so rare that they probably still exist only within reserves. Coffee (produced by *Coffea arabica*, a native of Ethiopia) is one of the world's most valuable trading commodities. The burgeoning interest in a healthy diet, which is such a feature of late twentieth-century western civilization, could lead to considerable interest in some of the wild Madagascan coffees, because their beans are said to be very low in caffeine. Their use in hybridization could also be vital in introducing disease resistance into the cultivated strains of coffee now widespread around the world.

Chapter 3
The Invertebrates

More than 90 per cent of the world's animal species are invertebrates — animals, such as insects or slugs, without backbones. The overwhelming majority of these belong to just one class, the insects, with a total number of species reaching anything up to 30 million, depending on whose estimate is believed. Even the more conservative assessments consider at least five million to be likely. Compare this with the mere 13,000 different species which the mammals and birds combined can muster, and you begin to appreciate why entomologists are only just beginning to come to grips with the insect life to be found just within Madagascar. Some of the other classes of invertebrates are even less well known than the insects, and the information given here tends to reflect the current state of our knowledge within each group.

Large colourful flatworms up to 6 inches (15 cm) long crawl around in the eastern rainforests during wet weather.

Worms and snails

Because they live underground, most annelid worms are seldom seen, the unwelcome exceptions being the myriads of tiny leeches which can make life in the eastern rainforests unpleasant during the wet season. Their small size enables these persistent pests to insinuate themselves through the narrowest of crannies in clothing, and the first evidence of their presence may be a spreading red stain across a shirt front or a squelchy feeling in the boots as blood from several wounds seeps into them. Unlike mosquitoes, leeches are just a nuisance rather than life threatening, because they do not transmit diseases. The main problem is the infuriatingly irritating itchiness around the site of the wound for a couple of days afterwards, inducing the sufferer to scratch the offending area – this is a common way to bring on a tropical sore which can be very unpleasant.

Much more conspicuous than the small grey leeches are various kinds of flamboyantly coloured flatworms (Planaria) which ooze their way across the damp rainforest floor during a tropical downpour. Some of these hammer-headed monsters, which can reach a length of 6 inches (15 cm), may be surprisingly beautiful with their black-and-red or mustard-and-brown striping.

Snails and slugs are also active during wet conditions, hiding away under leaves or in the soil during dry weather. Madagascar has one of the richest and most interesting land-snail faunas in the world, currently estimated at about 380 species, although this will undoubtedly rise in the future. No fewer than 361 of these are endemic, a status shared by 11 of the 56 genera, while the dominant families are completely different from those in nearby Africa. The lime-rich areas of the south, west and north hold the greatest number of species, especially the north, which boasts over half the known total. Here the richest and most valuable locality is the Tsaratanana massif where the endemic molluscan riches rival those of its flora.

The largest genus *Tropidophora* contains 89 species, 87 of which are endemic, varying widely in the shape of the shell, from elongate and conical to round and flat. More than 50 of these are of very narrow distribution, so would be threatened if a major alteration of their habitat, such as conversion to farmland or grassland, were to occur. *Clavator* contains 12 species of snails with elongated shells which are among the most characteristic snails of the island. Fossils in this genus are known from Africa, and are used to date geological strata. Unfortunately the snail most often seen by visitors is the introduced African giant snail *Achatina fulica*, which is now very widespread, and has also become a pernicious pest in vanilla plantations on the east coast. To make matters worse, predatory snails introduced in an effort to control *Achatina* could pose a severe threat to the rare indigenous snails.

Arachnids — spiders and scorpions

Scorpions are generally small and seldom seen in Madagascar, although one or two of the dozen or so

*Left: **The scorpion-spider Arachnura scorpionioides (Araneidae) is so-called because of the scorpion-like shape of its 'tail'. The function of this 'tail' is not to sting, however, but to disguise the spider's true nature by resembling a leaf stalk as it hangs head-downwards in its small web. This is usually placed near the ground on a fern-covered bank in rainforest. In this pose the spider lookes like a small shrivelled leaf caught in its web, the more so as it hangs beneath a string of strategically placed detritus consisting of the husks of former prey and one or two heavily disguised egg sacs. It is widespread in tropical Africa.***

*Below left: **There are numerous species of jumping spiders (Salticidae) in Madagascar. This small but pretty Thyena species is close to T. tamatavica from the east coast and may be a form of it. It was photographed in rainforest near Antananarivo and is an endemic.***

*Below: **The crab spider Phrynarachne rugosa (Thomisidae) sits in full view on rainforest leaves mimicking a brown bird dropping. Its deception is far more convincing to the naked eye than to the revealing combination of flash and macrolens used to take the photograph. This species is widespread in Africa and there are related species which also mimic bird droppings in Australasia.***

known species may make their presence felt rather than seen in the most painful way. This applies in particular to one or two small delicately built, brownish-yellow species from the western forests — their sting is traumatic. During two years at Ampijeroa, Don Read has been unlucky enough to be stung twice (once on the foot, once on the leg after kneeling down to catch a lizard) by one of these skinny little creatures. On both occasions this took place at night when the scorpions are active — during the day they hide away in crevices and are less of a risk. Don describes the pain as 'almost unsupportable', so bad in fact that he just did not know what to do to resist it, and spent the night walking up and down in an effort to ease the suffering. Similar symptoms are reported for another small species which crept under the groundsheets of a film crew camped in Ankarana Special Reserve and stung the unfortunate occupants through the sheet as they crawled inside. A mat spread over the bottom of the tent should solve this problem, and visitors to the dry forests are advised to check inside boots before putting them on and not to put hands into clothing or backpacks which have been left overnight where scorpions could crawl inside.

Spiders are far more conspicuous, and much more is known about them, although so much work still remains to be done that no reliable estimate is available of the total number of species in Madagascar. The current total of around 430 species in 39 families undoubtedly bears little resemblance to the real number. Even the number of families is open to question, because the absence of such characteristic widespread groups as the Linyphiidae and Mimetidae may be due to under collecting, rather than to a genuine lack. In this respect, it was only in quite recent times that two subfamilies of the Araneidae, the Cyrtarachninae and Mastophorinae were found to be present.

Recent efforts at thorough collecting in other groups has yielded some interesting results. The Archaeidae is one of the most ancient of the world's spider families, the type species having being described from Baltic amber several million years old, rather than from a living specimen! It is a tiny family, with seven species in Madagascar, one in South Africa, three in Australia, five in New Zealand and one (probably of this family) on the extreme southern tip of South America. This kind of distribution is exactly what would be expected from an ancient family dating from before the splitting up of Gondwanaland, and now hanging on only in small numbers in widely separated parts of the globe. Of the seven Madagascan species, one, *Archaea godfreyi* is also found in South Africa. Several of the others have only been recently described after intensive searches for members of this family on the island. They are among the most grotesque of all spiders, with grossly enlarged chelicerae (pincer-like appendages) jutting from a head which is itself perched atop a bizarre upward protrusion of the cephalothorax (head-body structure). Unfortunately, such intriguing physical eccentricity can be but little appreciated with the naked eye because

The green lynx spider Peucetia madagascariensis *(Oxyopidae) is found in the eastern rainforests. The similar-looking* P. lucasii *is more widespread, occurring widely in both wet and dry habitats. Both species are endemics.*

these strange little monsters are only about 0.14 inch (3.5 mm) long. *A. godfreyi* spends its life among leaf-litter on the ground, a habit also found in all the other species living outside Madagascar.

The Madagascan endemics are special in living on foliage in the forest shrub layer, often among a jumble of debris caught in the leaf bases of a pandan palm, or among a miniature forest of mosses and lichens. The sexes are very similar, a relatively unusual situation in spiders, and their prey consists exclusively of other spiders. The female totes her egg sac around attached to the foot of her third leg, until she senses that the young are about to hatch. She then fixes the egg sac to a twig and assists her babies' passage into the world by teasing open some of the sac's strongly woven threads. The number of eggs laid is quite small, only 6-16 being enclosed within the silken envelope. Several species of *Archaea* are widespread in the eastern rainforests, at Périnet, for example, although to find one requires considerable effort in searching. *A. paulini* is a recently recognized addition to the extensive endemic fauna of Andohahela.

The *Peucetia* green lynx-spiders are the largest and most attractive examples of the numerous endemic species of Oxyopidae. *P. lucasii* is very widespread in wet and dry habitats; while the very similar-looking *P. madagascariensis* is more typical of the shady eastern rainforests. Both of them are basically green, with varying amounts of red on the abdomen. The females build a nest among leaves and stand guard over their egg sacs, remaining on sentry duty over their fuzz of tiny, newly hatched babies until their first moult, when they disperse.

The most conspicuous spiders on the island are some of the large orb-web builders in the family

The endemic Argiope coquereli *is closely related to A.* lobata *which enjoys a very wide distribution in Africa. This large female was photographed in the Kirindy forest north of Morondava.*

Araneidae. The prize for the largest web of all is difficult to allocate because *Nephila madagascariensis* and various species of *Caerostris* are capable of spanning the most amazingly yawning gaps with their impressive silken handiwork. The squat brown species of *Caerostris* are particularly fond of placing their webs in the open sunny flight lines above forest streams. Thus, the airspace over the stream below *la grande cascade* in Montagne d'Ambre presents a considerable hazard to any flying insect, so densely is it packed with *Caerostris* webs glistening brightly above the turbulent waters. Anyone walking across the wooden bridge into Périnet reserve will probably notice the huge *Caerostris* webs spanning the slow-moving stream at this point. By taking measurements across the bridge, I calculated that the topmost strand of a nearby web measured nearly 16 feet (5 m) across. The plump spider usually sits head-downwards in the

Caerostris mitralis (Araneidae) is one of the commonest spiders in the eastern rainforests and even occurs in large numbers in Parc Tzimbazaza in Antananarivo. When at rest, this spider is particularly cryptic, mimicking a brown bump on a stem or leaf.

centre of these massive constructions, looking very much like a dead leaf which has become lodged in the web.

Nephila madagascariensis builds a large web of yellow silk. This is a much more handsome spider, at least the female is, and her large, sausage-shaped body, which is up to 1¼ inches (32 mm) long, is attractively patterned in black, white and pale yellow. The long gangly black legs are decorated with conspicuous tufts of hair. This jumbo-sized creature normally clings to the centre of her strong web, often accompanied by the tiny amber-coloured male. Few people would recognize his status as her consort, for he is a midget, perhaps only as little as a-thousandth of the female's weight. Not surprisingly, therefore, he looks like a completely different species. Yet his diminutive stature is his lifeline, for he fails to measure up to his fierce companion's minimum prey size, so she ignores him as he ambles casually around the web, even allowing him to scramble over her and to try to mate whenever he feels like it without showing so much as a tremor of reaction.

The tiny brown teardrop-shaped *Argyrodes* spiders (Theridiidae) which also live in her web in twos or threes are there only on sufferance, however. They are uninvited commensals that glean a risky living feeding at the ogress's table, sneaking up and latching on to her prey while she is too busily absorbed in her meal to notice their cautious arrival. As well as being the largest spider on the island, *N. madagascariensis* is also one of the commonest and most successful. It is particularly at home in clearings and along roadsides in the eastern rainforests, but it may also be very common on the hostile open grasslands of the Hauts Plateaux, wherever there are a few trees or bushes of sufficient stature to support the huge web.

Surprisingly, though, it is also found in mangrove swamps around the coast.

Members of the subfamily Gasteracanthinae are usually known as thorn spiders because of the spiky projections from the abdomen which are typical in most species. They are well represented in Madagascar, with several new species having been described within the last few years. The commonest species *Gasteracantha versicolor* is also found in Africa, and is one of a trio of closely related species which also includes the African *G. falcicornis* and *G. milvoides*. *G. versicolor* is very much a spider of the eastern rainforests, with just a single relict population in the forests on the Isalo mountains near Ranohira. The endemic subspecies *G. v. avaratrae* is widespread, and is common in the small patches of 'sacred woodlands' in the Hauts Plateaux near Anatananarivo; it is also quite at home in *Eucalyptus* plantations. The large web of *G. v. formosa* is a typical sight on the roadsides at Périnet and, on the whole, *G. versicolor* seems to prefer the more open spots in the forest.

The rather similar *G. sanguineolenta* is also widespread in Africa, and is so variable that 15 former specific names are now included in its synonymy. The subspecies *G. s. andrefanae* is widespread in Madagascar's western dry forests; *G. s. bigoti* lives in mangroves near Tulear; while *G. s. mangrovae* lives in the same habitat on Nosy Be. *G. rhomboidea madagascariensis* is another rainforest species, while *G. thorelli* is endemic to Nosy Be and Nosy Komba. The webs of all these larger species are often inhabited by the same *Argyrodes* commensals as are found in *Nephila* webs.

G. versicolor females lay up to 300 eggs in a single batch, although 180 is the average. They may not

The bizarre **Augusta glyphica** *(Araneaeidae : Gasteracanthinae) belongs to its own monotypic genus which is endemic to Madagascar. With its amazingly flattened body, it resembles a fleck of dead leaf which has become caught in an empty web. The web is placed on low vegetation in the eastern rainforests, generally in a shadier position than in the related* **Gasteracantha** *species.*

always manage even this, as they are taken by *Sceliphron* hunting wasps, which use the paralysed bodies of the spiders as 'stay-fresh' fodder for the developing larvae in their earthen cells. *Isoxya* is mainly an African and Madagascan genus with a single

The thorn spider **Gasteracantha versicolor formosa** *(Araneaeidae : Gasteracanthinae) is common in the more open parts of the forest and on roadsides at Périnet in the eastern rainforests. The species is found widely in Africa; the subspecies is endemic to Madagascar.*

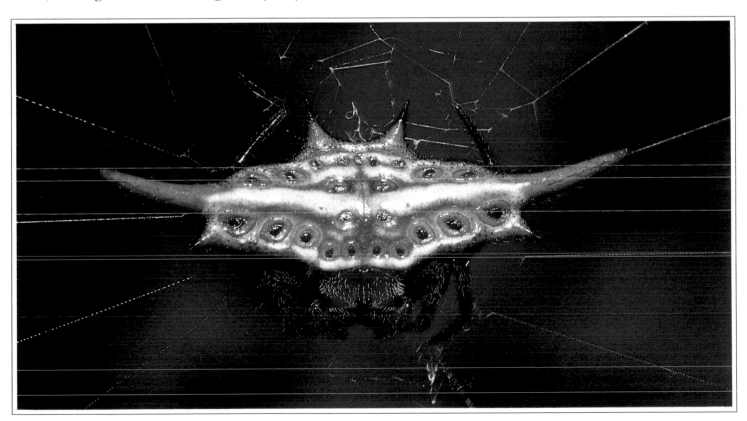

species in Sumatra and Java. The abdomen is more rounded than in *Gasteracantha*, and *Isoxya* are generally smaller spiders which build their webs in shadier places closer to the ground. *I. mahafalensis*, a close relative of the Angolan *I. mossamedensis*, lives in bushes in the far south, around Ampanihy, Fort Dauphin and Ambovombe. *I cowani* is widespread in the eastern rainforests, *I. milloti* is found only in Ankarana, and *I. renteri* is restricted to Lokobe reserve on Nosy Be and one or two localities on Nosy Komba. These two islands also provide the only known localities for *Madacantha nossibeana*, an endemic genus. It is widespread in the eastern rainforests and is the sole member of the genus in Madagascar, although there are two other species in Africa.

Some of the smallest members of the Araneidae are not without interest in a more cryptic kind of way. Several miniature species of *Cyclosa* contrive to make themselves as inconspicuous as possible within their webs. One rainforest species incorporates into the centre of its web a spiral of whitish silk which it decorates with bits of junk, such as the husks of former prey, and then settles down in such a position that its squat brown body resembles part of the confusing jumble of unappetizing garbage. A second species, with a much slimmer, rather elongated, grey-and-white body, constructs a vertical band of dense silk down the centre of its web, also integrating various cast-offs from its previous meals. One-third of the way down this band, the spider leaves a gap just wide enough to take its body as a snug fit when sitting head-downwards. The spider spends the day in full view in this pose, and anyone (or any predator) passing by would dismiss the web as empty. This spider is common in dry and in wet forests and similar kinds, which employ the same web-building strategy, are found in Africa and in South America.

One of the most celebrated spiders in Madagascar is the small *Olios coenobita* (Eusparassidae) which makes its home in snail shells on the dry Mahafaly plateau. As the shells litter the ground, and the spider lives up in bushes, it solves the housing problem by reeling in the chosen shell on a silken hoist.

Millipedes and centipedes

The 64 known species of chilopods or centipedes belong to 24 genera, most of which are widespread in tropical regions. Many of the smaller, more primitive, soil-living centipedes have close relatives in Australia, New Zealand, Polynesia and Chile — a typical Gondwanaland distribution. The large species of *Scolopendra* have been introduced and are found throughout the tropics; they are rather feared because they can administer a painful bite with their paired fangs which consist of modified front legs supplied with a hollow canal linked to venom sacs. In general, centipedes are seldom seen because they are strongly nocturnal, although my most abiding memory of these creatures in Madagascar is of a 2½-inch (6-cm) long, brilliant greenish-blue specimen running over my foot in broad daylight and quickly disappearing under a hut in the Kirindy forest near Morondava. This must

Giant millipedes up to 6 inches (15 cm) or more in length are a common sight in the eastern rainforests. Despite its bright warning coloration, this large species, which is an everyday sight in the rainforests at Ranomafana, is eaten by red-fronted lemurs. Every one of the numerous kinds of giant millipede is endemic to the island.

surely be one of the world's most spectacularly beautiful centipedes, and I regret that I was not able to photograph it.

Millipedes (Diplopoda) are seen far more often, and many extremely large kinds are a frequent sight as they meander slowly around through the forests during the day. The biggest of these can reach lengths of 6 inches (15 cm) or more, and may be decked out impressively in warning colours of black and orange. This bright uniform is supposed to be a memory prod to all-and-sundry, with 'millipedes-as-meals' on their minds, that the millipedes can fight back, by exuding droplets of poisons and distasteful quinones (in some species including hydrogen cyanide). This repulsive cocktail does not necessarily protect them from attack by brown lemurs (*see* Chapter 7), which have ways of making their unsavoury meal more palatable. When molested, the millipede reacts first by coiling up into a tight defensive spiral like a watch-spring, before

Huge **Sphaerotherium** *pill-millipedes the size of golf balls (when rolled-up defensively) abound in the west and in dry forests. This individual is grazing on rotten wood in gallery forest in the Berenty Private Reserve in the south-east.*

further rough handling stimulates the production of its nasty counter-measures.

Millipedes are harmless vegetarians, and these multilegged beasts trundle around over mossy logs and dead leaves looking for suitable vegetable matter to eat. Millipede taxonomy is so complex that it is difficult even to assign a genus with any degree of certainty, although the gaudy black-and-orange giant, which is particularly common in the rainforests at Ranomafana, is probably a species of *Aphistogoniulus*, while the genus *Spirostreptus* is well represented in Madagascar by numerous large species.

Huge *Sphaerotherium* pill-millipedes which, when rolled up, reach almost the size of a golf ball, abound in most Madagascan forests. They have much shorter, broader, more squatly profiled bodies and amble around very slowly to graze on rotten wood and algae. They are most reluctant to open up once they have rolled into a ball, a process in which the parts of the body fit so snugly together that the exterior is virtually smooth and chink-free. They come in a variety of colours, including russet, brownish black, black, brown and orange and deep bottle green. Despite their warning colours, they are also eaten by brown lemurs, which treat them with considerably greater relish than they manage with the longer kinds, crunching them up like rather tough and scaly figs.

The insects

The more research that is carried out on the Madagascan insect fauna, the more it is realized just how rich and unique it is. Insect evolution has been proceeding apace in Madagascar for a very long time and, with the island's large variety of available ecological niches, a huge number of species has arisen. Most of these are endemic to Madagascar, and there is an accompanying high rate of endemism to a particular locality. Insect numbers reach their peak during the wettest season from January to March, declining rapidly as the habitat dries out, so that the dry western and southern forests have little to offer during the long dry season, although there is always some insect activity to be seen in the eastern rainforests.

ODONATA — DRAGONFLIES AND DAMSELFLIES

This group is quite well represented in Madagascar, which is relatively much richer in these insects than any similar-sized African country. There are 76 species of dragonflies (Anisoptera) in 36 genera and rather more damselflies (Zygoptera), although much more work remains to be done on the latter, and numerous new species will probably be added.

Of the 76 dragonfly species, 39 are widespread in Africa, and many of these also enjoy a much wider distribution outside that continent. Of the genera, *Paragomphus, Phyllomacromia, Orthetrum, Trithemis* and *Zygonyx* are all widespread in Africa; *Hemicordulia* is of Oriental and New Guinean origin; *Nesocordulia* and *Libellulosoma* have affinities with the South American genera *Neocordulia* and *Aeschnosoma*. Visitors from Europe may be surprised

Madagascar is rich in members of the order Odonata, although the number of endemic damselflies (Zygoptera) far exceeds the total of endemic dragonflies (Anisoptera), many of which are wide-ranging migrants. Crocothemis sanguinolenta *is an endemic dragonfly from lakes in the eastern rainforests and on the Hauts Plateaux.*

to see the familiar blue form of the emperor dragonfly *Anax imperator* flashing past in some Madagascan forest glade; this species is very wide ranging. *Trithemis annulata* is found over the whole of Africa up to the Mediterranean and into Egypt, while *Pantala flavescens* is pantropical.

The rate of endemism in the Zygoptera is much higher, and all save eight species are restricted to Madagascar. This is not surprising, because damselflies are far weaker fliers than the powerfully aerobatic and often strongly migratory dragonflies, and less likely to stray far from their birthplace. Two of the damselflies, however, are particularly wide ranging: *Ischnura senegalensis* from Senegal to the Philippines; and *Ceriagrion glabrum* from Palestine, over the whole of Africa to Madagascar. The richness of the damselfly fauna is due partly to the unusually large numbers of *Pseudagrion* with 25 species. This genus seems to have undergone a vigorous speciation within Madagascar comparable to *Megalagrion* in the Hawaiian Islands, also with 25 species. Many of these damselflies are slim, brilliantly metallic insects gleaming in gold, red, blue or green. Anyone familiar with the limited dragonfly and damselfly fauna of temperate rivers and streams will be pleasantly surprised at the abundance and variety of these insects alongside running waters in the eastern rainforests. Many species breed only in still water, including the lake in Parc Tzimbazaza in Antananarivo, an excellent place for an initial introduction to Madagascar's fascinating array of Odonata.

A brief mention can be made here about the mayflies in the order Ephemeroptera. These have been little studied, but they are of considerable interest because of the presence of the huge archaic representatives of the genus *Euthyplocia*, known only from the massifs of Andringitra and Tsaratanana.

THE ORTHOPTEROIDS

Included here are stick insects, termites, cockroaches, grasshoppers, crickets and praying mantids.

Stick insects

The Madagascan stick insects (Phasmatodea) are undoubtedly among the most interesting and spectacular of their kind. There are over 80 species, all endemic, and there is little to rival the huge species of spiny *Achrioptera* which include some of the only warningly coloured examples of stick insects in the world, brilliantly garbed in bright sky-blue or metallic

Right: **Several kinds of Madagascan stick insects select a resting place among small bits of debris — moss, twigs or flaking bark — which have become lodged in the shrub layer as they descend from the canopy. In this position they are very difficult to spot, not least because the abdomen is also arched upwards over the back. Both these species are from the eastern rainforests.**

Below: **Circia stick insects are remarkable for the moss-like outgrowths on body and legs. This is probably C. madegassa from the rainforests of Ranomafana.**

Opposite: **This stick insect is noteworthy for its apparent ability not only to feed on an introduced plant, Australian Eucalyptus, but also to mimic its newly adopted host's stems to an amazing degree. I found several of these adaptable insects at Périnet, always on Eucalyptus, a plant in which the leaves are chemically defended with pungent oils. Madagascan insects seem to exhibit a remarkable tolerance for these. The bug Amberana marginata (Cercopidae) forms dense clusters on Eucalyptus at Périnet.**

green and orange and flashing equally gaudy wings in
a defensive display. These amazing creatures may
reach 10 inches (25 cm) in length, at least in the
females; the males are smaller and slighter as in all
phasmids. These colourful giants are typical of the dry
western forests, but alas, are seldom seen.

The much more humid environment of the eastern
rainforests, with the trees heavily garlanded with
mosses and lichens, is home to a plethora of
awesomely cryptic species which are impressively
modified to blend into their surroundings. In *Circia
multilobata* and *C. madegassa*, numerous flattened
outgrowths on the body and legs mimic the fronds of
mosses and lichens. The insect often rests among the
genuine article, but this is not absolutely necessary, for
the resemblance is so perfect that even a solitary
insect is convincing in its own right as a mossy stick.
The nymphs of several species are extraordinarily
adept at selecting a suitably cryptic resting place, often
hanging upside-down on bits of debris caught up on
lianas or twigs. Many of these have flattened segments
on the legs, resembling peeling bark, and curve the
abdomen upwards over the back. I have found stick
insects throughout the rainforests of the world, but
few can boast such flawless camouflage as these
Madagascan species.

Hissing cockroaches

In its *Elliptorhina* and *Gramphadorhina* hissing
cockroaches, Madagascar is also blessed with some of
the world's most fascinating members of the Blattodea.
The island is richly endowed with members of this
order, with over 100 species, all except four endemic.
Hissing cockroaches are large brown cockroaches in
which the males are the larger sex, an unusual
situation among insects. The males of *G. portentosa*

*Elliptorhina javanica **is one of a large number of handsome
heavy bodied hissing cockroaches which are endemic to
Madagascar. It was photographed while foraging at night
after rain in the Berenty Private Reserve in the south-east.***

may reach 4 inches (10 cm) in length, and some
species are attractively patterned with cream bands.
During the day, they hide away under loose bark and
in tree holes, sallying forth at night to forage for fallen
fruits and fungi; they are most active immediately after
an evening downpour.

There are numerous species scattered around the
island, particularly in the dry forests. They hiss loudly
when touched, producing a remarkable volume of
sound by the expulsion of air through the second pair
of abdominal spiracles. The males are usually very
aggressive towards one another, charging at rivals and
ramming them with their armoured, knobbed, pronotal
shields, hissing all the while. The victor is the one
which succeeds in pushing its opponent backwards,
the loser often being chased ignominiously from the
scene of battle. Such heavyweight engagements
probably establish a dominance hierarchy among the
males, and go a long way to explain why they should
be the larger sex. A more subdued hissing is also used
during courtship; it is such an essential ingredient that
males prevented from hissing fail to induce a receptive
mood in the females, and mating does not take place.
If things go well these cockroaches are unique in that
copulation begins back to back, a posture which, in
other cockroaches, is attained only after the female
has first mounted the male to couple, and then moved
sideways off his back.

Termites

The presence of termites in the order Isoptera is less
obvious in Madagascar than in many tropical
countries, because there are no species which make
large conspicuous earthen mounds, although one
species in the dry south does make small conical
mounds a foot or so (30 cm) high. These dot the
landscape in thousands in the savanna-like country
south of the Isalo mountains. Around 75 species (71
endemic) in 17 genera are currently known.

Mantids

Although it has no flower-mantids, as found in Africa
and Asia, Madagascar does boast a substantial share of
the world's most impressive dead-leaf and bark-
mimicking praying mantises in the order Mantodea.
The present total is 52 species, of which only six are
found outside the island, a rate of endemism of 88 per
cent. In addition, 13 of the 25 genera are endemic,
and most of these contain but a small number of
species, often only one. The majority of the
Madagascan mantids are of African affinities, with such
shared genera as *Tenodera, Galepsus, Phyllocrania,
Idolomorpha* and *Polyspilota*, the latter containing the
most frequently seen mantis on the island, the large
green *P. aeruginosa*, which is also found in Africa and
Asia. Some genera, such as *Brancsikia, Majanga* and
Liturgusella, are more closely related to the Asian
fauna, while *Tisma* is of South American affinity.

Most mantids, particularly the more interesting
endemic species, live in the eastern rainforests
although a few of these are also widespread in the
western dry forests. Successful colonizers of the

Above: **The nymph of the endemic praying mantis Danuriella irregularis *is a persuasive mimic of a dead stick, thanks in large measure to its posture, with its front legs stuck out in front of the head. The adult, although still stick-like, is easier to spot. This species is common in the eastern rainforests and not difficult to find on the roadsides at Périnet.***

Above right: **Majanga basiliaris *is a rare praying mantis from the eastern rainforests; the genus is endemic. It spends the day on the boles of small trees, in which position it is exceptionally difficult to spot, so is probably under-recorded. This specimen was photographed in Montagne d'Ambre National Park.***

Right: **The most commonly seen praying mantis on the island is the green Polyspilota aeruginosa *which is also widespread in Africa and Asia. It is abundant in Parc Tzimbazaza in Antananarivo and on the roadsides at Périnet. This nymph has adopted a defensive pose revealing the coloured markings on its front legs.***

degraded western savannas tend to be wide-ranging African species, such as *Polyspilota aeruginosa* and *Tenodera*, which are characteristic of African savannas. Certain easily accessible areas of the eastern rainforests, namely Périnet and Montagne d'Ambre, are notably rich in species. One of the best dead-leaf mimics, the endemic *Phyllocrania illudens*, is quite common along the roadsides and broader forest tracks at Périnet. Adults and nymphs are remarkably faithful mimics of fallen leaves, but of different kinds, the adult copying the more flattened variety, while the nymph passes itself off as a desiccated, crinkled leaf. Although they can sometimes be found sitting on top

*Opposite top: **The extraordinary** Phyllocrania illudens **praying mantis is a convincing mimic of a dead leaf. This is the adult, which is about 2.4 inches (6 cm) in length. This fascinating endemic species is found in eastern and in western forests, and is a paler, more silvery colour in the latter, copying the generally sun-dried nature of the leaves.***

*Opposite bottom: **The nymph of** Phyllocrania illudens **is, if anything, even more remarkable than the adult.***

of vegetation in the shrub layer, or actually walking around, all stages of this bizarre creature most typically hang in an inverted posture beneath a stem, thereby imitating a dead leaf which is still in position, with the twisted extension on top of the mantid's head looking like a shrivelled leaf tip. This species is not restricted to the rainforests, and also occurs in the dry western forests. Here it tends to be a lighter straw-coloured shade, in keeping with the paler tones of the dead leaves in these drier sun-crisped forests. The darker brown of the eastern form blends in well with the generally darker trend of the dead leaves in the wetter forests.

Species of *Brancsikia* are also extraordinarily good mimics of dead leaves, although they are much less often seen than *P. illudens*. The pronotum is extended into a broad, leaf-like plate which, in the short, squat *B. aeroplana*, is quite enormous, so that the whole mantis becomes the embodiment of a brown leaf. This species is also found at Périnet, and it is important to stress here that these dead-leaf mantids do not rest among a carpet of leaves on the forest floor, but rather live on bushes in the shrub layer. Photographs in books sometimes show such mantids from various countries artificially (and wrongly) posed among carefully chosen, similar-looking leaves on the forest floor, after they have been attracted to a light at night for photography.

Some species live cryptic lives among moss and lichen on tree trunks in the rainforests; these include *Liturgusella malagassa* with a mottled pattern which is very similar to the bark-inhabiting South American *Liturgusa*; and *Enicophlebia pallida*, a delicately built species with lace-like transparent wings. Several kinds, such as *Danuriella*, are superb mimics of twigs, especially in their nymphal stages.

GRASSHOPPERS, CRICKETS AND BUSH-CRICKETS

Grasshoppers, crickets and bush-crickets (called katydids in the United States) belong to the large order Orthoptera. The number of species in Madagascar is relatively low, although virtually all are endemics and, compared with Africa, there is a scarcity of brightly coloured species. The actual numbers of individuals also seem to be rather low. Much more work needs to be done on this group, however, so that the final species list is likely to be considerably longer. Within the large family Acrididae (true grasshoppers), two of the most familiar subfamilies in southern Africa, the bladder grasshoppers or flying gooseberries (Pneumorinae), and the widespread toad grasshoppers (Pamphaginae), are missing. The Madagascan acridids currently number some 149 species in 89 genera, of which 140 species (94 per cent) in 62 genera are

endemic. A few of the non-endemics have a vast distribution: *Cyrtacanthacris tricolor* ranges over the whole of tropical Africa and Asia as far east as the Philippines and Sumatra; and *Acrotylus patruelis* is found over all of Africa up into southern Europe and eastwards into Asia. The peripatetic migratory locust *Locusta migratoria* also includes Madagascar in its vast old-world range. The monkey-hoppers (Eumastacidae) are particularly well represented in Madagascar, and some of the species are among the largest in the family; almost all are endemic.

Most Madagascan grasshoppers tend to be small (by tropical standards) and fairly cryptic; this even applies to most of the 41 species of Pyrgomorphinae, a subfamily which, in Africa, includes a large number of flamboyant representatives. Most of the Madagascan members are quite drably coloured, with the exception of the large and impressively vivid *Phymateus saxosus* which, with its brilliant combination of blue, red and yellow, and its spiky pronotum, must be one of the world's most spectacular grasshoppers. Unfortunately, it does not seem to be very common in its dry western forest habitat. Its relative, *Phymateus madagassus*, is a much more dowdy, brownish insect and rather a disappointment for a *Phymateus*; as luck would have it, this less rewarding of the two is more common, mainly in the dry south and west.

BUGS

The bugs in the order Hemiptera are split into two easily recognized suborders. The Madagascan members of the suborder Homoptera are generally less entertainingly bizarre than in many tropical countries, mainly because of the puzzling absence of the fascinating and large family Membracidae. Rates of endemism in the families Cercopidae, Jassidae,

Most members of the Orthoptera in Madagascar are endemic. These mating Parasymbellia inermis *grasshoppers from Ankarafantsika's dry forests belong to the family Eumastacidae, richly represented in Madagascar.*

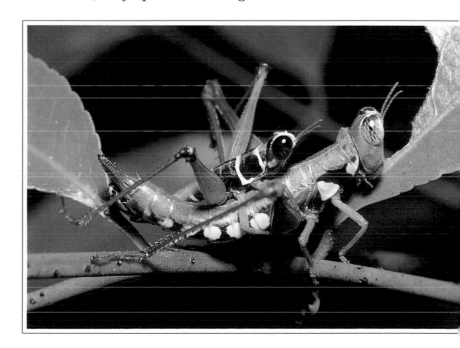

Opposite top left: **The nymphs of the bug Phromnia rosea (Flatidae) cluster on twigs and stems in the dry forests of the south and west. Their wispy 'tails' consist of a waxy substance which is thought to be unpalatable to predators.**

Opposite bottom left: **Yanga hearthii is a large, endemic cicada which gives vent to its deafening song from tree trunks in the southern dry forests.**

Opposite top right: **Clusters of Phromnia rosea adults resemble a spike of flowers. When a bird attempts to catch one of their number, the whole group explodes into flight, scattering in all directions, leaving the would-be assailant perplexed and still hungry.**

Opposite bottom right: **Agaeus bicolor is a warningly coloured shieldbug (Pentatomidae) from the dry western forests.**

Right: **Large clusters of adults and nymphs of the bug Libyaspis coccinelloides (Pentatomidae : Plataspinae) can be seen on tree trunks along the roadsides at Périnet in December. Note that the nymphs are cryptic, although they moult into warningly coloured adults.**

Below: **The endemic Piezodera rubra (Pyrrhocoridae) is warningly coloured, like most members of its family worldwide. This bug was photographed in the rainforests on the Montagne d'Ambre, one of the richest sites for insects on the whole island. The genus Piezodera is restricted to Madagascar.**

Flatidae and Cixiidae are very high, and there has been a great deal of recent study into the homopteran fauna, resulting in the description of a deluge of new species, mostly small and unlikely to be noticed by the non-specialist. Taking this into account, there is likely to be at least 1000 homopteran species on the island.

Much work also remains to be done on the second suborder, the Heteroptera. The best studied of these are the shield-bugs or stink-bugs in the family Pentatomidae. This family is well represented in Madagascar with over 220 species, some of which are not only large but among the most beautifully coloured members of their group. Pentatomids are

Top left: **Dysdercus flavidus cotton stainer bugs (Pyrrhocoridae)** *are a frequent sight feeding on seeds of the kapok tree* Ceiba pentandra *in the dry western forests. This is a group of warningly coloured nymphs, with a single adult. All stages are mimicked by the corresponding stages of a* Phonoctonus *species assassin bug (Reduviidae), which preys exclusively on this species of cotton stainer. This is one of several instances (mainly African) where an assassin bug predator mimics its cotton stainer prey.*

Centre left: **The** Phonoctonus *bug.*

Bottom left: **The endemic assassin bug** Velinus rotifer **(Reduviidae)** *is one of many small orange species from the eastern rainforests. Madagascar is extremely rich in these insects.*

Below: **Several species of large spectacular ant-lions (Neuroptera : Myrmeleonidae)** *are found in the savanna-like habitats of the west. This is* Palpares weelei, *one of many endemics in this genus and one of the few beneficiaries of people's creation of large areas of grasslands by destroying the original forests.*

Alus corpulentus is one of several species of large, spectacular, endemic click beetles (Elateridae) from Madagascar's forests. This individual was photographed in the Ampijeroa Forest Reserve in the north-west.

often implicated in damage to cultivated crops, such as *Antestia confusa* on coffee and *Diploxys fallax* on rice, although the many species of *Nezara* are less troublesome in Madagascar than other members of this genus are in Africa and elsewhere. Some of the peculiar beetle-like bugs in the subfamily Plataspinae also cause problems. *Plataspis coccinelloides* lives in dense aggregations on tree trunks and branches, especially on certain legumes such as *Albizzia*. The trees resist repeated attacks for several years before individual branches, and sometimes the whole tree, may succumb and die.

The water-bugs have been quite well studied and number more than 120 species, of which over 80 per cent are endemic. The largest bug in Madagascar is a species of *Belostoma* which can reach a length of 3 or 4 inches (8-10 cm).

The assassin bugs (Reduviidae) are also well represented, and many new species, mostly endemics, have been described over the last few years. Many of these are warningly coloured in shades of orange or red; the wingless *Mutillicoris* is interesting in mimicking persuasively some of the commoner species of mutillid wasps. An event of particular note was the discovery 40 years ago of a new species of bug *Systelloderes milloti* (Henicocephalidae) in

Madagascar. It belongs to a genus which had previously been known only from a dozen species scattered in the Americas, New Zealand and tropical Africa.

BEETLES

The Madagascan beetle fauna (order Coleoptera) is among the richest and best studied on the island, although certain families are still very neglected. The likely total of species is probably about 20,000. Many new species have been discovered and described over the past 50 years, and rates of endemism, both at the national and local level are remarkably high.

The jewel-beetles (Buprestidae) are extraordinarily diverse, with over 500 species, almost all endemic, including numerous large, metallic, kaleidoscopic *Polybothris*, many of which appear on the scene only briefly during the rainy season in the southern and western forests.

There are more than 600 described species of longhorn beetles (Cerambycidae), including many brightly coloured members of the subfamily Lamiinae. Some kinds, such as *Tlepolemoides vadoni* from Antalala, are densely hairy and the pile of this covering is quite luxuriant. This is also true of *Thaumastesthes penicillus* and *Atybe planti* from the eastern rainforests generally. Fallen trees in the rainforests often show plenty of evidence, in the form of exit-holes and little mounds of fresh sawdust, of the presence of longhorn larvae. The adult beetles can

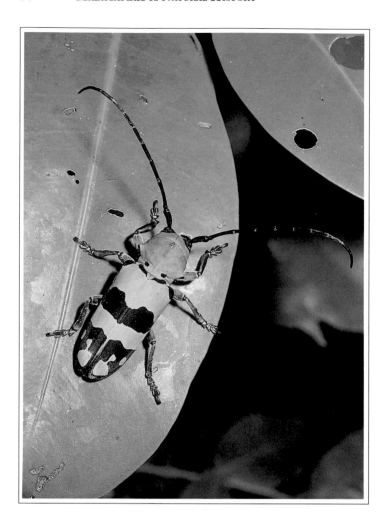

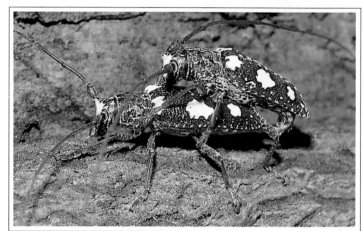

Opposite top left: The longhorn beetle Tragocephala juncunda (Cerambycidae) comes from the dry western forests. It is a member of a genus which is widely distributed in southern Africa, where there are numerous colourful representatives (eg T. variegata, T. ducalis) similar to this Madagascan endemic.

Opposite bottom: The endemic Helictopleurus quadripunctatus is one of the prettiest dung-roller beetles (Scarabaeidae) in the world. It is found in the dry south, but is only active after rain, when numerous individuals can be seen scurrying busily around in search of lemur dung. Not just any dung will do, however. Only the droppings of the sifaka Propithecus verreauxi are of the correct size and consistency to be rolled to the subterranean nest in one piece, without requiring any pre-forming into a ball. The larger, softer, more amorphous offerings of the ring-tailed lemur Lemur catta are therefore ignored, as a considerable amount of moulding would be needed to render them rollable. A different species of beetle is adapted for dealing with these. If the sifaka becomes extinct and its conveniently shaped dropping are no longer available, then H. quadripunctatus will also swiftly follow its benefactor into oblivion.

Opposite top right: The endemic Tragocephala crassicornis takes off from a leaf in the dry western forests near Morondava.

Opposite centre right: Protorrhopaia sexnotata is one of the commonest longhorn beetles of the eastern rainforests. Large numbers of this endemic beetle can often be found mating and laying eggs on fallen trees.

Below: The giraffe-necked weevil Trachelophorus giraffa (Attelabidae) is one of the most bizarre insects in Madagascar. Only the males have such long necks, the females being more conservative in this respect. These spectacular weevils can be seen sitting on leaves in open spots and roadsides in the eastern forests — eg it is common at Périnet.

also be seen mating and laying eggs if you are lucky enough to arrive at the right moment.

Most ground beetles (Carabidae) are less often seen because they live under leaf litter and debris but, with 1097 species, they are very prolific, and there are 1024 endemics, a rate of 92.5 per cent.

Tiger beetles (Cicindelinae) are active during the day and may be seen running rapidly across bare sand or a carpet of leaves. One species mimics a large black ant, another an orange-banded pompilid wasp.

Within the darkling beetles (Tenebrionidae), there is also a high rate of endemism, with 53 of 58 members of the Tentyrinae restricted to Madagascar. Many of these tenebrionids are small, and it is possible to find as many as half a dozen different species lurking within a single bracket fungus in the rainforests.

The scarabs and chafers (Scarabaeidae) are represented by a huge number of species. The rate of endemism may be very high — over 99 per cent in the Scarabaeinae. The most noticeable scarabs are the dung beetles, many of which are brightly coloured, and can be seen plodding along paths in the forests, rolling balls of lemur droppings before them. A single area of rainforest may be home to 10 or 12 different kinds of these beetles, belonging mainly to the large endemic genus *Helictopleurus* and specializing in lemur dung. As a result, these beetles are just as vulnerable to forest destruction as the lemurs themselves are.

Left: **Beetles of the family Anthribidae are usually found on tree trunks. This is the endemic** Phloeotragus albicans *from gallery forest in Berenty Private Reserve in the south of Madagascar.*

Below left: **Lixus barbiger is one of many large, hairy weevils which inhabit the eastern rainforests. The genus** Lixus *is represented by many species in Africa, often yellow in colour, but lacking the extraordinary hirsute ornamentation seen in many of their Madagascan relatives.*

Bottom left: **Lithinus weevils also resemble small mobile brushes. This is probably L. sepioides from the eastern rainforests; it mimics a small crinkled leaf.**

Weevils (Curculionidae) are among the most frequently encountered Madagascan beetles and, with more than 1300 species on the island, only three or four of which are not endemic, this is hardly surprising. In its many bizarre species of large hairy *Lithinus* and *Lixus*, Madagascar boasts some of the most extraordinary weevils in the world. *Lithinus hildebrandi* is called the lichen weevil because of its extraordinary similarity to a tuft of lichen. Undoubtedly, many more species await discovery, for many areas are rich in localized endemics and, at the turn of the century, one collector found more than 200 new weevils in the forests on the Montagne d'Ambre alone.

TRUE FLIES

Flies (order Diptera) may not be to everyone's liking, and few visitors to Madagascar would probably pay attention to any apart from the irritating mosquitoes or the hoards of large black horse-flies (Tabanidae) which descend upon you towards dusk in the dry forests near Morondava; they may gather in such numbers that they make a living cloak upon your back. Fortunately, they are incapable of forcing their rather stout proboscis through the material of a shirt or trousers. No doubt, there are still exciting discoveries still to be made by specialists studying Madagascar's flies. Until 1962, only six members of the family Conopidae were known; then seven species were added, six of them new to science and two of these unique and not at all closely related to any other members of the family.

There are more than 200 species of craneflies (Tipulidae), mostly endemic and described mainly in the last 20 years.

Of 15 species of picture-winged flies (Tephritidae) collected at Ranomafana in 1988, no fewer then 12 proved to be new to science; and some of these represent new genera as well. These kinds of discoveries are most stimulating for the specialists concerned, and none more so than finding a new species of net-winged midge (Blepharoceridae) belonging to the primitive subfamily Edwardsininae. Before 1952 members of this relict subfamily had been known only from a single genus *Edwardsina*, with a few species from Chile, Argentina, Tasmania and Australia. The Madagascan specimen merited a new genus and was described as *Pauliniana* in honour of the deputy director of the Institut Scientifique de Madagascar.

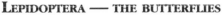

LEPIDOPTERA — THE BUTTERFLIES

Compared with that of many tropical countries, the butterfly fauna of Madagascar is rather impoverished. Some continental faunas can be remarkably rich, as in the 13, 585 acres (5500 ha) of lowland tropical rainforest in the Tambopata Natural Reserve in Peru, where more than 1300 different species of butterflies have been recorded. Set beside this impressive figure, Madagascar's tally of less than 300 species seems disappointing. Presumably, this has occurred because relatively few species were able to cross the seas in the first place to make up the founding stock. It seems certain that butterflies were not present in Madagascar before it split from the mainland because, at that time, butterflies as a group had probably not yet diverged from the ancestral stock.

The eastern rainforests hold the bulk of the species, although the best place to see butterflies is probably in the Montagne d'Ambre National Park, particularly around the Grand Cascade, where the humid air is usually alive with the brightly coloured wings of large swallowtails and nymphalids, spiralling up among the spray-drenched trees or flapping lazily above the turbulent river.

Despite their relatively low diversity, the butterflies of Madagascar are still of great interest for the entomologist, mostly because of the generally high rate of endemism, but also because of the origin of some of the species. The actual rate of endemism varies markedly from family to family. In the Papilionidae it is 77 per cent. In the Pieridae, a family

Above left: **Graphium cyrnus** *is a swallowtail (Papilionidae) without a tail. Males are often seen 'puddling' on damp sand beside rivers and roads in the eastern and in the western forests.*

Top: Although it is endemic to Madagascar, the kite swallow-tail **Graphium evombar** *(Papilionidae) is common over most of the island. It has the long slim 'tails' typical of its genus.*

Above: The spectacular **Atrophaneura antenor** *(Papilionidae) is the largest butterfly in Madagascar. It flaunts a typical warning pattern resulting from the caterpillar's diet of poisonous plants in the Aristolochia family. A strong flier, it is common and widespread over much of the island; this mating pair is perched on planted teak in Ampijeroa Forest Reserve.*

containing generally peripatetic butterflies, several of which are noted migrants, this falls to 34 per cent. It rises to 78 per cent in the Nymphalidae, a mixed bunch but containing two genera of 'browns' (Satyrinae), *Henotesia* and *Strabena*, which have speciated exuberantly in Madagascar. This phenomenon also occurs among members of the group from other parts of the world, such as in *Erebia* in the European mountains, especially in the Alps. In the Lycaenidae the rate is 58 per cent.

The overall affinity with the African fauna is obvious, and many of the genera and a few of the species are shared with Africa although, within Madagascar, many of these have diverged into well-defined endemic subspecies. There also exists an oriental connection, the most notable example being Madagascar's largest, most spectacular and most beautiful butterfly, *Atrophaneura antenor*. This splendid insect is a member of the swallowtail family, Papilionidae, with 12 further representatives in Madagascar, all showing clear African affinities. *Atrophaneura* stands alone as the most westerly member of a genus typically found in the East. As such, it is the sole representative of the tribe Troidini within the whole Afro-tropical subregion.

The caterpillars of this tribe normally feed on members of the Aristolochia family, plants which are well distributed throughout Madagascar in many different habitats, hence this butterfly's wide distribution within the island. Apart from its sheer size, its long-tailed wings, with their black-and-silver chequered pattern contrasting with the bright red body, combine to make it a very conspicuous butterfly. This is no accident, for *Atrophaneura* wears the classic 'warning' uniform in common with other members of the tribe, such as *Troides* in Asia, and *Parides* and *Battus* in South America. Plants of the Aristolochia family generally contain toxic defensive chemicals, which are sequestered by the butterfly caterpillar as it feeds, and then redeployed in its defence through to the adult stage. Predators soon learn to make the mental connection between the butterfly's bright colours and its nauseating taste, and leave it alone.

Atrophaneura often flies very strongly at quite a height and, on one occasion, I mistook one for a bird as the insect powered strongly along the beach on the hot dry coast at Morondava. With its widespread distribution and lack of fussiness over habitat, this magnificent butterfly is not under imminent threat from environmental changes caused by humans, although it is taken by commercial collectors, whose activities should perhaps be kept under surveillance.

The other members of the Papilionidae belong to two different genera: *Graphium*, the kite swallowtails; and *Papilio*, the swallowtails proper. Two species of kite swallowtails, *Graphium evombar* and *G. cyrnus*, are widespread in humid and in dry forests over most of the island, and neither species is at risk. *G. cyrnus* males regularly seek out mineral-charged deposits on riverbanks, particularly where animals have urinated, the sodium-rich salts in the urine being a great attraction. They may form part of a mixed band, comprising several kinds of pierids and lycaenids, as well as one or more additional species of papilionid. A large butterfly, such as *G. cyrnus*, pumps up the enriched liquid at such a rate through its long, slim proboscis that drops of water are regularly squirted forcibly out of the rear end, a process known as 'puddling'. The third species, *G. endochus*, seems to be much rarer than the other two, and is confined to rainforests, although it is common at Montagne d'Ambre.

The brown and yellow citrus swallowtail *Papilio demodocus* has been introduced accidentally from Africa. Since then, it has rapidly become a minor pest of citrus in Madagascar, where its large caterpillars can often be found on the leaves of orange or lime trees in gardens. It has also colonized such native habitats as rainforests, and its larvae are common on the naturalized citrus trees scattered around the forests of the Montagne d'Ambre. The adult of *P. demodocus* could perhaps be easily confused with three other members of the genus *Papilio* which are endemic to Madagascar. Of these, the large, handsome *P. erithonioides* is fairly common and widespread, but the two others are more restricted. *P. grosesmithi* is found only in a number of deciduous forests in western Madagascar, including Ankarafantsika, the forests near Morondava and the Androvonory forest east of Tulear. *P. morondavana*, the Madagascar emperor swallowtail, is one of the rarest of Madagascar's endemic butterflies, with much the same distribution as the last species, but on a far more localized basis. It is collected commercially, but the main threat comes from habitat destruction caused by fire and by the removal of the forest for agriculture.

The remaining endemic swallowtails are fairly common. They are among the most frequently seen and conspicuous of rainforest butterflies because of their large size, bright colours and habit of flying strongly in the more open spots. The attractive black-and-blue *Papilio oribazus* and *P. epiphorbas* are commonly seen flapping around in glades and over rivers in the eastern rainforests, often accompanied by the pale cream-and-black *P. delalandei*, which resembles the much rarer *P. mangoura* that is so prized by commercial collectors for its scarcity and consequent high price.

The widespread African mocker swallowtail *Papilio dardanus* occurs in Madagascar as *P. d. meriones*. The creamy yellow males are common in Montagne d'Ambre where they can readily be seen flying along the main tracks. They are also fond of drinking on the rocks above the river near the Grand Cascade. These rocks are constantly bathed by a slippery film of mineral-rich water which seeps from the steep slope above. The mocker swallowtail is found widely in Africa, but only in Madagascar does the female resemble the male in colour and in wing shape. In Africa, the hindwings of the females lack the tails so that, overall, they look quite different from the males. These females are mimics of a variety of warningly coloured butterflies, such as the black-and-white *Amauris niavius* and the black-and-orange plain tiger *Danaus chrysippus*. The latter is common throughout Madagascar, yet it is never mimicked by the females of the mocker swallowtail. Indeed, the absence of the complex mimicry rings, which are such an intriguing phenomenon in Africa, is one of the most notable characteristics of the Madagascan butterfly fauna.

The family Nymphalidae contains some of the most abundant and wide ranging of Madagascan butterflies. Two of these are widespread African species present in Madagascar as subspecies: the eyed pansy *Precis oenone* as *P. o. epiclelia* and the rather inappropriately named yellow pansy (in Africa and Madagascar the dominant colour is orange) *Precis hierta* as *P. h. paris*. Both fly mainly in disturbed areas, such as forest edges, gardens and waste ground, over most of the island. With their liking for open weedy places, they

Top: Anyone who has visited Africa will be familiar with the blue pansy butterfly Precis oenone. *This is* P. o. epiclelia *which is endemic to Madagascar. It prefers open spots along roadsides and degraded areas in the eastern rainforests.*

Above: The eyed pansy Precis orithya *is perhaps the commonest butterfly in Madagascar in every kind of habitat, reflecting its wide range and catholic habits over the African continent.*

Top right: The orange pansy Precis hierta *is also a widespread and familiar butterfly in Africa.* P. h. paris *is a Madagascan endemic, seen here drinking on damp ground on the bottom of a pond which was rapidly drying out in April in the Kirindy forest near Morondava.*

Above centre right: Precis rhadama *is one of the most beautiful of Madagascar's endemic butterflies. Fortunately, it is common and widespread, and its beauty can be seen even without leaving Antananarivo, as it is abundant in Parc Tzimbazaza.*

Right: The strikingly marked undersides of Charaxes andara *are obvious in this photograph, taken on a dirt road in the Kirindy forest near Morondava, where the butterfly was feeding on the smelly corpse of a squashed tortoise. This endemic species is widespread in the dry western forests, but is absent from the eastern humid forests, which are the sole haunt of several rare species of* Charaxes.

Left: **The endemic Precis andremiaja** *is found in the eastern rainforests.*

Below left: **The leaf-like undersides of Charaxes zoolina** *are unusual within the genus, as is this butterfly's small size. This is C. z. betsimaraka which is endemic to Madagascar, where it occurs widely in all types of forest.*

Bottom left: **Neptidiopsis fulgurata (Nymphalidae) is widespread in eastern Africa. The nominate subspecies N. f. fulgurata** *is endemic to Madagascar, where it is wideranging. In its typical sleeping posture it is very hard to spot, sitting as it does head-downwards with its wings widely spread. In this posture it resembles the kind of silver-blotched dead leaf which is a common segment of the forest environment.*

have probably thrived from human destruction of the rainforest, when scrubby regrowth replaces the original closed forest.

With its lustrous royal-blue wings, the endemic *Precis rhadama* is one of the most handsome butterflies in the island. It is also one of the most common, and is found in all types of forest and even in the centre of Antananarivo, where it haunts the gardens of the Parc Tzimbazaza, together with *P. andremiaja*, another endemic usually found in the eastern rainforests. The eyed pansy *Precis orithya*, a blue-and-black butterfly with several eye spots near the margins of the hindwings, is a widespread African species which also occurs generally in Madagascar. It is a typical resident of paths, roadsides and open spots in the dry western forests.

Most of the eight Madagascan representatives of the large, mainly African genus *Charaxes* are inhabitants of the eastern rainforests. They are big handsome butterflies with prominent pointed tails on the hindwings, said to be used by the males as lances during a kind of gladiatorial combat. The undersides are usually elegantly decorated with a complex pattern, making these butterflies very prized by collectors. An exception is the rather small *Charaxes zoolina* ssp *betsimaraka*, an endemic subspecies of a widespread African butterfly, in which the undersides resemble a dead leaf. It is quite abundant in the forests of Ankarafantsika, where the males frequently land on perspiring visitors because they are attracted by the film of sweat on skin and clothes. Few of the other *Charaxes* make themselves so obvious, spending much of their time out of sight up in the canopy. They are trapped by commercial collectors using a bait consisting of fermenting fruit or rotting flesh, to which the males are greatly attracted, although a corpse squashed on the road will prove equally acceptable. *Charaxes* are also very fond of animal droppings, particularly those of small carnivores, such as mongooses.

Several other nymphalids also mimic dead leaves. Some exhibit a degree of authenticity which is most impressive; others are less accurate, but are still persuasive enough to remain invisible against a carpet of the genuine article. The latter category includes *Aterica rabena*, the butterfly most likely to be noticed by anyone walking through the eastern and the western forests. It seems to be particularly fond of forest paths, and frequently flutters up from beneath a

Above: **Gnophodes betsimena** *(Nymphalidae : Satyrinae) is a widespread 'brown' in Africa, the nominate subspecies G. b. betsimena being a Madagascan endemic. It skulks on the ground in the gloomiest parts of the rainforests, where its resemblance to a dead leaf ensures that it is missed unless disturbed by one's footsteps. It is particularly common on the Montagne d'Ambre.*

Above right and right: **Aterica rabena** *(Nymphalidae) is one of the most commonly seen butterflies in Madagascar's forested areas. It is particularly fond of sitting on a carpet of leaves along forest tracks. With its wings closed it is a passable mimic of a dead leaf.*

walker's feet, usually settling again quickly only a short distance away. The males devote long, frustrating hours to fruitless courtship of the indifferent-seeming females. The scenario always seems to follow the same pattern. The male settles beside his chosen mate, trying to stimulate some interest by stroking her with a fluttering action of his wings and antennae. Her usual reaction is disappointingly negative, and she flies off a little way, closely shadowed by her suitor in hot pursuit. The male now repeats the same routine, and may do so over and over again, doggedly pressing his case until either the female abruptly breaks off the engagement by making a rapid and final getaway, or he finally wearies of his thankless task and settles down with outspread wings. In this posture he is easy to spot but, if he senses danger, he quickly snaps his wings shut and is instantly transformed into a quite convincing dead leaf.

Gnophodes betsimena, a widespread African butterfly (Satyrinae) with *G. b. betsimena* endemic to Madagascar, haunts the gloomiest parts of the

rainforest understorey, skulking anonymously among the drab carpet of debris, its brown-patterned undersides making it just one more dead leaf among millions. Only when it flutters out unexpectedly from beneath one's descending foot does it reveal its presence. This cryptic species is very common along the shady paths on the Montagne d'Ambre, often accompanied by another dead-leaf mimic, the endemic *Salamis anteva.* This is a much more colourful butterfly, widespread in the humid forests, and with a liking for perching in sunspots along the paths, its wings spread wide, revealing the rufous uppersides shot through with the subtlest hint of a purple shimmer; the tips of the forewings are black with white chevrons. It often potters around on the forest floor, with a peculiar jerky action, searching for fallen

Top and above: **Salamis anteva (Nymphalidae) is a widespread endemic of the eastern rainforests. When at rest with closed wings it is a remarkable mimic of a dead leaf.**

Top right and above right: **The Madagascar diadem Hypolimnas dexithea is one of the largest and most spectacular members of the Nymphalidae on the island. It flies in glades and above rivers in the eastern rainforests, seeking a roosting site beneath a leaf in the late afternoon. It is particularly common in Montagne d'Ambre National Park.**

fruits on which to dine. If disturbed, it darts quickly into the undergrowth, performing a head-flip as it lands, to end up with its head pointing downwards. Then, only the leaf-like undersides are visible, while the inverted pose can be seen to have placed the tapered tips of the hindwings in such a position as to resemble a leaf stalk. Unless the landing site has been

noted carefully, the motionless butterfly is impossible to distinguish from the jumble of natural vegetation on which it rests.

The broad tracks in Montagne d'Ambre are also the favourite haunt of the endemic Madagascar diadem *Hypolimnas dexithea.* This magnificent butterfly is considerably larger and more impressive than most of the African representatives of the genus. The males patrol up and down the forest rides, occasionally dropping in to refuel from a flower: a favourite is *Lantana camara,* a native of Mexico which now forms dense pungent thickets alongside many of the tracks in the park. In the evening, the males cease their restless activity and can be seen searching for a place to roost, inspecting leaf after leaf before finally choosing one and flipping upside down into the roosting position. The leaf above now functions as an umbrella, giving protection from any torrential tropical downpour which may batter the forest during the night. This butterfly is also common around the Grand Cascade in Montagne d'Ambre, often coming down to drink at the same seepages beloved of the mocker swallowtails. Fortunately, *H. dexithea* is widespread in the eastern rainforests, although mostly in small numbers, often merely giving one the most tantalizingly fleeting of glimpses as it dashes rapidly along above some forest stream, in contrast to the close-up views easily obtainable in Montagne d'Ambre.

Of the four other species of *Hypolimnas* which occur in Madagascar, two, *H. bolina* and *H. misippus*, are not only pan-African, but even extend as far as the Oriental and Australian regions. By contrast, *Euxanthe madagascariensis* is endemic, and the sole representative of its genus on the island, where it is widespread but local in the forested areas. The males are among the most strongly and belligerently territorial of all butterflies, staking out a position on the trunk of a sapling and mounting frequent sorties to intercept and investigate not only other butterflies trespassing within the territory, but even birds or passing humans. This butterfly invariably perches with its wings shut, so only the brown undersides, marked with blotches of the palest blue, are normally visible.

The endemic genus of 'browns' Strabena (Nymphalidae: Satyrinae) has speciated vigorously in Madagascar. This species, S. batesii, is found in the rainforests of Ranomafana.

It is attracted to the sap oozing from injured trees trunks, where it may spend long periods so thoroughly absorbed in its feeding that it can easily be picked up. The fermenting nature of much of this sap may help to explain this lack of nervousness!

With their narrow, often rather drably coloured wings, members of the subfamily Acraeinae are unlikely to attract the attention of any but the

Most members of the subfamily Acraeinae (Nymphalidae) are rather small, dull, narrow-winged butterflies. Acraea zitja is one of the smallest but, with its sumptuous orange tints, it is one of the prettiest. It is endemic in marshy areas throughout Madagascar; this one was on the roadside at Périnet.

The three members of the endemic genus Saribia are the only members of the butterfly family Riodinidae in Madagascar. All three are similar in appearance and difficult to separate. They are classic 'false-head' mimics which perform a quick about-turn upon landing and are commonly seen in the eastern rainforests, particularly along the edges of paths.

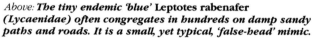

Above: **The tiny endemic 'blue' Leptotes rabenafer (Lycaenidae) often congregates in hundreds on damp sandy paths and roads. It is a small, yet typical, 'false-head' mimic.**

Above right: **From its handful of records, this unusually flamboyant skipper Malaza empyreus (Hesperiidae) appears to be one of the rarest of the endemic Madagascan butterflies. It was photographed at Périnet, an outstandingly rich area of forest holding many rare, local species of fauna.**

dedicated lepidopterist. Several endemic species occur in Madagascar, perhaps the prettiest being the small, flame-coloured *Acraea zitja* which is found in marshy areas throughout the island; it is common along the roadsides at Périnet. The Satyrinae contains a bunch of even drabber butterflies, collectively called 'browns'. To the professional entomologist, these undistinguished-looking insects are among the most interesting members of Madagascar's butterfly fauna. This is because two genera have shown a remarkable degree of speciation within Madagascar. There are no fewer than 41 endemic species of *Henotesia*, all rather typical 'browns', being dull butterflies with small eye spots near the wing margins. Most of the species are confusingly similar, and are unlikely to excite the attention of the non-specialist. Strangely enough, the endemic genus *Strabena* also boasts 41 species, although these are often more attractive than *Henotesia* because of the frequency in many species of attractive white markings on the undersides.

The metalmark family, Riodinidae (often also seen as a subfamily of the Lycaenidae), attains its peak of abundance in South America. Relatively few species occur in Africa and only three in Madagascar, all belonging to the endemic genus *Saribia*. These

butterflies are common along paths in the eastern forests, such as at Périnet and Ranomafana, typically perching on a leaf with the wings almost, but not quite, closed so as to leave a gap between them. The undersides are brown, and there are two pointed tails on the tips of each hindwing, accompanied by two blue-and-black spots. The effect of this combination of spots and tails is to mimic the butterfly's own head, complete with 'eyes' (the spots) and 'antennae' (the tails). To reinforce the illusion and increase the confusion, should an enemy have its eye on the butterfly and follow its movements, the *Saribia* does a rapid, scarcely noticeable about-turn as it alights on a leaf, thus placing its false head exactly where a pursuing bird would expect the real head to be. A quick peck aimed at the 'head', and intended to deal an instantly mortal blow, would thus merely yield a few useless shards of broken wing as the butterfly, with its real head still in one piece, makes good its escape.

Clusters of butterflies, puddling on the damp earth of riverbanks or on dirt roads, are as much a part of the Madagascan scene as in any other part of the tropics. As already mentioned, *Graphium cyrnus* often occurs singly in these aggregations, along with pierids, such as species of *Belenois*. These are often heavily outnumbered by hordes of 'blues' (Lycaenidae), the main participant commonly being the small, endemic *Leptotes rabenafer* which is another example of a 'false-head mimic', a phenomenon which is frequent in tropical lycaenids. These are some of the few butterflies which are characteristic of the drier southern part of Madagascar, such as the 'spiny desert', the least productive area for butterflies as a whole.

Our knowledge of the moths is growing apace as collecting becomes more intensive. Many new species have been described in the last 20 years, almost all endemic, but no doubt the number of species yet to be discovered and described runs into the thousands. Because most moths are nocturnal, they attract attention only when they come to light and, even in Antananarivo, large, splendid green-and-brown

Right: **The endemic hawkmoth** Panogena lingens *is the sole pollinator of the orchid* Angraecum arachnites*. The moth occurs in two forms, one with a 2.8-inch (7-cm) proboscis, and one in which the proboscis reaches 4.7 inches (12 cm) in length. It is this latter form only which visits the orchids. During the day the moth rests in full view on a tree trunk in the rainforest, relying on its cryptic pattern to keep it safe from prying eyes.*

Below: **Batocnema coquereli** *is an endemic hawkmoth from the humid forests. This specimen was photographed sitting in the open on a leaf on the Montagne d'Ambre.*

Below right: **The hawkmoth** Panogena jasmini *occurs in two forms on the island. In the humid east, the wings are heavily suffused with dark grey, blending in with the general tone of the tree trunks in the wetter forests. In the south, the wings are almost white and less densely streaked with deeper black lines. This corresponds to the generally paler bark of the southern forests' trees. This specimen was spotted in its daytime resting pose on a tree in Parc Tzimbazaza in Antananarivo.*

hawkmoths wander into buildings after dark. The majority of moths abound in the eastern rainforests, where they may be found resting during the day on tree trunks or among debris and leaves. Caterpillars are difficult, or impossible, to identify unless one has the time to collect and breed them through to the adult stage. On Montagne d'Ambre I found a remarkable large black-and-white hawkmoth caterpillar (Sphingidae) which responded to a gentle prod by jerking its front end back and forth and giving vent to a loud squeaking-creaking sound. Another surprise was a colourful slug-moth caterpillar (Limacodidae) seen happily feeding on castor-oil *Ricinus communis* leaves, one of the world's most poisonous plants and usually immune to attack by insects.

One of the most brilliantly jewel-like of all moths,

Chrysiridia madagascariensis (Uraniidae), is a large, endemic, day-flying species which most people would mistake for a swallowtail butterfly. It is said to be common, and to migrate across the island in huge groups although, in six months on the island, I was not lucky enough to come across even a single lonely specimen, although thousands have been collected over the years for inclusion in display boxes. The same applies to the huge comet moth *Argema mittrei* (Saturniidae), one of the world's biggest moths, in which the males may reach almost 8 inches (20 cm) in length, measured down to the tips of the long 'tails' which form extensions to the hindwings. Fortunately, the larvae eat a wide variety of plants, so this gargantuan species is less likely to be destroyed by commercial collecting than would be the case if just a single foodplant were acceptable.

Opposite top left: **This endemic moth Achaea imperatrix (Noctuidae) exhibits a highly stylized resting posture, with its head pointing downwards and just a single front leg sticking out to one side to function as a brace. In this pose it closely resembles a dead leaf, with the silver spots copying fungal damage. Don't be fooled by the clarity revealed by the flash — only many years of experience in seeing through the superb camouflage of forest insects around the tropical world enabled me to spot this specimen lurking in the gloomy understorey of the forests on the Montagne d'Ambre.**

Opposite bottom: **This moth larva (Arctiidae) from the eastern rainforests exactly mimicks a clump of lichen. Many insects from these forests are similarly cryptic and to find them requires considerable experience.**

Opposite top right: **Temnora argyropeza is one of the smallest hawkmoths (Sphingidae) in Madagascar. The adults spend the day in full view, usually carefully selecting a resting site on or near a dead leaf. In this position the moth itself closely resembles a dead leaf. It is common in the eastern rainforests; this one was at Périnet.**

Opposite centre right: **Euchromia folletii is an endemic warningly coloured, day-flying moth in the family Arctiidae. It is common in the lowland forests — including disturbed areas — near Maroansetra.**

Below: **Like many hawkmoth caterpillars (Sphingidae) around the world, this Madagascan species tucks its head into its underside and exposes two eye-like spots in a defensive display.**

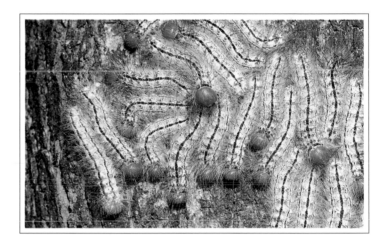

Above: **Groups of furry moth caterpillars are a common sight on tree trunks in the eastern and in the western forests. At night they form a procession which worms its way up into the canopy to feed.**

Below: **This warningly-coloured moth caterpillar from the eastern rainforests is one of many which are impossible to identify unless one has time to rear them through to the adult stage.**

Below right: **These moth caterpillars on a leaf near Diégo Suarez appear to be warningly coloured, a defensive strategy which is particularly common in the tropics.**

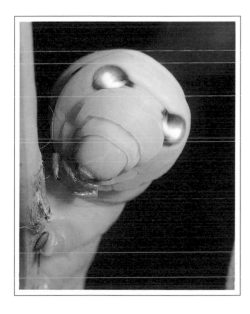

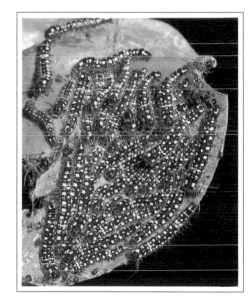

Above left: **Female sand-wasps are a frequent sight through-out the world dragging an outsize caterpillar across some sandy track. This is** Ammophila beniniense, **a widespread African species with A. b. imerinae** endemic to Madagascar. **These wasps are typical of the dry forests of the south and west.**

Above: **The nests of the endemic social wasp** Ropalidia anarchica **are characteristic features of Madagascar's forests. This nest was being exposed to strong sunlight as the sun set, leading several of its inhabitants to resort to some furious fanning of their wings to cool things down a little.**

Left: **This attractive species of** Polistes **social wasp seems to be close to the endemic P. fastidiosus and may be merely a form of it. It was photographed in the dry forest of Kirindy near Morondava, an area which is rich in species of wasp.**

Below left: **The sombre-toned mud-dauber wasp** Sceliphron fuscum **is a common sight around houses near Maroansetra, often trying to build its earthen nests on clothes hanging out to dry. This endemic wasp more normally chooses a building site on the trunk of a tree or beneath a rock overhang. The female makes repeated visits to the nest carrying a pellet of mud in her jaws. She skilfully moulds this plastic material into a cluster of cells which she stocks with paralysed spiders (including** Gasteracantha versicolor — **see** plate**).**

Opposite: **Madagascar's beautiful green social wasps are unique in all the world. This appears to be a form of** Ropalidia pomicolor **photographed in the dry forests at Ampijeroa. With its cluster of inhabitants, the nest is remarkably cryptic, resembling a multi-lobed fruit (of which there are several kinds on the island) hanging from the tip of a twig. Could this indeed be a remarkable example of fruit mimicry?**

BEES, WASPS AND ANTS

Bees, wasps and ants all belong to the huge order Hymenoptera. Some of these groups are among the best-studied insects in Madagascar. Hundreds of new species of parasitic wasps, in the families Chalcididae and Ichneumonidae, have been described in recent years — most of them endemic — but these are of little interest to the non-specialist. Much work still remains to be done on the social and solitary wasps which are undoubtedly very rich in Madagascar. All 10 species of *Belonogaster* skinny paper wasps are endemic, some of them turned out in beautiful shades of green. The nest is usually a single hanging comb, in which the exposed cells form a more-or-less oval grouping, although *B. brevipetiolata* suspends its cells in long threads, often below some rock overhang by a

river in the eastern rainforests. Similarly attractive and striking shades of green are also seen in certain species of *Ropalidia* and, in fact, the frequent occurrence of this colour in Madagascan species makes them unique among the world's wasps.

Certain Madagascan bees, in the family Anthophoridae, also shimmer in lustrous shades of brilliantly metallic green which, coupled with their rapid, darting flight, makes them look confusingly similar to some of the euglossine bees from South America.

Ants (Formicidae) are far less evident in Madagascar than in Africa, Asia or South America because such conspicuous (often with painful bites) types as the army and driver ants, leaf-cutting ants and tailor ants are absent.

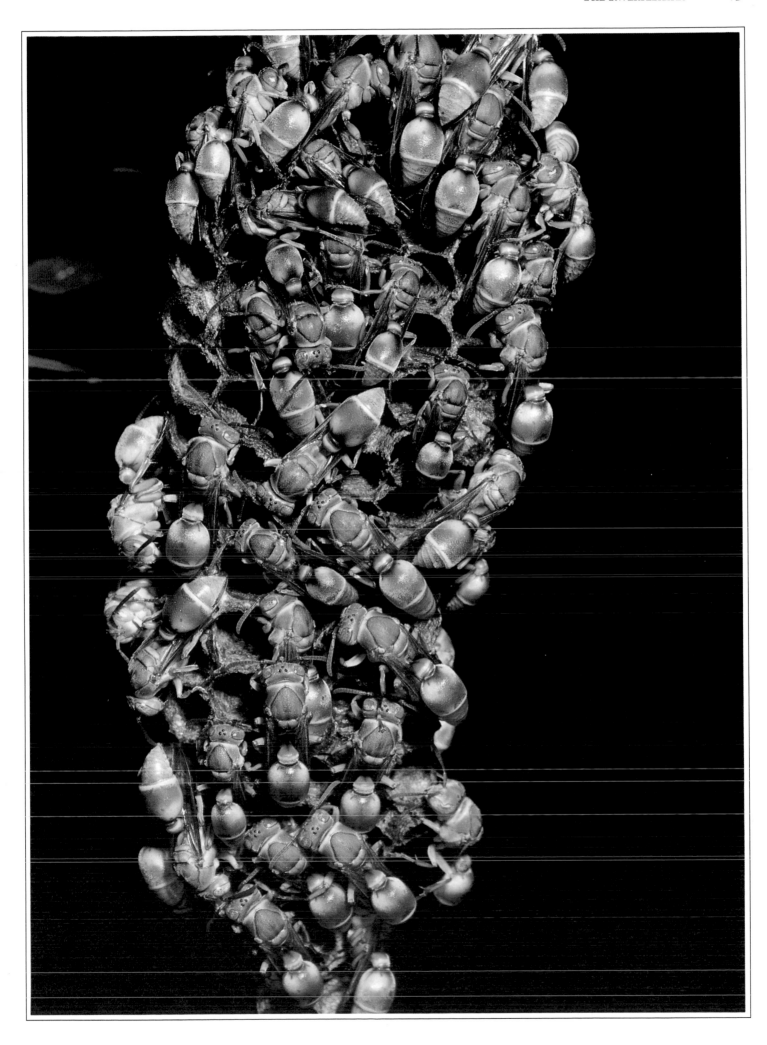

Chapter 4
Amphibians and Reptiles

The amphibians

Madagascar is rich in amphibians, and about 150 species have been recorded to date. Forty of these have been described since 1970, and new species are even now regularly turning up. In common with most other groups of Madagascan animals, however, the amphibians are represented by a large number of species belonging to only a small number of families, with some surprising and major omissions. There are no caecilians (present in much of Africa as well as the Seychelles), and even such familiar animals as newts and salamanders (Salamandridae) are wanting, as well as toads (Bufonidae), a family of wide distribution, otherwise absent only from Australia, New Guinea and New Zealand. Yet, despite this lack of diversity, the amphibians are of extreme interest for the herpetologist, because of the very high rate of endemism. Only two of the 150 species are found elsewhere. *Ptychadena mascareniensis* also occurs in East Africa, while *Rana tigrina*, the Asian bullfrog, has been deliberately introduced and is spreading throughout the island, particularly on the Hauts Plateaux where it finds the rice fields to its liking.

The majority of Madagascan frogs are forest dwellers which are intolerant of any major modification of their habitat. Only around 10 per cent of the endemic frogs are thought to be capable of adapting to artificially induced habitat change, so the long-term survival of some of the more localized species — and these are many — must be in doubt if their particular neck of the woods comes under the

Mantidactylus aglavei (Ranidae) from the eastern rainforests spends the day on a mossy branch. This individual was only spotted when one of the Duke University primatologists leaned against a tree and the frog jumped out from beneath his shoulder! Note the moss-like fringes on the hind legs.

axe. Certain areas of forest are remarkably rich in species. Perhaps the most accessible and best-known locality is the mosaic of primary forest, secondary formations and exotic plantations at Périnet. This area contains a wide variety of biotypes, including temporary rainy-season pools in open grassy swards, sunlit swampy patches with abundant *Pandanus* palms, Stygian shaded pools in dense forest, numerous tiny rivulets, small fast-flowing streams and a large river. More than 50 species of frogs have been found here, the most famous being the golden mantella *Mantella aurantiaca* which is currently known from nowhere else. Not surprisingly, the drier areas of the south and west are rather poor in frogs although they do provide the favoured habitat for certain characteristic species.

Little is known about the breeding habits of many Madagascan frogs, but it does seem that most of the more bizarre and interesting customs seen in other parts of the world are absent. Thus, there are no mouth-brooders, no marsupial species, no males ferrying tadpoles on their backs, and no examples of foam-nesters. On the whole, the Madagascan frogs seem to be rather a conventional lot, opting for basically uncomplicated breeding methods in still or running water.

FAMILY HYPEROLIIDAE

There are some nine Madagascan representatives of this family which is centred on sub-Saharan Africa but which also occurs in the Seychelles. Most of the 290-odd species are arboreal, and many African *Hyperolius* sedge frogs are among the most eye-catching and brightly coloured amphibians in the world. The Madagascan members of the family, all in a single genus, *Heterixalus*, are less spectacular but some species, such as *Heterixalus tricolor*, are a most attractive shade of greenish gold. This small frog can be very common along the east coast in open areas such as dunes, the sedgy areas around lakes and on scrubby cleared forest. During the day, it crouches down low on a leaf near the waterside, its underside close to the surface and its legs clasped tightly to its sides. In this posture, it seems to be very resistant to desiccation and often chooses a position which is fully exposed to the sun and wind. In such an open situation, these golden frogs contrast strongly with the darker green of the leaves, and it is a mystery how they avoid heavy predation by birds such as herons. *Heterixalus boettgeri* is similar (it was once considered synonymous with *H. tricolor*) but is a slightly darker green, which serves as better camouflage during its similarly exposed daytime torpor. It is particularly common in the open swamps near Fort Dauphin where it inhabits the same ground as the pitcher plant *Nepenthes madagascariensis*.

With their liking for open habitats and resistance to drying out, most *Heterixalus* are better adapted to survive artificial habitat modification. It is hardly surprising that one of the commonest frogs on the Hauts Plateaux is *H. betsileo* which is quite at home in the savanna-like landscape here and further to the

Top: **Heterixalus tricolor (Hyperoliidae)** *in its typical exposed daytime resting position.*

Above: **Heterixalus boettgeri** *is commonly seen perched on leaves in the swampy areas near Fort Dauphin. Until 1982, it was included in the synonymy of* H. tricolor.

west. At the start of the wet season in the dry western forests, the males appear like magic from the previously crisp-dried landscape, and can be heard calling in hundreds around the rapidly filling lakes and ponds. The eggs are laid in masses on vegetation just above the water where further rainfall will be sure to bring about their inundation.

FAMILY MICROHYLIDAE

Often called narrow-mouthed frogs, this family has a very wide distribution in the Americas, Africa, Asia and the Australian region. There are over 280 species worldwide of which some 41 are endemic to Madagascar. These are divided into four subfamilies; three endemic, the Scaphiophryninae, Dyscophinae and Cophylinae, and one, the Microhylinae very

Above: **The spectacular large tomato frog Dyscophus antongili (Microbylidae) is a warningly coloured diurnal species which can secrete copious quantities of poisonous white mucus. It is common enough around Maroansetra but its total area of distribution is very restricted.**

Left: **Platypelis grandis (Microbylidae) exhibits a remarkable ability to select a suitable background on which to spend the day. Note how this male has carefully arranged himself on the edge of a patch of similarly patterned lichen.**

widespread. In common with the worldwide trend, the majority of the Madagascan species tend to be cryptically coloured in greens and browns although this family also contains some of the most striking of Madagascan frogs. The most impressive is the tomato frog *Dyscophus antongili* (Dyscophinae) a large, corpulent beast (it will nearly cover the palm of a hand) conspicuously coloured in shades of red, sometimes verging on salmon-pink, but often a glowing vermilion. This florid creature is restricted to the region around the Bay of Antongil and near Tamatave although it is probably more widespread in forests in the area than is currently realized. It is found within the town of Maroansetra where it apparently breeds in pools in gardens. It also occurs abundantly in a plantation of *Eucalyptus* nearby where it lays masses of eggs in small shallow pools trapped in hollows beneath the trees. In late April and early May, such pools may be virtually clogged with these eggs and, despite being originally an inhabitant of primary rainforest, the tomato frog has obviously been capable of adapting to radical alterations of its habitat. With its bold red uniform, it is similar to some of the famous South American poison-arrow frogs (Dendrobatidae). The tomato frog is, however, very much larger and more dramatic than any of these, but it shares their diurnal habits, a universal feature in amphibians flaunting warning colours. When picked up and roughly handled, the tomato frog exudes copious quantities of a white fluid which is probably toxic, although this has not been tested in detail.

Pseudohemisus madagascariensis is a smaller but attractive species, decked out in various shades of olive or bluish green and with a series of wavy brown stripes along its back. This is one of a plethora of Madagascan frogs that have very restricted distributions, in this case just the Andringitra mountains. It has recently been demonstrated that, in anatomical features, *Pseudohemisus* tadpoles lie midway between the families Ranidae and Microhylidae. This discovery perhaps brings into question the present placement of the subfamily Scaphiophryninae, and possibly even the wisdom of maintaining the families as separate entities. Relict species exhibiting primitive ancestral features, which have since diverged more positively in continental faunas, however, are typical of long-isolated islands such as Madagascar.

Most members of the Cophylinae are typical examples of arboreal breeders. The tadpoles do not feed during their development and are guarded by the male. In species such as *Platypelis grandis* of the eastern rainforests, the toes are prominently inflated into broad, almost circular suckers, which efficiently 'glue' the frog to a tree trunk. During the day, males have been collected from beneath debris, but they may also sit in full view on bark in a damp shady part of the forest. Their pattern is rather variable, but is often mottled so as to resemble lichens. It is noteworthy that these frogs actually seem to exercise considerable discrimination in their choice of resting place, as males have been found displayed against isolated splodges of lichen which the frogs matched very closely in appearance. At night, during early spring in September and October, the males utter their penetrating calls from the shelter of a tree hole, which may also possibly function as an amplifier. Holes in large, broad-stemmed bamboos are particularly favoured. Females are attracted to the calling males and the 100 or so eggs are laid and fertilized within the nesting chamber. The female deserts the nest several days later, leaving the male alone at his post to guard the developing tadpoles. The male sticks to his task for around five weeks, during which time the copious amount of yolk in the notably large eggs is absorbed by the growing tadpoles. This yolk-reservoir fuels the entire process for the tadpoles fast throughout the whole period of their development, and eventually metamorphose into minute froglets less than 0.4 inch (1 cm) long.

The presence of the father does more than merely shield his developing progeny from attack by small predators. Indeed, this could even be of minor significance, for his main function may be to provide fungicidal secretions. In their enclosed stagnant environment the tadpoles quickly moulder and die if the father is removed. The need for close parental presence to prevent fungal infection is also known in other unrelated groups of animals. These include insects, such as earwigs (Dermaptera) and mole crickets (Orthoptera: Gryllotalpidae), in which the eggs rapidly become covered in a fungal mould if the attendant female is removed. Some members of the Cophylinae have burrowing habits and spend most of their lives in a burrow. Breeding is carried out in small cavities which become filled with water during the wet season. Here, too, the father remains on sentry duty with the developing non-feeding young. Ants typically seem to constitute the food of many members of the subfamily, although beetles have been found in the stomachs of some.

FAMILY RANIDAE

The so-called true frogs belong to a practically worldwide family with over 600 species, of which 63 are found in Madagascar, thus making this the major group of frogs on the island. Of these, only three belong to the non-endemic subfamily Raninae. The widespread *Ptychadena mascareniensis* and introduced *Rana tigrina* have already been mentioned. The third species, *Tomopterna labrosa*, is a burrowing frog and one of the select band which prefers the drier western and southern regions.

The rest belong to the endemic subfamily Mantellinae, mostly small to very small frogs which are among the most familiar and frequently seen of Madagascan amphibians. The calling and piping of the males are characteristic features of the night in the eastern rainforests. The best-known species is the golden mantella *Mantella aurantiaca*. This frog is active during the day and often swarms on the forest floor at the beginning of the rains in its home at Périnet. The vivid, egg-yolk yellow of its skin contrasts

The tiny golden mantella Mantella aurantiaca *(Ranidae) is perhaps the best known of Madagascan frogs as it has been extensively exploited for the pet trade. Despite this, it still remains common at Périnet, its only locality.*

strongly with the dull browns and blacks of its surroundings. As in *Dyscophus antongili*, this flamboyant exterior is thought to advertise the presence of toxins secreted by the skin, so it is a powerful visual 'keep off' message. Unlike the robust tomato frog, however, the golden mantella would fit comfortably on to a thumbnail, a smallness of stature also typical of many of the warningly coloured poison-arrow frogs from South America. Unfortunately, the majority of the Mantellinae are small drab frogs which only come to notice when they hop out from under a descending boot in damp spots in the rainforests. Although the two largest species, *Mantidactylus femoralis* and *M. lugubris*, are just brown spotted with black, they are handsome in a subdued way. They always seem to live near to fast-flowing streams in forests, often clinging to rocks next to the foaming waters, held firmly in position by the large suckers on hands and feet. Both species are widespread in the eastern region. When disturbed, they may leap into the swirling waters but are generally most tolerant of having a light shone on them.

Some species of *Mantella* and *Mantidactylus* deposit their eggs on the ground near water, where further rain will wash them into the water or subsequently submerge them. The most interesting habits are shown by species which place their eggs in masses on leaves well above the water level. In some *Mantidactylus* species, the act of fertilization and egg laying is remarkably brief, taking perhaps a mere ten minutes or so. In this time, a gelatinous blob of eggs is attached to a leaf overhanging a shaded shallow pool. While carrying out his procreative duties, the male stands in a most unusual position over the female, with his thighs level with the back of her neck. Species which deposit their eggs on leaves above water include *Mantidactylus blommersae*, *M. depressiceps*, *M. liber*, *M. tornieri* and *M. wittei*. At first, the gelatinous packaging containing the eggs is viscous and holds them firmly in place against the erosive effects of even torrential rain. Gradually, the viscosity decreases as the tadpoles develop, head uppermost, until finally they tumble off the leaf and into the water where the rest of their development is normal. This form of reproduction closely parallels that seen in many non-Madagascan tree frogs of the family Hylidae.

Several other *Mantidactylus* also lay their eggs on leaves, but the tadpoles complete their entire development in their aerial home, making do with the minuscule reservoir of water trapped in the leaf axils of such plants as *Pandanus* palms and the traveller's palm *Ravenala madagascariensis*. The tadpoles are characterized by their wide, horny, multitoothed beaks with which they rasp off the carpet of algae that often encrusts the palm leaves. When times get tough and their miniature pools are about to dry up and leave them stranded, they may stave off disaster by using their very muscular tails to flip themselves out of their home. If their luck holds, they will land in or near a lower axil where water is more likely to be present. These obligate tree dwellers are typical denizens of the eastern rainforests. Their muted croaking is often heard during the day in groves of *Pandanus* palms. Although they are easy enough to hear, the perpetrators of these gentle duets can be frustratingly difficult to find. They often call from 16 feet (5 m) or more above the ground, surrounded by a spiky stockade of leaves which must afford them at least some protection against predators.

In two species of Mantellinae, the tadpoles probably develop directly in the absence of free water. *Mantidactylus asper* males call only during the height of the rainy season when the air and ground are permanently saturated with moisture. These are just the conditions dreaded by human visitors to the forest when the fungal disease known as trench foot may strike painfully, camera lenses become smothered in a filigree of fungal hyphae, electronic equipment ceases to operate and leather boots moulder and fall apart after a month. Such high humidity is perfect for *M. asper* tadpoles, however, and their development probably takes place among sopping green drifts of moss on branches well away from standing water. The rainy season also stimulates the appearance of a multitude of small invertebrates, just when the developing froglets need a food supply of small animals. Circumstantial evidence also indicates that *M. eiselti* (known only from the type locality at Périnet) also develops in the same way although it is possible that some kind of parental care, so far unobserved, may also be involved.

FAMILY RHACOPHORIDAE
This family of just under 200 species is distributed in widely separated parts of sub-Saharan Africa and, more commonly, in south-east Asia. Typically, non-Madagascan species lay their eggs in foam nests on or above the ground. Some amazing Asian species of *Rhacophorus* are known as flying frogs because of their prowess in gliding. The Madagascan representatives belong to two genera, *Aglyptodactylus* (one species) and *Boophis* (28 species), none of which flies nor creates foam nests. They are mainly small, cryptic frogs which deposit their eggs in water, usually in fast-flowing forest streams, although some species prefer stagnant water, sometimes in the open. In fact, among Madagascar's frogs, *Boophis* are probably the most quintessential stream breeders. At night in the rainy season, the males are drawn from every corner of the forest towards their breeding sites alongside swiftly flowing streams, some of which enjoy but a brief flurry of life and cease to run during the dry season. Chorusing males add their lusty concert to the patter of raindrops and incessant gurgling of the water as they seek to attract a mate to lay her eggs.

In most species, the eggs are attached to water plants within the stream. *Boophis goudoti* affixes batches of 30 or so eggs to rocks in the midst of the surging waters, the tadpoles later developing in the

Boophis luteus (Rhacophoridae) lives beside fast-running streams in the eastern rainforests.

slower backwaters and associated pools. This is one of the most widespread frogs in Madagascar, common near stagnant ponds or slow-moving streams, not only in forests, but in unnatural habitats such as rice fields. The adults seem adept at catching large prey, such as grasshoppers and insect larvae, while the frogs themselves form part of the diet for the local people, and are prized as a delicacy. The tadpoles of some species, such as *Boophis erythrodactylus*, have a streamlined profile and powerful sucker-like beak for clinging to rocks in the midst of the maelstrom. The majority of *Boophis* tadpoles are more rotund, however, and adapted for a more tranquil life in the less violent parts of the streams.

Most species undergo their final metamorphosis and emerge on to dry land at the start of the summer rains in September and October. The frog which initially emerges may not necessarily bear much resemblance to the adult because, in many *Boophis*, there is a marked juvenile coloration, generally some shade of green. This dissimilarity reaches a climax in *Boophis madagascariensis*. The adult is a large brown frog which spends the day crouched down on the forest floor, where its resemblance to a dead leaf renders it virtually undetectable. Leaf-like projections on the tips of the elbows and heels help to merge the legs smoothly into the general body outline, and contribute significantly to the overall effect. Yet the young froglets are an attractive pale green, patterned on the back with black, and on the head with white

Boophis madagascariensis (Rhacophoridae) is one of several treefrogs which spend the day on the forest floor where they resemble dead leaves.

spots. Such is the difference from the adult that these striking juveniles were originally classified as a separate species, although such striking dichromatism is also found outside Madagascar, for example, in *Hyla geographica* (Hylidae) from Brazil.

Some *Boophis* species are restricted to mountains, where the tadpoles take two years to develop fully in the cold clear waters at these higher altitudes. *B. williamsi* has been found only on the Ambohimirandana and Ankaratra mountains at 7200 feet (2200 m) and above. The tadpoles live in crystal-clear mountain rivulets running over stony beds through forested countryside. *B. microtympanum* is restricted to the mountains of Ankaratra and Andringitra where it lives along similar streams, attaching its eggs in batches of 100 or so to twigs partly submerged in the swirling waters.

The reptiles

For its area of 226,739 square miles (587 000 sq km), Madagascar is very rich in reptiles, with about 260 species described to date. It is interesting to compare this with the six species native to the 121, 655 square miles (314 950 sq km) of the British Isles. Over 30 of Madagascar's total have been described during the 1970s, and new species are regularly being discovered as herpetologists penetrate into some of the more remote areas of the island. At over 90 per cent, the rate of endemism is among the highest for any group of animals, reflecting the long evolutionary history of the reptiles in Madagascar. As in many other animal groups in Madagascar, this marked endemism is accompanied by a richness at the specific level and a poverty in the number of families and genera. In addition, there are strong differences between the overall composition of the Madagascan fauna compared with that of the neighbouring African landmass.

The Madagascan reptiles can broadly be separated into two sharply contrasting groups. Group 1 contains a small number of genera each with a meagre number of species. These seem to be relict forms, survivors of an ancient ancestry dating from the time before the initial break-up of Gondwanaland. Examples are the boid snakes and iguanid lizards. Group 2 contains genera which are outstandingly rich in species, seemingly derived from adaptive radiations arising from a number of separate, widely spaced immigrations which took place after the formation of the Mozambique channel. The chameleons are good examples of this.

CROCODILIANS

The only crocodilian is the Nile crocodile *Crocodilus niloticus*, the widespread crocodile of Africa. How much longer this animal will survive in Madagascar is open to question, because it has been extensively hunted for its skins, and crocodile-leather belts and other artefacts are sold openly to tourists in the streets of Antananarivo. As a result, it has become very rare and elusive, although a few survivors still lurk in the subterranean rivers of the Ankarana massif and elsewhere. In Lake Anivorano between Diégo Suarez and Ambilobe the crocodiles are held sacred and protected by a *fady*, but they generally seem to shun attention and most tourists hoping for a glimpse are doomed to disappointment.

TORTOISES AND TURTLES

Four species of sea turtles in the family Cheloniidae are found in Madagascan waters. The loggerhead *Caretta caretta* nests in small numbers, probably in the low hundreds, mainly in the south-east corner around Tulear and in a few places on the west coast as far north as Morondava. A few green turtles *Chelonia mydas* also nest. The hawksbill *Eretmochelys imbricata* still hauls ashore in good numbers but it is heavily persecuted by the Malagasy people and in excess of 2000 a year are probably taken for local consumption. This has led to a continuing and possibly terminal decline in the numbers arriving each year. The olive Ridley turtle *Lepidochelys olivacea* is said to breed sporadically in the north-west, but the luth turtle *Dermochelys coriacea* (family Dermochelyidae) is purely a vagrant in Madagascan waters. The long-term future for the successful breeding of any species of marine turtles in Madagascar seems uncertain, although important nesting beaches for the green and hawksbill turtles are

now subject to official protection, and all forms of exploitation are forbidden.

The land tortoises in the family Testudinidae are especially interesting. There are five species, four endemics and one, *Kinixys belliana*, which was imported from Africa and is now established in the north-west. The four endemic tortoises are very handsome beasts, although all have suffered a decline in numbers in recent years. The most severely threatened — indeed it is one of the world's most endangered reptiles — is the angonoka or plowshare tortoise *Geochelone yniphora*. It is a large tortoise with a strongly domed shell 18 inches (45 cm) long, neatly patterned with yellow and brown reticulations. It has probably always been very localized, restricted to three small peninsular forests in the Baly Bay area of north-west Madagascar. But, within this small enclave, it must once have been quite abundant, because, from the seventeenth to the nineteenth centuries, large numbers were collected for export as food. Since then, the habitat has been increasingly modified by people and currently consists of a mosaic of tropical dry forest with a tangled understorey of bamboo, alternating with patches of grassland and scrub. It is a difficult habitat to search because the plant life gets in the way, and, when the tortoise is active during the summer, the region is very hot. This makes it very difficult to make a precise count of the remaining numbers. An estimate based on extensive searching in the 38.6 square miles (100 sq km) of remaining habitat, however, suggests a surviving population of between 100 and 400 animals.

In view of the probability of further degradation of the habitat by burning and conversion to agricultural uses, coupled with the likelihood that the abundant feral pigs are responsible for decimating the vulnerable eggs and juveniles, a decision was made to establish a captive breeding colony using animals already in captivity. The site chosen was the Ampijeroa Forest Station south of Mahajanga. This programme is now enjoying increasing success with each passing year, as experience is amassed on the breeding and feeding requirements of this tortoise in captivity. In particular, it has not always been easy to find adequate supplies of local plants which are relished by the tiny babies, while variations in nesting time, and the resulting higher or lower nest temperatures, have probably been the reason for a number of failed nests, where no hatching took place. Each successive year sees a greater proportion of young successfully hatching, while survival of those which do is at an encouragingly high level, thanks largely to the dedicated care of the project leader, Don Reid, and his Madagascan assistant.

In the past, some authorities have blamed the rapid decline in this tortoise's fortunes on the 'plowshare' or gular plate, a projection from the underside of the carapace which, in the males, extends forwards for several centimetres under the head and neck. During the mating season, the males become highly antagonistic and engage in noisy bouts of jousting, rushing headlong towards one another to collide spectacularly with a crash of shells. Each combatant then tries his best to render his opponent impotent by tilting him on to his back, using the plowshare as a lever. It has been suggested that the gradual extension of the gular plate to its present extravagant proportions has proved to be an evolutionary time bomb, ticking away until eventually exerting its fatal effect when it finally became too long for its owner to be capable of feeding properly. After all, this argument goes, it is not easy to grab a tasty mouthful of herbage if you cannot stretch your neck down over an enormous plate which keeps on getting in the way. Captive males seem to feed without too much difficulty, however, and the reasons for the angonoka's decline can, as with so many Malagasy animals, be blamed firmly on human destructive influence. The captive breeding programme is proposed as part of an overall scheme to save this species from extinction. It is also hoped to establish a reserve on the Cape Sada Peninsula. This would provide an ideal habitat for the species and has the advantage of being relatively inaccessible and easily wardened. Being a peninsula, it should also be possible to seal off the area from wild pigs.

The other impressively large tortoise in Madagascar is the radiated tortoise *Geochelone radiata*. It is bigger than the angonoka, reaching a shell length of 15 inches (38 cm) and a weight of 29 pounds (13 kg). It is found in the dry south and south-west where it inhabits the 'spiny desert', as well as the remaining areas of gallery forest along the major rivers. It is an attractive animal, the yellow of the shell strikingly patterned with black sunbursts, although some individuals are rather drab as the black almost masks the yellow. This tortoise has been exterminated from the vicinity of Fort Dauphin and Tulear but it is still abundant in parts of the 'spiny desert', especially on the Mahafaly plateau. In this area a local *fady* has proved very effective in protecting the animal from exploitation for food by the local Antandroy and Mahafaly people. Unfortunately, visitors from outside this region have no such taboos and often collect the tortoises for food, stopping their cars to pick them up from the roadside. A large population exists in the Beza-Mahafaly reserve, where scientists have painted large numerals on their shells to enable research on their ecology and longevity to be carried out. The diet probably consists of a mixture of grass, tender young leaves and fruits. These are all in short supply during the long dry season, although this tortoise is certainly still active in July, when the cold winter nights restrict the daily activities to a short period from the late morning until about 4.00 pm.

The continued survival of this splendid tortoise has no doubt been assisted by its inclusion on Appendix 1 of the Convention on International Trade in

A splendidly marked specimen of the rare radiated tortoise **Geochelone radiata** *plods through gallery forest in Beza-Mahafaly reserve in the dry south.*

Endangered Species of Wild Fauna and Flora (CITES). Implementation of this convention by Madagascar and by the importing countries (mainly in Europe) has seemingly all but stopped the once thriving trade in exported polished shells. These days the purchase of such a grisly trophy is no longer a practical proposition for tourists visiting Madagascar, although some visitors are still 'caught' by smooth-tongued local vendors, and buy a shell before they realize that they have no legal way of taking it out of the country or into their own.

Both the other tortoises are much smaller. The Madagascar spider tortoise *Pyxis arachnoides* is a small [6-inch (15-cm)] species with a rather flattened carapace. It is restricted to dry areas of the south and south-west, not occurring more than 30 miles (50 km) from the sea. Its most northerly limit is near Morombe, extending down to Amboasary in the south, not far from Fort Dauphin. Populations are fragmented and it is split into three subspecies: *P. a. arachnoides* in the south-west; *P. a. matzi* in the south; and *P. a. brygooi* in the west. In parts of the south, it occurs in the same habitat as the radiated tortoise. The spider tortoise is thought to be declining rapidly, partly as a result of destruction, and partly because of collecting for the pet trade. Replacement of individuals lost from a population would seem to be slow, because the female lays only a single large egg, although the number produced each year is unknown. The prolonged dry period is spent underground, so the breeding season is fairly short.

The Madagascar flat-tailed tortoise *Pyxis planicauda* is even rarer and its plight almost as dire as the angonoka's. It is found only in the Andranomena forest, a mere 40 square miles (100 sq km) of refuge near Morondava. Luckily, some of the remaining habitat occurs within the Analabe private reserve, although it is surrounded by a wide area of agricultural development. It is the smallest Madagascan tortoise [carapace 5 inches (12.5 cm) long] and little is known of its ecology although, as in *Pyxis arachnoides*, only one large egg at a time is laid. It, too, is the subject of a captive breeding programme at Ampijeroa but, at the time of writing, without the success enjoyed with the angonoka.

The only endemic freshwater turtle, the Madagascar side-neck turtle *Erymnochelys madagascariensis*, is a species of great zoological interest. It is very closely related to the turtles of the South American genus *Podocnemis* and, indeed, until recently was included in that genus. Fossil *Podocnemis* have been found in Africa, but not even closely related forms are now found there. This relict species is declining in Madagascar as a result of extensive exploitation for food and because its nesting areas are being turned over to rice growing. It is a large grey turtle which can attain a length of 20 inches (50 cm) and a weight of 33 pounds (15 kg). Its favoured habitat comprises the quiet backwaters of large rivers, as well as lakes and ponds, but only in the west and north-west of the island. Three smaller species, *Pelomedusa subrufa*, *Pelusios castanoides* and *Pelusios subniger*, are not endemic and are widely distributed in neighbouring Africa. They are most often seen squashed on roads, but otherwise seldom encountered.

SAURIA — THE LIZARDS

With over 180 species, Madagascar is undeniably rich in lizards. These species are crammed into only five families, however: Gekkonidae (geckoes); Iguanidae; Cordylidae; Chamaeleontidae (chameleons); and Scincidae (skinks). Oddly, the most widespread, colourful and conspicuous of African lizards, the agamids, are absent, as are the large monitor lizards (Varanidae) which are such a frequent sight lumbering throughout much of the African bush. Yet more absentees are the generally small lizards in the Lacertidae, which are so familiar in Europe and which are also found in Africa. Nevertheless, it must be stressed that Madagascar is a very rich and exciting place in which to search for lizards.

Family Gekkonidae — the geckoes

There are 63 species of geckoes in Madagascar of which 53 are endemic to the island. These range from the world's most superbly camouflaged lizard, *Uroplatus fimbriatus*, to the most flamboyantly

The leaf-tailed gecko Uroplatus fimbriatus *is probably the world's most perfectly camouflaged bark-living lizard. It seems mainly to favour trees of the size shown in the picture, spending the day in a head-downwards posture, blending perfectly into the bark using the frill along the underside of the body.*

Left: **Sometimes** Uroplatus fimbriatus *selects a small sapling and then it is easier to spot.*

Above: **The frill beneath the head of the leaf-tailed gecko** Uroplatus fimbriatus **is particularly deep and well developed.**

beautiful of the entire clan, the day geckoes in the genus *Phelsuma*.

There are six species of *Uroplatus*, a genus endemic to Madagascar, of which the largest is the Madagascar leaf-tailed gecko *Uroplatus fimbriatus* which can attain a length of 11_4 inches (29 cm). It spends the day sitting head-downwards in full view on a tree trunk. It is not particularly fussy about the width of the trunk, electing to stretch out against anything from broad boles nearly 3 feet (1 m) in diameter to saplings so slim that its body protrudes on either side. A ragged-bordered fringe of skin forms a valance along the underside of the body; it is flounced out more generously beneath the chin and continues in a less elaborate manner along the undersides of the legs and body. The effect is to blend the outline of the body smoothly and imperceptibly into the bark of the tree, at the same time completely eliminating the tell-tale shadow which would be cast by an unbalanced profile. The very broad, flattened feet are splayed out against the bark,

and the back legs are held up vertically at the rear, where they are often almost concealed beneath the spatula-like tail. In this position, even a large specimen of this amazing gecko is extremely difficult to spot in the dappled light beneath the canopy. *U. fimbriatus* can even change colour to match the substrate; shades of green when sitting on moss or lichens; silver-grey for trunks covered with encrusting lichens; black for sombre-barked, lichen-free wood.

This accomplished quick-change artist can alter its appearance with incredible speed, too, for, if a whitish specimen is disturbed from its closely matching background and runs upwards to a moss-covered area, it will assume a corresponding shade of green in a matter of seconds. Its choice of colour is not always infallible, however, and bad matches do occur where a dark lizard is posed against a light background and vice versa. Sometimes, it may take several attempts to get the match right. I noted an almost black individual standing out conspicuously on a pale-brown, lichen-free trunk. The next day the lizard had moved to an adjacent trunk encrusted with white lichens. Yet it was still conspicuous, because it had changed to green! Only on the third day, after it had moved again, this time to a nearby dark-brown trunk, did it finally achieve a suitably corresponding shade. This was on the island of Nosy Mangabe, where the lizard is so abundant that I found 29 individuals in the space of a few days. This high density is probably due to the low predation pressures on this isolated island, from which the fossa (a primitive civet) is absent and where birds of prey noticeably rare. On the mainland, *Uroplatus fimbriatus* is very widespread and is probably present wherever there remains enough natural forest although it is absent from the dry south and south-west. In all regions, except Nosy Mangabe, it always seems to exist in low (sometimes very low) densities, probably because of the ubiquitous presence of the fossa and the abundance of raptors and arboreal snakes.

If its superb camouflage fails to keep it safe from prying eyes, *U. fimbriatus* can still fall back on a remarkable defensive ploy. If it is touched or picked up suddenly, it raises its tail abruptly above its back and opens its mouth wide to reveal a startling scarlet tongue protruding in a rather intimidating manner. Such a sudden transformation from harmless cryptic lizard to fearsome-looking, open-mouthed demon is presumably designed to unnerve a potential enemy. The scarcity of *Uroplatus* in many areas, however, perhaps indicates that this last-ditch display often fails to save the animal's life.

Uroplatus guentheri is similar, but smaller and less impressive, lacking the sophisticated frill on the underside. For many years it was known only from a single specimen of unknown origin, but it has now been discovered in one or two localities, including the Forestry Station of Ampijeroa. The adaptive ingenuity shown by these trunk-dwelling *Uroplatus* is not the end of the story, however. Whereas *U. fimbriatus* is the world's most perfect bark-mimicking lizard, *U. alluaudi* and *U. ebenaui* are the best examples of dead leaf mimicry, even to the extent of having extravagant leaf-like outgrowths on the legs and body. These incredible mimics spend the day resting invisibly on bushes, and finding them is really practical only at night when they perch in a more prominent position and can more easily be picked out in a beam of light. *Uroplatus* are typical wait-and-see predators, sitting tight in one place and biding their time until their large bulbous eyes spot a suitable insect walking within range.

The reverse of this unpretentious cryptic lifestyle is exemplified by the numerous species of *Phelsuma* day geckoes which are the most ornately garbed and eye-catching members of the Gekkonidae. With its 13 described species, Madagascar ranks top in the *Phelsuma* league table, although this total may change because the classification of these lizards is somewhat confused owing to their variability. This may result in one or two names being dropped, while new names may be erected for species previously unrecognized.

Phelsuma is thought to have evolved in Madagascar and subsequently spread to other parts of the Indian Ocean, including the Comoro Islands, Mauritius, Réunion, the Seychelles and as far east as the Andaman Islands in the Bay of Bengal. These living jewels among geckoes are active only during the day and employ their ostentatious colours in courtship displays involving vigorous head bobbing and tail waving.

The most widespread, as well as the largest, of the Madagascan species is *P. madagascariensis*. As in many *Phelsuma*, its basic colour is a brilliant emerald green which, in this species, is emblazoned with contrasting dayglo orange splashes. The intensity of the hues is very variable; it is linked to the wide distribution of the lizard around Madagascar, extending to virtually every kind of habitat save the sterile Hauts Plateaux and the higher mountains, although its occurrence is often very local. Over this large range, it is far more beautiful in some areas than in others. It is disappointingly dull in the forests of Ankarafantsika, but dazzlingly sumptuous in the area around Diégo Suarez where it is very common. This

If it is suddenly touched, U. fimbriatus *goes into a ritualized defensive routine, turning towards its antagonist and gaping widely to reveal a starling red tongue, while simultaneously raising the tail up above the back. Whether a fierce predator, such as a fossa* Cryptoprocta ferox, *would be intimidated by such a display is doubtful but presumably it must be effective sometimes, or it would never have evolved.*

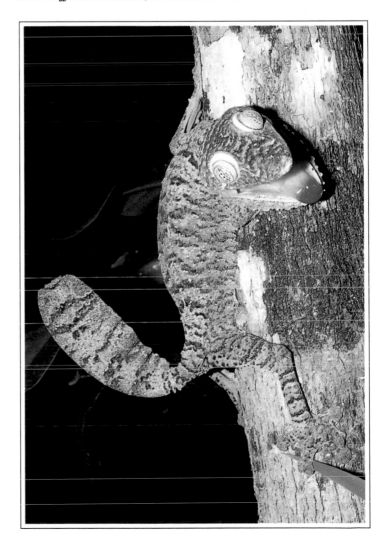

Above: **Although widespread throughout the island, the large day gecko** Phelsuma madagascariensis **presents a far more gaudy spectacle in some areas than in others. This is the most spectacular form of all, from the dry forests in Ankarana Special Reserve.**

Below: **Phelsuma quadriocellata** *is a day gecko from the forests of the central and south-east regions; it is common at Ranomafana.*

Above right: **Phelsuma guttata** *is one of the smaller day geckoes from the eastern rainforests. This specimen, photographed on Nosy Mangabe, has recently shed its tail which will be re-grown in a stubbier, less elegant form.*

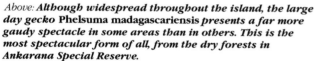

northern form is also the biggest. Anyone driving along the rough back road from Ambilobe to Matsaborimanga (heading for the Ankarana Special Reserve) is bound to spy these lizards from some considerable distance. They pose garishly on the trunks of the large shade-trees planted in the small villages. In contrast to many geckoes this species seems always to sit head uppermost. It is a mystery how such a conspicuous creature, presenting such an apparently easy target for every predator in the vicinity, manages to avoid being picked off and its populations decimated, when such cryptic lizards as *Uroplatus* seem to suffer heavy predation. Perhaps a simple combination of keen eyesight and fleetness-of-foot is the key to its survival.

Compared with these lurid giants, some of the smaller *Phelsuma* require closer inspection before the true beauty and brilliance of their livery become evident. Getting a good view is not always difficult, for several species regularly live close to human habitations. In Duke University's encampment in the forests at Ranomafana, a pretty little *P. quadriocellata* took up residence on the log platform used for draining freshly washed dishes, while others pattered around on the roofs of the tents. Not all the species are so conspicuously colourful, however. Several, such as the small [only 4 inches (10 cm) long] *P. mutabilis*, are drably mottled in a cryptic pattern which is more typical of the Gekkonidae. It is common on tree trunks in the dry forests of the western region, even occurring abundantly in the centres of towns such as Morondava. The small, but beautiful blue-green *P. lineata* can often be seen peeping out from among *Agave* or palm fronds in gardens along the east coast. *Phelsuma* are also wait-and-see predators, although it seems that the prey needs to be moving and reasonably conspicuous to attract attention. A *P. madagascariensis*, resident on a tree trunk in the Ankarana forest, was seen several times to walk right over a flattened bug (family Flatidae) resting cryptically on the bark. Several times the lizard's head came to within a hair's breadth of this potential meal; but the bug remained immobile and stayed alive.

Members of the endemic genus *Geckolepis* are rather broad-bodied, fish-like, shiny grey geckoes clad in very flat, rounded, overlapping scales. These slippery customers must be handled with great care because tails and scales are easily detached. Like many tree-living geckoes, they frequently come into houses, hiding behind the furniture during the day and coming out at night to feed. *Paroedura* contains some attractively marked nocturnal geckoes with thin legs and large heads, from which protrude large bulbous eyes. Several species are quite restricted in distribution and seldom seen although *P. pictus* is common along paths and dirt tracks in the Kirindy forest north of Morondava. The many species of *Lygodactylus* are small, cryptic, bark-inhabiting geckoes which are derived from African stock. Several of them are superficially very similar to *L. capensis* from South Africa. *Homopholis* has similar habits but is generally

Left: **Phelsuma mutabilis** *is one of several small species of day geckoes which are cryptically coloured in greys and browns. It is abundant on tree trunks in the Kirindy forest near Morondava, and even occurs in the centre of the town.*

Above: **The gecko** **Homopholis antongilensis** *is endemic to the rainforests around Antongil Bay.*

Below: **The attractive gecko** **Paroedura pictus** *is quite common in the western dry forests.*

larger and more flattened. *H. antongilensis* occurs in the area around the Bay of Antongil. It perches head-down on tree trunks in much the same manner as *Uroplatus fimbriatus*, and is almost as difficult to spot when on a suitably chosen background.

Geckoes lay large, white, hard-shelled eggs of which the true nature may be something of a mystery to those unfamiliar with reptilian reproduction. Sometimes they arouse curiosity by being attached to bark in quite conspicuous places.

Family Iguanidae — the iguanids

The presence of this family in Madagascar is something of an enigma. Most iguanids are found in Central and South America, where the family reaches its peak, but there are isolated outliers in Fiji and Tonga in the Pacific, as well as in Madagascar. There are no iguanids in Africa, yet the widespread African agamids, which uncannily resemble some of the Madagascan iguanids, have never reached Madagascar. It seems logical to assume that ancient iguanids were present in that part of Gondwanaland which contained Madagascar before the break-up of the supercontinent, but were either not present on the segment destined to be Africa or died out there at a very early stage. If this assumption is true, then the Madagascan representatives have undergone a humble degree of speciation during their long isolation on the island, especially when compared with groups presumed to be of more recent immigration, such as the species-rich chameleons.

Typically, the Madagascan iguanids are inhabitants of hot dry areas and they are absent from the eastern rainforests. The sole member of the endemic genus *Chalaradon*, the 'langalia' *C. madagascariensis*, is very common on sandy soils in the south, south-east and west. In the west, it is patchy, and absent from apparently suitable parts of the Kirindy forest, yet it swarms all over the place on small oases of sand surrounded by buildings and constant human disturbance on the seafront in Morondava. It is by far the most common reptile in the 'spiny desert', which leads to its playing an important, if involuntary, role in the economy of the predators in this area. During December, a pair of nesting Madagascan kestrels *Falco newtoni* in Berenty Reserve fed their young almost exclusively on a diet of these lizards. The rate of attrition was considerable, as the hard-working male kestrel presented a limp, lifeless *Chalaradon* to his waiting mate every 25 to 75 minutes throughout the day. This sharp-eyed killer had little difficulty in picking out his well-camouflaged prey against its sandy background. His task was obviously simplified by his prey's habits, for *Chalaradon* is very much a sun-loving lizard which spends most of its time basking right out in the open on patches of bare sand. Thus preoccupied, they are also ambushed by snakes

Above left: **Chalaradon madagascariensis** *is by far the most abundant member of the Iguanidae in the dry south. This charming little lizard abounds in Berenty Private Nature Reserve where the photograph was taken.*

Left *The large* **Oplurus cuvieri** *is the typical iguanid lizard of the dry western forests. It is common in the Kirindy forest near Morondava and at the Ampijeroa Forest Reserve further north. Note the spiky tail which is used to close off the entrance to the lizard's lair, usually in a crevice in a tree trunk.*

Left: **Oplurus cuvieri** *is often infested with tiny scarlet mites, usually situated on or near the head.*

Above: An iguanid lizard was discovered by Don Read on isolated sand reefs in Ampijeroa Forest Reserve in 1989. It is thought to be a form of **Oplurus cyclurus** *but is very widely separated from the nearest populations of that species and may prove to be something quite new.*

such as *Mimophis mahafalensis* which, despite its small size and slim build, can easily tackle a full-grown *Chalaradon*. *Chalaradon* remains very common throughout the south, however. During the summer breeding season, each male establishes a territory and parades up and down inside it, proclaiming ownership by making frequent head-bobbing movements. These also prove extremely provocative to neighbouring males, and pent-up aggression may lead to mad-cap chases across the shimmering sands. Ritualized posturing between rival males often degenerates rapidly into pugnacious combats, during which the opponents grapple with one another in a free-for-all. The procedure seems to be to hang on to anything which can be grabbed with the jaws, and then stubbornly refuse to let go until one or other emerges as the victor; or perhaps until a marauding kestrel decides the outcome. At this season the males increase their vulnerability to predators by breaking out into a bright breeding dress. This renders them even more conspicuous than at other times, just when their avian enemies need a high kill rate to satisfy their nestlings' ravenous appetites.

The six species of *Oplurus* are generally greyish or grey-brown, day-active lizards which perch openly on a tree trunk, fallen log or rock. *Oplurus cuvieri* is a western species, just as much a part of the scenery in the Ankarafantsika forest near Mahajanga as in the dry forests near Morondava much further south. In its typical pose, it sits in an alert attitude, head

uppermost, 6-10 feet (2-3 m) up on a tree trunk; but it also perches on fallen logs near ground level and often adopts a head-downwards posture on vertical trunks, with its head held up well away from the substrate at an angle of nearly 90 degrees. It is a handsome lizard with a conspicuous black 'collar', while the long, tapering tail is remarkable for its dense array of spiky embellishments. In habits and appearance, it closely resembles many African agamids, such as the common *Agama atricollis*, even though it is in a different family.

Oplurus cuvieri is a perfect example of a wait-and-see predator, patiently biding its time until a meal happens to walk past. Just how often a potential victim wanders along within striking distance each day is unknown. In Ankarafantsika I watched a robust *O. cuvieri* stuffing down an extremely large cockroach in broad daylight. This was a surprise, because cockroaches are normally nocturnal, and not usually to be found blundering within range of a hungry lizard's jaws in daylight. Large, easily won meals such as this, taken at long intervals, probably suffice to fuel the lizard's relaxed lifestyle. Its relaxed approach even extends to possible enemies, and *O. cuvieri* must be one of the world's tamest lizards, only summoning up the energy to move a short distance into hiding if strongly provoked. Individuals are often faithful to the same spot day after day, month in month out, usually within handy reach of a bolt hole. This is normally a crevice in the bark, its entrance securely closed off by the lizard's portable security door, its thorny tail!

The juveniles are often quite thick on the ground in April. They are paler-coloured miniatures of the adults but, unlike an adult, the juvenile has a conspicuous black spot in the centre of the forehead marking the location of the third (pineal) eye; this primitive feature disappears as the lizard matures. The juveniles usually perch head-downwards and pounce on anything which moves, launching themselves into space with great agility to snap up aerial prey such as flies. Insects are also plucked off the bark with such speed that they never know what hit them, giving them no chance to take advantage of their quick reactions and make a rapid getaway.

Oplurus cyclurus slightly resembles *O. cuvieri* but it is a less handsome species which lives in the dry south of the island. In 1989, an isolated population thought to be of this species was found by Don Read at the Ampijeroa Forest Reserve in the north. At this locality, the lizards are confined to tiny outcrops of white sand which form 'reefs' among the surrounding sea of tropical dry forest. The presence of such specialized drought-tolerant plants as *Pachypodium rosulatum rosulatum* and an *Aloe* species on this isolated outcrop is in itself of considerable interest. But the presence of *O. cyclurus* is baffling because it is difficult to imagine how this tiny cut-off population arrived in such a secluded spot, so far from their southern kin. Here, not only is the lizard confined to the small scattered trees of the open sun-baked sand reef, never venturing even a foot or two inside the forest, it is even restricted to the warmest north-facing slopes, and is absent from similar-looking slopes facing south. Because it differs in a number of small ways from *O. cyclurus*, there is also the additional possibility that it might prove to be a new species.

O. grandidieri is a characteristic species of the granite inselbergs in the south-centre, particularly between Ambalavao and Ihosy, where it is very common. It spends a lot of time basking on the smooth grey rock, retreating quickly inside a fissure when disturbed. The similar-looking *O. saxicola* also spends the day relaxing on granite, but only in the extreme south-east, particularly near Beraketa where it shares its rocky home with the special endemic plant of that region, *Pachypodium rosulatum horombense*. It is a dark-coloured lizard which blends well with the substrate. It spends the night sleeping in a crack in the rocks, and up to 20 may be wedged into a particularly suitable crevice. This species is unique in the development of a breeding dress by the males during the rainy season. The greyish-green *O. fierinensis* is another species with a very spiny tail; it lives in the arid bush on the Mahafaly plateau.

Family Chamaeleontidae — the chameleons

There are two aspects of Madagascar's fauna which appeal to most visitors even if they are not especially interested in natural history. The first priority is to see some lemurs; the second is to find a chameleon or two. The local Malagasy people have not been slow to recognize and to capitalize on the curiosity of the white-skinned visitors. The mere sight of a tourist displaying an interest in any natural feature, whether it be bird, butterfly or flower, will usually trigger the belief that chameleons are the quarry; and, of course, in many cases they are. So the subsequent arrival of a smiling villager, proudly bearing a chameleon clinging

sullen-faced to the end of a stick, is often greeted with warm enthusiasm. After all, the appearance of such a gift does away with the lengthy and irksome searching necessary for unaccustomed European eyes to pick out the cryptic reptile as it lurks in the undergrowth. The expected reward of a few francs in return for such a 'useless' creature is welcomed but does little to enhance the villagers' opinion of the white visitors' sense.

Although the Malagasy people undoubtedly relish the chance to profit from such a lowly creature, which to them is both commonplace and of little practical use, they often find it impossible to conceal their amusement that a tourist is actually willing to pay good money just to admire and to photograph a mere lizard. So the handing-over of the chameleon may be accompanied by scarcely concealed giggles or even outbursts of helpless mirth. Similar bursts of merriment may also erupt from passing groups of young girls when they realize that the tall white stranger is wasting his time on a hot day carefully combing the roadside vegetation for chameleons. Yes, chameleons! Yet their own attitudes are not entirely neutral for, strangely enough, most Malagasy people are terrified of actually touching these harmless lizards. Instead, a stick is used to prod the animal off its branch and into some kind of container. And, when the white stranger actually picks up the dreaded creature and carelessly handles it, such boldness and folly are greeted with surprised gasps and still more amusement.

Few Malagasy villagers realize that their island is also home to no fewer than two-thirds of all the world's species of chameleons. In fact, chameleons have a rather limited distribution, from India (with only a single species) through the Arabian peninsula and into the whole of Africa. Only one species has managed to achieve a precarious toe-hold in Europe, on the southernmost tip of Spain and in Crete, but none lives in Asia east of India, nor in Australasia and the vast extent of the Americas. The Chamaeleontidae contains four genera. *Rhampholeon* and *Bradypodion* are dwarf chameleons from Africa. The equivalent genus of small chameleons in Madagascar is *Brookesia*, the endemic stump-tailed chameleons. Madagascar also boasts the bulk of the species in the genus *Chamaeleo* which contains the only European and Indian representatives of the family. The number of species so far described from Madagascar is 20 for *Brookesia* and 34 for *Chamaeleo*. Several new species have been described in both genera over the last 20 or so years, however, and it is possible that more might be discovered. To set against this there are three species, *C. furcifer*, *C. monoceras* and *C. tuzetae* known only from the originally described specimen; they may prove merely to be abnormal forms of some more familiar species.

The *Brookesia* chameleons are among the most difficult of all Madagascan animals to find. Their impressively cryptic appearance, in various shades of brown or grey, enables them to merge unseen into their forest environment. In addition, they may bear bony projections and ornamentations on the body,

Above: The stump-tailed chameleon Brookesia superciliaris, *which lives among dead leaves on the rainforest floor, is a convincing mimic of its surroundings. This individual only betrayed its presence to me by moving.*

Right: Brookesia stumpffi *is the most widely distributed of the stump-tailed chameleons on the island, although its actual localities are very scattered. It spends the day clinging to twigs in the gloomiest understorey of the rainforest, where the bark-like texture of its skin renders it virtually invisible.*

Below: Chamaeleo balteatus *has a very restricted distribution in the south-central region of the eastern rainforests such as at Ranomafana. This is a female; the male has a prominent bifid appendage on his nose.*

In this picture of a female **Chamaeleo balteatus***, the bifid, clamp-like nature of the twig-gripping feet is obvious. This species has a restricted distribution in the south-central region of the eastern rainforests such as at Ranomafana. The male has a prominent pair of nasal appendages.*

often coupled with a rough, bark-like texture which makes them look like part of the scenery when resting on a twig or rotting stump. Others are perfectly shaped and textured for a life on a carpet of dead leaves, for many *Brookesia* are ground living. This contrasts with the strongly arboreal habits of *Chamaeleo*, although even these specialized tree dwellers will descend earthwards to cross a road or the open ground between well-spaced trees. Some species of *Brookesia* are dark olive green and live among the moss cloaking the trees in the eastern rainforests. As their name suggests, stump-tailed chameleons have short tails, very different from the long prehensile appendages found in *Chamaeleo*. The largest species, *B. perarmata*, is only 4.3 inches (11 cm) long including the tail while the smallest, *B. minima*, reaches a mere 1.3 inches (3.2 cm) so their small size makes *Brookesia* chameleons even harder to spot. *Brookesia* shows quite a high degree of local endemism, with individual species often being restricted to just one isolated area.

The visitor to Madagascar could easily spend many weeks wandering in the forests without ever setting eyes on a *Brookesia*. Yet even a brief visit will usually yield one or more kinds of *Chamaeleo*. This is partly

because most of these are larger and more brightly coloured than in *Brookesia*, and partly because several species of *Chamaeleo* commonly haunt such easily accessible habitats as roadsides or gardens. A *Chamaeleo* is superbly adapted for an arboreal existence. The lateral flattening of its body helps the animal to balance on narrow twigs, which are firmly gripped in the clamp-like, two-lobed feet. These are formed from two closely knit toes opposing three others, which are also fused to function as one. The soles are provided with a series of ridges which ensures a secure, non-slip grip on smooth-barked twigs. The tail is very rare among lizards in that it is prehensile, contributing in effect a strong enough fifth 'hand' to allow a chameleon to hang quite safely by it alone. Rather like a butterfly's proboscis, the chameleon's tail is coiled up neatly out of the way when not in use. The only other lizards with similar prehensile tails are the small *Bradypodion* chameleons from South Africa.

A chameleon's hesitant method of walking, with its peculiar fore-and-aft swaying action, helps it to avoid detection (it resembles a leaf blowing in the wind) and to judge distances. The chameleon's vision is excellent, for the conical eyes can move independently of each other, swivelling like miniature gun-turrets through almost 180 degrees in the vertical and longitudinal planes to examine the surroundings, without any need to move the head. A chameleon is thus in the singular position of being able to look forwards and backwards at the same time. Just how the brain copes with two completely different and independent, non-overlapping images arriving simultaneously cannot be imagined, but the system certainly works well, for juvenile chameleons grow at an amazingly rapid rate, something which is possible only when adequate prey can be located and caught.

Such an acutely tuned and flexible form of target location as a chameleon's pivoting eyes can only prove its worth when it is backed up by an equally efficient method of capturing the prey. Slow-moving lizards, such as chameleons, are obviously unsuited to the rapid, leaping 'capture-dart' used by more agile reptiles. Yet the chameleons lose nothing by their lack of athleticism, for they have at their disposal a vastly more sophisticated method which is arguably the slickest and most effective technique of prey-capture evolved by any animal. With both eyes focused forwards to give binocular vision, the chameleon can judge the distance to its target with great accuracy. When the victim is within striking distance, the chameleon unleashes its long, flexible tongue which can extend to a length equal to the entire body. The tongue is, in effect, a telescopic lasso, designed to pick off and haul in prey from a stand-off position. At its tip, the tongue bears a sticky pad which adheres tenaciously to any kind of surface, from shiny bodied beetle to densely scaled moth, to yank it back to the capacious mouth. The whole procedure takes a mere 40 milliseconds, and the chameleon seldom needs to strike twice for the prey is plucked off its feet with such lightning speed that it has no chance to see what

is coming. Surprisingly large prey can be dealt with and, although the target's movements play a key part in attracting the chameleon's attention, even stationary targets may be recognized and summarily dealt with. On Nosy Mangabe I watched a small juvenile *Chamaeleo pardalis* stalk a motionless skipper butterfly (family Hesperiidae) which was nearly as big as the chameleon. Such a bulky insect would seem to present quite a burden for the slim elastic tongue yet the unsuspecting butterfly ended up between the gaping jaws in a split second, and was quickly swallowed with a series of chewing and gulping movements.

Madagascar boasts the largest species in the genus, *Chamaeleo oustaleti*, which may measure almost

Top: **Chamaeleo nasutus** *is the smallest member of its genus. It is widespread and common throughout the eastern rainforests.*

Above left: **Chamaeleo oustaleti** *is the largest of all chameleons and the most widespread species in Madagascar. It is not, however, one of the most beautiful species, the males usually being a rather subdued shade of grey.*

Above: ***The females of* Chamaeleo oustaleti *are much prettier, usually occurring in this delicate shade of green with white spots along the sides.***

27 inches (68 cm) long; and also the smallest, *C. nasutus*, which normally reaches about 4 inches (10 cm) in length and weighs a mere 3-4 grams (an ounce or so). Although it holds the record for length, the rather drab, greyish-brown males of *C. oustaleti* are

Male *C. parsonii* are usually coloured a shade of green, often a beautiful bluish hue, mixed with light brown. The females lack the nasal adornments and are smaller and drabber, often a mixture of dull greens and browns which makes them harder to spot in the forest. Despite its size, this is not an easy species to find although it has a wide distribution in the eastern rainforests as far north as Montagne d'Ambre, and even on Nosy Be on the west coast. Watching these large chameleons moving stealthily around in the trees at Périnet or elsewhere emphasizes the purely mythical nature of the idea that chameleons constantly switch colours as they move around to match the changing background and retain a perfect camouflage. Although this belief has long persisted, it has no basis in reality. A chameleon may stubbornly maintain the same colour as it moves from shaded tree trunk to leafy branch or rust-red laterite road throughout Madagascar.

Chameleons can change colour with astonishing speed, but not in response to a changing background. They are very territorial animals, usually living widely

neither as attractive nor as bulky as the nominally smaller and often strikingly beautiful *C. parsonii.* Whereas the male *C. oustaleti* has a prominent rather elongated casque on the head, that of *C. parsonii* is more pointed, and two short, blunt, diverging 'horns' project conspicuously from its nose. Such 'horns', either singly or in pairs, are found on a number of male Madagascan chameleons, although they are never as long and impressively rhino-like as in certain African chameleons, such as the three-horned *C. jacksoni.* They are employed by the males as jousting pieces during head-to-head combat, but how often this happens in nature is open to question. Chameleons are solitary, highly territorial creatures and meetings between individuals are relatively infrequent.

spaced out within a given habitat. This not only helps to ensure that predators cannot easily form a search image which would result in the rapid decimation of a crowded population, it also guarantees that neighbours seldom stumble across one another. This is just as well, for if a male bumps into another male, the result is usually fairly explosive. The instantly heightened tension is expressed in a number of ways: audibly, in the form of hissing; or physically, in the form of lunging. But the initial and primary reaction is visual, as of a brilliant intensification of colour, coupled with puffing up the body. This is designed to impress and unnerve a rival to such a degree that he retreats in defeat without the need for combat. Similar tactics are also employed during encounters between the sexes, during which a male responds instantly by turning up the brightness on his skin to impress the female. Her response may be unenthusiastic, and this too is communicated visually, so that a kind of motionless and soundless colour battle is instigated which can be most impressive.

Below: The females of Chamaeleo labordi *are very variable but always extremely colourful — in fact, few people would connect such an extravagant display of showiness with a 'cryptic' chameleon. As in many chameleons, there is little resemblance to the males which, seen in isolation, could easily be taken for a different species.*

Right: Chamaeleo labordi, *only recently removed from the synonymy of C. rhinoceratus, is endemic to a localized area of forest in the south-west such as the Kirindy forest where it is common. The males have a single prominent 'horn'.*

The female *C. labordi*, for example, is a strikingly beautiful creature clad in a complex mosaic of blue, mauve and green, contrasting with her bright orange back and red throat. Many people expect chameleons to be camouflaged in drab greens and browns so this boldly coloured creature often comes as a complete surprise. Yet the transformation which sweeps across her body when she spies an unwelcome male is extraordinary indeed; for, in an instant, he is confronted by a coal-black creature on which the uniform darkness is broken only by a scatter of small mauve spots. This is a superb exhibition of the power of mood to induce a dramatic change in colour; yet the same female could walk across a dozen different backgrounds without the slightest change of colour.

Left: **Chamaeleo rhinoceratus** *is found in scattered localities in the forests of the west; it is common in Ampijeroa Forest Reserve. The male has a single nasal appendage and is quite unlike the female.*

Above: *The wet-season nuptial livery of this female* **Chamaeleo rhinoceratus** *is just beginning to fade at the beginning of May. At its peak, the shade of purple would be more intense than in the photograph and the tail a bright shade of orange.*

The male *C. labordi* is not only larger than the female but looks very different. Basically, he is a mixture of olive green and white and sports a prominent nasal appendage. Such marked differences between the sexes are common among the Madagascan chameleons so that, unless you see them mating or you have a good reference book, it is not easy to place them in the same species. The showiest liveries, often flaunted by males and by females, are best seen at the height of the breeding season, coinciding with the rainy austral summer from December to March. After this the bright nuptial colours gradually begin to fade, and a more subdued and cryptic pattern prevails until the arrival of next year's rains. Although they are present throughout the year, chameleons (and, indeed, all lizards) are thin on the ground during the dry season, becoming far more prominent during the rains, when the arrival

of numerous juveniles also swells the numbers.

Some of the largest and most attractive chameleons actually seem to have prospered as a result of human interference with the native habitat, and are more abundant in farmland, the scrubby regrowth in degraded areas, gardens and along roadsides than in natural undisturbed forest. A typical example is *C. pardalis*, which commonly lives on cultivated trees in gardens around Maroansetra; it is also particularly abundant around Diégo Suarez where it is often seen crossing the roads. In this area it seems to be quite rare in the natural forests on Montagne d'Ambre, yet is easy enough to spot on the weedy roadsides and in gardens in nearby Joffreville. The female is brown with orange spots, a dull creature compared with the larger male which revels in an almost luminous shade of lime green. On Nosy Mangabe I watched a female of this species lay her eggs. She selected a tiny patch

Left: *The males of* **Chamaeleo pardalis** *are usually this superb shade of lime green, contrasting strongly with the much smaller, drabber females. This large chameleon is particularly common in farmland and degraded areas around Diégo Suarez, but is rare in the undisturbed forests of the region.*

Below: *This female* **Chamaeleo pardalis** *is using her front feet to rake soil back over a nest in which she has just deposited a clutch of eggs.*

Chamaeleo brevicornis is rather a variable species from the eastern forests. It is common at Périnet.

of bare damp earth on the edge of the forest and excavated a small hole, using her front feet to rake out the earth. With the hole dug to her liking, she turned and deposited her eggs, remaining motionless for several minutes. She then began to fill in the hole, raking the earth inwards with her front feet, and using her rear pair to tread it down. With all the loose earth back in place she turned and firmed down the whole area with a kneading action of her front feet. With their bifid, twig-gripping shape, the feet looked quite unsuited to the task, although it was soon accomplished to her satisfaction.

Chameleons are found in virtually every habitat throughout Madagascar, although the driest areas of the south are rather unrewarding, while certain areas of upland rainforest are particularly rich. Some isolated mountain massifs are endowed with their own endemic species, such as *C. tsaratananensis* from the Tsaratanana massif and *Brookesia karchei* and *C. peyrieresi* from the Marojejy massif. Most of the grassy, windswept uplands of the Hauts Plateaux are as devoid of chameleons as of most other forms of native wildlife. Where even a few trees remain, however, such as in the valley bottoms, chameleons may still be able to scrape a living, even in the centre of Antananarivo, where *C. lateralis* thrives in the

mixture of alien and native trees growing in the grounds of the zoological gardens at Parc Tsimbazaza. This is the second most common and widespread of Madagascan chameleons (after *C. oustaleti*) and one of the most variable, and every individual seems to possess its own personal colour pattern. Some forms are extremely striking, especially when a row of pale-blue spots provides an ostentatious decoration along both sides. Small animals such as chameleons are, of course, capable of surviving and even prospering in small areas of degraded forest, from which larger animals, such as lemurs, would long since have disappeared. By no means all chameleons can tolerate even minor modification of their habitat, however, and all the *Brookesia*, in particular, require relatively undisturbed primary forest.

Family Scincidae — the skinks

Madagascar is home to 48 described species of skinks in 10 genera. Of these, only a single species, *Cryptoblepharus* (= *Ablepharus*) *boutonii*, is not endemic, and is widespread within and outside Madagascar. It is a small, lithe, dainty, black lizard with a pale stripe down either side of its back. It has a strange habitat preference for it is restricted to rocks on the shore, often within the tidal zone where it is covered with water at each high tide, when it takes refuge in holes in the cliffs.

Chamaeleo lateralis *is one of the most widespread and abundant chameleons in Madagascar. It is also one of the most variably coloured, as is shown by this selection of individuals all photographed in the grounds of Parc Tzimbazaza in Antananarivo, where this species is common.*

There are 22 endemic species in the genus *Amphiglossus*, only removed from *Scelotes*, a genus of mainly African distribution, in fairly recent times. Some of the species are rather poorly documented and inadequately known, including: *A. andranovahensis* known only from the original specimen; and *A. ankodabensis* with only two recorded specimens. They are mostly rather drab, glossy brownish-yellow lizards although there are exceptions, such as the widespread *A. splendidus*, which is instantly recognizable by its attractive pattern of dark transverse stripes across a pale-brown background. *Amphiglossus poecilops*, from the eastern rainforests, is one of several species with very reduced legs; this group also includes *A. decaryi*, found on coastal rocks near Fort Dauphin and known only from the original specimen. *Androngo elongatus*, a slim, brownish-yellow lizard from the north near Ambilobe and Diégo Suarez also has tiny, twig-like legs; and *Androngo crenni* is known from only two specimens and is unusual in

having vestigial legs with just two fingers on the front feet and three on the hind feet.

Limb reduction is taken one step further in the almost worm-like *Voeltzkowia* (= *Grandidierina*) *fierinensis* from the dry south-west, in which the front legs are missing, while the rear ones, if present at all, are tiny and functionally redundant, often with the fingers absent. Finally, *Paracaontia*, which is a rarely seen burrowing form, lacks legs altogether.

There are six species in the mainly African genus *Mabuya*, of which *M. gravenhorsti* is by far the most often seen. It is very common in the dry forests of the west as well as in a variety of other habitats throughout much of the island. It may be increasing due to the replacement of the original closed-canopy forest by the more open secondary vegetation which it prefers. It is very similar to *M. elegans* which also ranges over a wide spectrum of habitats, and there are persuasive suggestions that they are merely different forms of a single rather variable species.

Family Cordylidae (formerly Gerrbosauridae) — girdle-tailed lizards

Madagascar is home to 12 species (11 endemic) in two genera of this family of rather large lizards. The family's other representatives are all confined to Africa south of the Sahara. *Tracheloptychus madagascariensis* is widespread but scattered in the east, south-east, south and west, with one isolated record from the north near Nasatra. It is a lithe, brownish-olive lizard with three pale stripes down its back and pale spots on the flanks. *T. petersi* is similar but has only two broader stripes bordered on either side with white. It is restricted to the south-west, near Morombe and Tsivanoha. The ten species of *Zonosaurus* are handsome glossy lizards which occupy a spread of habitats around the island. Two species are limited to dry environments in the south, *Z. trilineatus* near Ambovombe and *Z. quadrilineatus* in the south-west generally. The latter is quite decoratively marked with four yellowish stripes spaced at regular intervals along the dark reddish-brown back. *Z. karsteni* is a very handsome species which is common in the baobab forests near Morondava.

The small skink Mabuya elegans is one of the most widely distributed lizards on the island, partly because it is expanding its range into the increasing areas of degraded habitat. It is particularly abundant in the dry western forests.

During the breeding season, coinciding with the arrival of the rains in November-December, the males become particularly handsome and glossy with a lustrous polished sheen. They establish territories, often around a jumble of fallen logs, offering plenty of bolt holes when danger threatens. They fiercely chase away any intruding rivals, scampering noisily across the carpet of dry leaves and sounding like far larger animals than mere lizards.

Z. laticaudatus is a very widespread, large sedentary species which normally sets up home on a hollow log and spends all day just sitting outside its entrance, waiting for a meal to wander along. In this respect, it is similar to *Oplurus cuvieri*, and the two are often found living close together in the same forests.

Z. ornatus is rather smaller and plumper but very attractive, its dark shiny body decorated with contrasting spots and lines of yellow and pale brown. It is basically a forest species, but generally shuns the shadiest spots, preferring craggy outcrops and sunny riverbanks within the forest. This species also favours artificial habitats, such as roadsides; it is, for example, very common along the road and on the riverside rocks at Ranomafana. At 24 inches (60 cm) long, *Z. maximus* is the largest species. It is a brownish-black lizard with pale blotches along both flanks and a touch of red on the throat. *Z. maximus* also often

Left: **Zonosaurus karsteni** *is an elegant member of the Cordylidae from the western dry forests. Unfortunately it is far more timid and less approachable than several of the other species, which can be ridiculously tame.*

Below left: The large Zonosaurus laticaudatus *(Cordylidae) leads very much a stay-at-home kind of lifestyle, rarely straying far from its favourite hollow log, on which it can be seen basking day after day. It is widespread but rather local; this pair is from the Ampijeroa Forest Reserve.*

Bottom left: **Zonosaurus elegans** *is probably the most attractively patterned of the Madagascan members of the Cordylidae. It is common in the eastern rainforests, preferring roadsides and open rocky riverbanks and shunning the densest shadier spots.*

inhabits forests, particularly alongside rivers and water courses, where it searches for earthworms in deep leaf litter. It also frequently enters the water in search of aquatic organisms.

Z. madagascariensis is one of the smallest species and of rather sombre aspect, the dark brownish black of its ground colour relieved only by a pair of rather faint, whitish, brown-bordered bands down either side of the back. It probably occurs at higher densities than any of the others, and is very abundant in natural forest and in disturbed habitats, such as secondary forest. It can also be particularly common in gardens. For example, it is an everyday resident in Maroansetra, where it is often an uninvited visitor in buildings and outhouses. In such crowded habitats, rival males often bump into one another, provoking territorial disputes which flare up into savage fighting. Ignoring the feet of anyone standing near, the two antagonists engage in a running battle, viciously biting and scratching one another, and turning over and over in a frantic scramble which may result in one combatant losing his tail. This enticing appendage, vigorously wiggling with a temporary vitality after its abrupt separation from its owner, will be seized upon and greedily bolted down by the victor. He, indeed, has won a treble victory. Not only has he put his rival to flight. He has also deprived him of his tail, and to grow that back again will soak up vital resources. And, of course, the winner benefits from the extra resources yielded by his meal.

SERPENTES — THE SNAKES

In Costa Rica, primatologists making daily observations of monkey behaviour have to wear thick leather leg protectors. This is to guard against the high risk of being bitten by one of several deadly snakes which are very common in Central and South America, and which could easily be trodden on while attention is concentrated on events taking place overhead. Primate studies in Africa and Asia also demand constant attention to the ground in front, for the same reasons. Researchers observing lemur behaviour in Madagascar's forests have no such worries. They can relax and enjoy their work, safe in the knowledge that

Opposite: **The boa** Sanzinia madagascariensis *is one of Madagascar's commonest snakes and is a frequent sight by day and by night in the eastern rainforests. It is supposed to be arboreal, but is often seen on the ground. This is the typical colour and pattern for the species.*

whatever they might accidentally step on, it can do them no harm. There are no dangerous snakes in Madagascar. There are no members of the Elapidae, so no lethal snakes with rapidly acting neurotoxic venom, such as the African and Asian cobras, the African mambas or the South American coral snakes. Nor are there any members of the Viperidae with their mainly haemotoxic (blood-acting) venom; this family includes the gaboon and saw-scaled vipers and puff adder of Africa, bushmaster and fer-de-lance of South America, and the numerous species of American rattlesnakes. This leaves only three families of snakes known from Madagascar: the Typhlopidae or blind snakes; the Boidae or boas; and the Colubridae, with no widely accepted common name although 'harmless snakes' has been suggested.

The Typhlopidae has nine representatives, eight of them endemic, contained in two genera. They are very slim, cylindrical snakes, usually grey or black, with indistinct heads and reduced eyes hidden beneath head plates. They spend almost their entire lives burrowing beneath the ground, feeding on soft-bodied invertebrates. Not surprisingly, very little is known of their habits in the wild and, in general, they are among the most seldom seen of all Madagascar's reptiles.

The presence of the Boidae in Madagascar parallels the occurrence of the Iguanidae in the island. The boas, too, are a relict group in Madagascar, and have

Some individuals of **Sanzinia madagascariensis** *are suffused with a beautiful blue sheen — it even extends on to the tongue.*

existed there, without showing any strong tendencies towards a wide adaptive radiation, since the early break up of Gondwanaland. Nowadays, the closest relatives of Madagascar's three endemic species of boas live in South America where the great majority of the family resides. Similar boas occur in Africa only as fossils. The African and Asian sand boas are not closely related, having been separated from the rest of the family for more than 50 million years, and are often included in a separate family, the Erycidae. The pythons (Pythonidae), the typical large constricting snakes of Africa, are absent from Madagascar. Madagascar's largest snakes are the two species of *Acrantophis*, *A. dumerilii* and *A. madagascariensis*, which can reach a length of almost 6 feet (1.8 m). The latter is the more widespread of the two, and is well distributed in the more northerly part of the island and in the east; while *A. dumerilii* is restricted to the south and south-west. Both species seem to have similar requirements, thriving in damp habitats along the edges of streams and water courses. Being large and relatively placid, they are likely to be killed by the local people, and they also suffer from the usual problems of habitat destruction. *Sanzinia madagascariensis* is smaller but very much more common, occurring wherever reasonable cover still exists. It is normally considered to be a tree dweller, but it is often seen on the ground and, indeed, its frequent terrestrial forays make this one of the two or three snakes most likely to be seen on a visit to Madagascar. Its normal colour is a beautiful delicate shade of greyish green. The back is slightly darker while, along the sides, there is a row of darker

markings picked out with white. A beautiful purplish-blue tinge is often present as an ephemeral flicker appearing and disappearing when the snake moves. Sometimes, this beautiful tint is intensified to such a degree that the whole snake is a shimmering blue, and even the tongue is a bright shade of aquamarine. Some texts have described this handsome snake as 'small and aggressive' but, in my experience, most specimens seem to be very passive. It probably catches a wide variety of prey, including lizards, rodents and small tenrecs — even the spiny ones.

The 50 or so species of Colubridae, contained in 16 genera, are a varied bunch. Only one genus, *Geodipsas*, is also found in Africa although the two Madagascan members are endemics, while two species of *Lycodryas*, which also reach the Comoro Islands, are the only non-endemic species. This family includes some of the most commonly seen snakes of Madagascar, as well as some strikingly coloured species. It also includes a number of extremely rare snakes, often known only from a single specimen or locality. Examples include *Alluaudina mocquardi*, known only from the type specimen from Ankara cave; *Lycodryas inornatus*, known from only three specimens; *L. maculatus*, known in Madagascar only from the type from an unknown locality; *Pararhadinea albignaci*, known solely from the original specimen picked up dead off the road near Périnet in 1970 and never seen alive in its forest home; *Pseudoxyrhopus ambreensis*, known only from the holotype from Montagne d'Ambre; *P. occipitalis* and *P. tritaeniatus*, known only from the original specimens; and *L. apperti* described from a single specimen discovered in 1968 in deciduous forest between Tulear and Morombe. This forest has now been virtually destroyed and it is doubtful that this snake still survives.

In addition, there are several other species which have not been seen for many years, including *Pseudoxyrhopus heterurus* from Nosy Mangabe and *P. microps* from the Betsileo region. On the other hand, several species previously known only from one or two old records have been seen again more recently, often in new localities. This more positive news applies to such species as *Alluaudina bellyi*, formerly known only from the original specimen discovered in Montagne d'Ambre in the late nineteenth century. Recently, it has been found not only in the original locality but also from forests near Sambava and Ambatonutatao. *Heteroliodon torquatus* was originally known only from the type, found near Tulear in the early part of this century. Again recently, single specimens were found north of Tulear and much further north in the Kinkony forest south of Morondava. *Liopholidophis grandidieri*, for many years confined to the original specimen from the mouth of the River Saint Augustin in the south-west, is now known from three new specimens discovered, perhaps surprisingly, in the eastern forests. These rediscoveries, as well as finding such new species as *Pararhadinea albignaci* and *Liophidium apperti* (*see* above), *L. therezeni* (described from two specimens collected in

1966 and 1969), and *L. chabaudi* (described in 1983 from three specimens discovered in the south-west) reflect the increasing amount of field work carried out on Madagascan reptiles. No doubt more species will come to light as long as suitable habitat still exists.

Many snakes are common and widespread, of course. One, the Madagascan giant hog-nosed snake, *Leioheterodon madagascariensis*, occurs throughout most of the island. With its strictly diurnal habits and large size — up to 5 feet (1.5 m) — it is perhaps the most frequently encountered snake in habitats as diverse as the baobab forests near Morondava, the dry forests of Ankarafantsika and the rainforests on the slopes of the Montagne d'Ambre. It is a very handsome snake, neatly combining a mixture of yellow, pale brown and black in a kind of chequerboard pattern. Although this snake is often seen basking beside some forest track, it is more usual to spot one crawling unhurriedly across a carpet of leaves in a painstaking quest for food. With constantly flicking tongue, it meticulously peeps and prys its way across the forest floor. Promising areas, such as piles of fallen logs, come in for an especially thorough investigation, the head probing hopefully into every nook and cranny. This species usually becomes so absorbed in its search that it will allow a human observer to follow along at arm's length, only raising its head 6-8 inches (15-20 cm) off the ground for a good look around if it is alarmed suddenly by an incautious movement, or a heavy footfall which disturbs the ground.

North of Morondava in April 1990, I observed a fascinating sequence of interactions between this snake, a related species and the local Malagasy people. I was waiting for birds to come down to drink by a small lake. Only one shade tree was available and, beneath this, there also sat several men, women and children, hoping to sell fruit from a small roadside stall. Although they spoke no French, and I spoke no Malgache, a nudge on the arm by one of the men was enough to alert me to the unobtrusive arrival of a large *Leioheterodon madagascariensis* which had slipped quietly out of the surrounding forest and was making its way directly towards the group. Ignoring the assembled humans completely, it advanced smoothly until it was beneath the same tree. Here it paused on a table-sized patch of damp sand; it was only a yard (less than 1 m) away from me. It quickly set to work, devoting some considerable time to gouging a hole in the sand, using its blunt nose in a rotating action as an auger to force the sand aside until about 6 inches (15 cm) of its head and body had disappeared from view. Suddenly, a muffled croaking issued from the depths, and the snake started to inch backwards out of the hole. As its head emerged, it was obvious that the snake was swallowing, and the legs of its protesting victim, a small frog, were still sticking out of the sides of the serpent's mouth until, after a few more gulps, they disappeared from view. The frog's vocal protests continued unabated for some distance down the length of the sinuous body until, finally, they were abruptly silenced. The snake now moved forwards, its

hidden in its depths, were frogs which had buried themselves for the duration of the long dry season. The snakes' subsequent actions indicated their ability to locate these frogs precisely from above using the sensitive tongue. If such productive hunting sessions took place on a regular basis, it is interesting to speculate how many frogs, if any, in that particular patch of sand, might manage to escape detection and emerge to breed when the rains came six months later. Almost as fascinating was the attitude of the onlookers to these reptilian goings-on. In the chapter on reptiles in his book *Key Environments — Madagascar*, Charles P Blanc states that *L. madagascariensis* terrifies the local people. This might be true in some areas, but hardly so in the Kirindy forest. In fact, there must be few places in the world where such a large snake could go quietly about its business for an hour or more, right next to a group of people, without even being disturbed, let alone killed. Even the children were quite unperturbed and played in the dirt very close to the supposedly intimidating serpents. And, when they scattered before the *L. madagascariensis*, it was obvious that this was more

tongue flicking out to stroke the damp surface, before it selected a spot and started digging again. Four holes and four frogs later, this successful hunter was joined by a somewhat smaller, brownish-grey snake *Leioheterodon modestus*, a common species found throughout the island. The new arrival immediately followed the identical procedure, and its tunnelling efforts were soon rewarded with a croaking frog. The two snakes were now within 20 inches (50 cm) or so of one another, but each was apparently unaware of the other's presence. This peacefully neutral state of affairs ended when the *L. modestus* edged across to search a new area, suddenly bringing the two snakes face to face no more than 8 inches (20 cm) apart. The two startled reptiles froze for a second or two before the larger of the pair, the *L. madagascariensis*, turned tail and sped off, sending the bystanders running and jumping wildly in all directions, sparking off delighted peals of laughter from those too far away to be directly involved.

These events have been described in such detail because they illustrate a number of important points. Firstly, each of the snakes had obviously made tracks directly for the sand patch in the knowledge that,

Above right: **Leioheterodon madagascariensis (left)** *and* **L. modestus** *meet face-to-face while digging for frogs in the Kirindy forest. The outcome? The larger of the two on the left beat a hasty retreat, sending several local onlookers scattering in all directions.*

Right: **Leioheterodon modestus** *after a succesful hunt, swallowing a small frog which it has just dug out of the damp sand.*

the natural reaction of any bare-footed, bare-legged human to the rapid advance of a large snake, rather than real fear. The hoots of laughter by all concerned (including those who scattered) confirmed this.

Mimophis mahafalensis is a slim, agile, brown-and-white snake which is widespread and common, particularly in the dry south. It is active during the day, so it is seen often, and it feeds on other snakes. *Liopholidophis lateralis* is another slim species which is found over most of the island — it is even able to

The small, slim **Dromicodryas bernieri** *is perhaps the commonest snake on the island in every kind of habitat. Here in the gallery forest of Berenty Private Nature Reserve one of these elegant little snakes has enveloped a* **Paroedura bastardi** *gecko in its coils; within a few moments the lizard was dead.*

survive on the Hauts Plateaux where it is often found in gardens and parks, including the grounds of the zoological gardens in Antananarivo. *L. sexlineatus* also makes a success of life on the Hauts Plateaux, mainly because it prefers open, marshy habitats and is very much at home in the rice fields of the Betsileo region. A number of other slender-bodied, fast-moving, day-active snakes are also common, and superficially rather similar. These include *Dromicodryas quadrilineatus* which is often found with its head poking out of the entrance to some large subterranean ants' nest. The females are attracted here to lay their eggs, apparently unworried by the presence of the hostile hordes of rightful residents. Similar habits are found in *Madagascarophis colubrina*, its Malagasy name of *Renivitsika* translating as 'mother of ants'. It is

a thicker-bodied snake about 40 inches (1 m) in length, its yellowish skin patterned with brown rectangles, each having a spot on each corner and one in the centre.

The award for weirdest Madagascan snake undoubtedly belongs to *Langaha nasuta*, a long, pencil-thin species which lives in forested areas throughout the island. The female is a strange creature, indeed, for her nose is extended into a bizarre leaf-shaped structure adorned with scales and small tooth-like projections. In the male, which has a bright yellow underside, the nose is drawn out to form a long, tapering, pliant 'thorn'. This species is a classic mimic of twigs, the nasal extensions probably serving to make the deception more convincing. When suddenly taken unawares on a road or elsewhere in the open, *L. nasuta* will dart rapidly for the nearest bush or jumble of dead sticks. As soon as it reaches this haven, however, it does not go to ground and hide immediately, as most snakes do. Instead, it abruptly abandons its headlong rush and stealthily begins to weave its way up among the twigs and branches. Now its whole demeanour changes as it creeps gradually upwards, all the time gently swaying its head to-and-fro and from side to side, stealthily insinuating its body among the twigs until snake and plant are almost indistinguishable. It may now lie still, relying on its camouflage to escape detection, or else slowly make its way further from the scene. Many aspects of this procedure are reminiscent of the behaviour of chameleons under similar circumstances. A second species, *Langaha alluaudi*, is also widespread but only the female boasts a nasal extension.

Another unusual snake, partly because of its colour and partly for the superstition surrounding it, is *Ithycyphus miniatus*, a widespread species with a rather scattered distribution. Its very slender body reaches about 40 inches (1 m) in length, most of which is a a drab shade of brown, that helps to conceal it in the forest canopy. The fairly long tail is painted a brilliant red, however, as if dipped in blood, presumably giving rise to the belief that its favourite habit is to drop tail-first from a tree, as rigid as a lance, to pierce and transfix a zebu passing innocently beneath.

A final comment is worth making. Madagascar is probably one of the best countries in the world in which to see reptiles in their natural habitat. Snakes in particular are far less elusive than in many countries, such that my six months in Madagascar yielded more encounters with these attractive creatures (all harmless of course, so always pleasurable) than in four years of travels in Africa, Asia and South America. Add to this the abundance of spectacular chameleons and day geckoes and you have a herpetologist's paradise.

Below left: **Dromicodryas quadrilineatus** *is almost as widespread as the previous species. The females often lay their eggs in the nests of ants. Here, one is peeping out at the photographer from its subterranean retreat.*

Below and bottom: *The bizarre* **Langaha nasuta** *is a superb mimic of a dry twig. The slender extension which the male sports on his nose looks thorn-like but is in fact soft and pliant. This snake is widespread but local in forests throughout the island.*

Chapter 5
Birds

Whatever its other natural assets (and they are many), unless you are interested in tracking down certain endemic species, Madagascar is not a good place to see birds. For a mainly tropical country boasting a wide variety of habitats, Madagascar has a remarkably impoverished avifauna. The total number of bird species recorded from the island is only some 250, of which just 197 are resident breeding species, an incredibly small number for any tropical land. To set this in its worldwide context, consider that in one 50,000-acre (20,000-ha) reserve in lowland rainforest in Peru, well over 500 species of breeding birds are known — and this just in a single kind of habitat, primary rainforest. Nearer to Madagascar, a keen birdwatcher in Kenya determined to amass a large total in a hurry could approach Madagascar's 250 known species in a single day; and without even covering more than one or two kinds of habitat. By comparison, in Madagascar, even a well-worked and notably rich area of rainforest, such as the reserve at Périnet, can only manage 111 species, while other productive areas of rainforest can muster totals of merely 70 or 80. Not surprisingly, this poverty in species is accompanied by a general scarcity of birds which can make Madagascar a strangely quiet place to visit. This is especially striking for the visitor arriving directly from Africa, where the teeming and colourful bird life is so much in evidence everywhere from suburban parks and gardens to remote deserts, forests or mountain tops. After such riches, the first thought on arriving in Madagascar tends to be 'Where have all the birds gone?'. Even on the tropical east coast, it is possible to walk through a patchwork of gardens, forest remnants and scrubby areas — habitats which, in Africa, would throng with a glittering array of rollers, sunbirds, weavers, bee-eaters, fire-finches and gaudy metallic starlings — and yet see nothing save a fleeting glimpse of one or two small brown birds. In fact, 'little brown jobs' are also the most likely source of the tantalizing calls emanating from the undergrowth in the rainforests, and it has to be admitted that, in general, Madagascar's birds are far less colourful than those of other tropical countries.

That said, however, it is true that some of the island's commonest birds are also among the prettiest, including the red fody and the olive bee-eater. Neither of these is numbered among the 106 species endemic to Madagascar, although a further 25 species occur outside Madagascar only in the nearby Comoro Islands. Thus, there are 131 species of birds which can be most conveniently seen in Madagascar, especially by those seeking to tick off on a list as many names as possible. This will require a fair degree of travel within the island, for the native birds are not uniformly distributed. For a start, wide areas of the the Hauts Plateaux are virtually devoid of bird life, what there is confined to ponds, lakes, rice fields and the few surviving patches of forest. The dry, deciduous forests of the western region support 52 endemic birds, of which only two are confined to this kind of habitat; the majority overlap into habitats which are wetter or grade into semidesert. The dry region of the south, with its spectacular 'spiny desert', hosts fewer endemics, only 42 species; but a high proportion (ten in all) is found nowhere else. A visit to the south would therefore be a must for any keen birdwatcher, although human encroachment is increasing in this region, and there is a growing necessity for establishing reserves for the major biotypes and their associated birds. The Sambirano area in the north is home to 49 species, none of which is restricted to the area, leaving the eastern rainforests with 83 endemic species, 30 of which are found nowhere else. In addition, endemics from the northern or western regions also often occur in the eastern forests which thus form a 'treasure house' containing nearly 80 per cent of Madagascar's endemic species of avifauna.

The endemic families

Madagascar is home not only to 106 endemic species of birds; there are also five families endemic to the subregion (including the Comoros), and it is these which are of interest to ornithologists. The Mesitornithidae (mesites) contains just three species which are superficially similar to the rails. All three are difficult to see because of their subdued coloration and habit of skulking in deep cover. The white-breasted mesite *Mesitornis variegata* is one of the rarest birds in Madagascar, if not in the world. It was discovered in 1834 without any record of the exact locality, and almost a century was to pass before a second bird turned up, in the Ankarafantsika forest, now a reserve. This was followed by regular sightings in the same area, as well as its discovery further north in the Ankarana massif (in 1930); and then, much more recently, many miles to the south near Morondava. The continuing survival of this bird in the Ankarana Special Reserve was confirmed in 1986, when a scientific expedition discovered a thriving population distributed widely throughout the massif's forests.

The white-breasted mesite is a ground-dwelling

bird which seems very reluctant to take to the air, preferring to run from danger. The nest is placed a short distance above the ground, however. Birds are usually seen in pairs, pecking around on the forest floor for insects and fruits. The brown mesite *Mesitornis unicolor* has similar habits although it is perhaps even more of a skulker in dark places, and is probably much more common and widespread in the eastern rainforests than current records suggest. Its streaked brown plumage blends so well into the carpet of dead leaves that the birds are virtually invisible, as long as they remain completely motionless.

The subdesert mesite *Monias benschi*, which occupies the drier south-west, is by far the easiest of the trio to observe, and may also be the most numerous. Its range lies between the Mangoky and Fierenana rivers, where it is restricted to a 44-mile (70-km) wide band along the coast. Within this area, it may be quite common locally, possibly because it does not seem to be too fussy about the exact nature of its habitat. Its main requirement seems to be a reasonable depth and extent of leaf litter, giving it enough scope to scratch around for seeds and insects. It also has the strange habit of pecking pieces from certain orchids. It is its gregarious behaviour, particularly, which makes this species more easy to spot than the other two. Groups of four to six are common, while flocks of ten have been recorded. This mesite places its nest higher than the brown mesite does, usually about 3-6 feet (1-2 m) up in a tree or stump, although always in such a position that the bird can climb rather than fly into it. Groups of these birds seem often to be accompanied by a number of Lefresnaye's vangas *Xenopirostris xenopirostris* in an apparently mutually beneficial relationship. The mesites are effective at putting up insects such as grasshoppers — often the most abundant large insects on the ground in dry areas — which escape in a vigorous but short flight, presumably straight into the waiting beaks of the grateful vangas watching the scene closely from the trees above. In return, the vangas' elevated position and sharp eyesight enable them to spot approaching danger and sound the alarm long before the ground-hugging mesites would be aware of it.

The five endemic species of ground-rollers in the family Brachypteracidae are often as difficult to detect as the mesites. Of these, the four species resident in the eastern rainforests present the greatest challenge because of their general rarity, retiring nature, and habit of living in remote and dense forest. The short-legged ground-roller *Brachypteracias leptosomus* is an attractive bird with a purplish head and nape, greenish back and brown upper breast speckled with white. It is restricted to just two distinct areas; in the north-east in the forests from Marojejy to Maroansetra and in the forests in the east central region inland from Tamatave. Although the bird is not entirely terrestrial, it spends much of its time on the ground in gloomy damp rainforest, preferring areas where the shade is so continuous that the moist earth has little or no

cover. It probably feeds mainly around dusk and dawn and perhaps at night, scratching among the mouldering debris on the forest floor and searching among low vegetation for its wide diet of worms, beetles, insect larvae, ants, millipedes and larger vertebrate animals such as small snakes and chameleons. Such painstaking terrestrial foraging habits would presumably make this species an enemy of the ground-dwelling, dead-leaf-mimicking *Brookesia superciliaris* chameleon which favours a similar habitat. Nesting takes place in rainy December when each pair excavates a tunnel around about 3 feet (almost 1 m) long in a bank. This species is found in the nature reserve at Périnet and also lives in the forests at Ranomafana, where it is often seen walking sedately along the paths.

The scaly ground-roller *Brachypteracias squamiger* occurs throughout the eastern rainforests, although it is apparently always scattered and rare. It is more terrestrial than the previous species but inhabits the same kinds of gloomy places, where it gleans a similar diet by fossicking among the carpet of dead leaves with its beak. The rufous-headed ground-roller *Atelornis crossleyi* is another attractive species with a russet head and breast, a black bib speckled with white and a greenish back. It is the rarest and least known of the group, seemingly occurring in discrete parts of the north and central areas. It is found in at least two nature reserves but its behaviour and ecology are little known, although probably similar in most respects to the other ground-rollers. The beautiful blue-headed ground-roller *Atelornis pittoides* was once also thought to be rare but is now known to be widespread throughout the entire eastern forests, including several reserves, as well as on the Montagne d'Ambre in the north. These rainforest ground-rollers are probably all really less rare than is currently thought, because they are quiet birds, seldom betraying their presence by calling, and generally very furtive.

The long-tailed ground-roller *Uratelornis chimaera* is a distinctive bird with its long, magpie-like brown tail edged with blue and its white breast bearing an inverted black U-shaped collar beneath the chin. It is remarkable in that it is closely linked to the occurrence of *Didierea* forests in a narrow coastal strip between the Mangoky and Fiherenana rivers in the south-west. It would be difficult to imagine a habitat more radically different from the dense, rain-soaked forests favoured by the other four species. Its range is much the same as for the subdesert mesite, although the ground-roller is more restricted in its choice of habitat. There has been a good deal of argument about how rare this bird really is, ranging from assertions that it is one of the rarest birds in the world, to less pessimistic assessments that it may even be fairly abundant in certain *Didierea* forests to the north of Tulear. It seems to need a sandy, easily worked soil in which to dig its long [up to 4 feet (1.2 m)] nest

The endemic sicklebill vanga Falculea palliata *is a noisy and unmistakable denizen of the dry western forests.*

burrows, which are excavated in flat or slightly sloping ground, rather than in the steep banks favoured by the other species. It is strongly terrestrial, ransacking the leaf litter for ground-living insects, such as beetles, grasshoppers and ants, although it may not be averse to aping a flycatcher to snap a butterfly out of the air.

The third endemic family, the Leptosomatidae (cuckoo-rollers), contains but a single species, the coural *Leptosomus discolor* which is also found in the Comoro Islands. In Madagascar it is a highly successful bird, found almost everywhere as long as there is some kind of reasonable cover, and even degraded forests are widely utilized. It has the habit of bringing attention to itself by uttering its loud and melodius call from a prominent perch so, when present, it is not easily missed.

The Philepittidae (asities and sunbird asities) is yet another very small family containing just four species. The velvet asity *Philepitta castanea* and Schlegel's asity *P. schlegeli* are both about 6 inches (15 cm) long, with rather short beaks adapted for a diet of fruit. The drab, greenish-yellow females of each species can be confused but the males are easily separated, for *P. castanea* is almost wholly black while *P. schlegeli* has a mainly yellow and olive plumage with a black head. During the breeding season, the males of both species develop conspicuous naked patches of bright blue skin on the sides of the head. The velvet asity is common over the eastern part of the island and north-west into the Sambirano region.

Although primarily a species of undisturbed forest, it adapts well to interference, and is often found in secondary formations. Schlegel's asity is confined to the west, mainly in the Sambirano and is a species of thick forest.

The two sunbird asities are so called because they were once confused with the true sunbirds of the family Nectariniidae. This is hardly surprising in view of the long, slim, downward-curved beaks common to both, an adaptation for probing flowers for nectar. Although much smaller than the asities, and of a superficially different appearance, sunbird asities show their affinities with the other members of the family in that the males develop bare blue skin on the sides of the head in the breeding season. The wattled sunbird asity *Neodrepanis coruscans* is locally abundant in various places in the eastern rainforests, mainly at higher altitudes, from Vendrozo northwards as far as Tsaratanana. The yellow-bellied sunbird asity *N. hypoxantha* is probably one of the rarest birds in the world. Before 1933, it was not regarded as a separate species because it does look very similar to *N. coruscans*. At that time, it was known only from 12 specimens, all collected before 1930. This remained

The giant coua **Coua gigas** *is the largest of the couas. This impressive endemic is found mainly in the dry south-west but extends eastwards as far as the Berenty Private Nature Reserve and the Andobabela Strict Nature Reserve. It spends most of its time picking around on the forest floor for insects.*

the situation until 1973, when a nesting pair was discovered in rainforest near Périnet. More sightings in the same area have followed, but the species is undoubtedly very localized, although almost certainly under-recorded.

The final endemic family, the Vangidae, contains 14 species, one of which is also found in the Comoros. Their main food consists of insects and, if you look at the beak of each species, you can see clearly how it is adapted for a particular feeding method. Fortunately, several species are common, and some are very conspicuous birds, easily seen by any visitor to Madagascar. The sicklebill *Falculea palliata* often announces its presence by perching high up on a branch and repeatedly giving vent to its raucous call. In the breeding season, ushered in by the coming of the rains to the sicklebill's dry western and southern habitat, several birds often sit and call loudly against one another. In addition to its conspicuous voice, the sicklebill's black-and-white plumage makes it easy to spot among the foliage. During the dry season, it forms noisy foraging flocks which can scarcely be missed. The long, down-curved bill is designed for winkling out insects from holes in trees. In the shape of its bill, its noisy gregarious habits and method of prey capture, the sicklebill parallels closely the wood-hoopoes and scimitar-bills (family Phoeniculidae) which are such a characteristic sight inching up tree trunks in search of insects over much of Africa. The sicklebill is mainly a western species, common in forests such as Ankarafantsika and in the Beza-Mahafaly reserve in the south-west.

The hook-billed vanga *Vanga curvirostris* has a shorter, thicker, much heavier bill in which the upper mandible bears a down-curved hook at the tip. It is a successful species, widespread throughout the east and the west, adapting to life in degraded forests and plantations of alien trees. Chabert's vanga *Leptopterus chabert* is even more successful, and is found throughout most of the east and west, even adapting to life in rice fields. It has a short, heavy bill and usually forages in conspicuous flocks. The three species of *Xenopirostris*, Pollen's vanga *X. polleni*, Van Dam's vanga *X. damii* and Lefresnaye's vanga *X. xenopirostris*, are all very similar-looking birds with strong bills and a general resemblance to the shrikes (family Laniidae), such typical birds of the African bush yet absent from Madagascar.

Lefresnaye's vanga is restricted to the desert-like environment of the south-west, where it lives mainly in the forests of *Didierea* and woody succulent *Euphorbia* near the coast. Pollen's vanga is scattered widely in the eastern rainforests, where it appears generally to be rather local and rare. It seems to hunt for insects, small lizards and frogs in dense primary rainforest, in company with other birds. Such mixed foraging flocks are common in rainforests around the world. Van Dam's vanga is very similar to Lefresnaye's vanga (and considered by some people to be a north-western form of it) and is extremely rare, known only from the dry western forest of Ankarafantsika. It is reported to be quite abundant in undisturbed forest in

this area which, fortunately, is a nature reserve.

The most beautiful vanga is the blue vanga *Leptopterus madagascarinus*, a large striking bird, especially the male with his white breast and dark blue back. This is the only vanga which is also found in the Comoros. In Madagascar, it is common in forest and scrubby places in the east, and in the far north on the Montagne d'Ambre. It is rarer in the dry western forests, and penetrates only to the edge of the semi-desert areas of the south. It survives well in degraded areas and is often seen in mixed parties with other species. The most bizarre of the vangas is the helmet bird *Euryceros prevostii*. Its huge beak, with its very deep upper mandible, rather resembles a somewhat stubby version of the enormous beaks seen in the African hornbills. This strange bird is confined to rainforest in the north-east where its total population is thought to be declining mostly because, unlike some of the other vangas, it seems unable to adapt to any major alteration of its rainforest home. Visitors to Périnet or other areas of the eastern rainforests may spot a smallish, red-billed, brown bird moving intermittently up a tree trunk in search of insects in crannies in the bark. At first glance, it looks and behaves like a nuthatch (*Sitta*) of Europe and North America. Nuthatches are absent from Madagascar and from Africa, however, and the bird with the same mannerisms as this familiar temperate species is another vanga, the coral-billed nuthatch-vanga *Hypositta corallirostris*, which is common enough throughout the rainforests.

Although the couas represent only a subfamily (Couinae) within the large cuckoo family (Cuculidae), the nine species endemic to Madagascar comprise such an attractive and special group that they are included here together with the endemic families. Unlike the vangas, in which the 14 species are divided among no fewer than ten different genera, the couas all belong to the single genus *Coua*. Whereas the bill of the vangas has responded to adaptive pressures with a remarkable flexibility, resulting in a variety of shapes suited for specific tasks, in the couas, it has remained much the same throughout. The couas all have one feature in common, a patch of bare skin, usually some shade of blue, around the eyes. Strangely enough, this is similar to the facial adornment also seen in the unrelated asities. The largest of the tribe is the giant coua *Coua gigas*, a stately grey bird which can reach a length of 24-25 inches (60-62 cm). Usually solitary, it spends the day stalking patiently around on the forest floor, hunting for insects and fallen fruit among the dead leaves. It will also pick insects from tree trunks and bushes, even deftly snapping up large, powerful fliers such as the plump grey *Yanga hearthi* cicadas which screech so piercingly from tree trunks in the southern gallery forests. When dealing with this kind of large, vigorous prey, the coua holds the struggling insect down with one foot and pecks off the wings, neatly taking away any chance of escape. The giant coua is widespread in the west, from Tulear northwards to Mampikony. It is also found in a few places in the east, such as in

The crested coua Coua cristata *is a widespread and familiar endemic bird which is most common in the western forests but it is extending its range into the increasingly degraded eastern forests. Its loud ringing call is very much a feature of the Madagascan landscape.* Above: *This individual is searching for insects on a tree in the 'spiny desert' in Beza-Mahafaly reserve in the dry south.* Right: *This bird is sunning itself soon after sunrise on a cool winter's morning in Beza-Mahafaly reserve.*

Berenty nature reserve where some individuals are very approachable.

The species most likely to be seen in dry forests throughout Madagascar, and increasingly in degraded forests in the east, is the crested coua *Coua cristata*. Smaller than the giant coua, this soft-plumaged, grey bird often startles the passer-by with its sudden shrill, ringing call, given repeatedly from the crown of a nearby tree. This is one of the most penetrating and characteristic bird sounds in Madagascar, although it usually emanates from cover and the caller can be remarkably difficult to spot until it flies off. In parts of the north-west, where the crested coua is found with the crowned lemur *Lemur coronatus*, the similarity between their calls can be very confusing. The crested coua seeks insects in trees rather than on the ground, as does Verreaux's coua *C. verreauxi*, the smallest of the group and the rarest — it is restricted to a coastal zone in the dry south-west. The running coua *Coua cursor* leads a mainly terrestrial life in desert scrub and dry forests from Morondava as far round as Cap Ste Marie in the south, while three species live in the very different habitat of the eastern rainforests. The red-breasted coua *C. serriana* is found only in the northern part, although it is common enough within this limited area. It spends most of its time on the ground, pottering around in search of fallen fruit and, to a lesser degree, insects. Reynaud's coua *C. reynaudii* has a similar lifestyle but concentrates its attentions on insects rather than fruit. It is common over a wide area of the east and penetrates westwards to the Sambirano region.

The blue coua *Coua caerulea* spends most of its time in the trees; its distribution parallels that of the previous species, but extends further to the south. The apparently extinct snail-eating coua *Coua delalandei* was only marginally smaller than the giant coua; it seems that it made its living by smashing open snails against stones. This bird was unfortunate in being confined to Ile Ste Marie off the east coast, now a popular holiday venue, where the native forest has been totally destroyed, together with the snail-eating coua and other interesting endemics. There has been a number of rumours that the bird also existed on the nearby mainland, where suitable forest still exists, so there is perhaps even now a very slim chance that this fascinating bird may still be bashing busily away at snails in some remote forest.

In common with those other independent members of the Cuculidae, the coucals, the couas make their own nests and rear their young themselves, rather than foisting their offspring on some other species of bird, as cuckoos do. Typically, a coua's nest consists of a mass of twigs formed into an open cup. Even among mainly terrestrial species, this is usually placed above the ground.

Ducks and wading birds

Madagascar is relatively well off for waterbirds, with 58 species, although some of the most commonly seen of these tend to be familiar African species, such as the red-knobbed coot *Fulica cristata*, the now almost universal cattle egret *Bubulcus ibis*, and the little grebe *Podiceps ruficollis*. The latter has undergone a population explosion in recent years because, it is thought, of the relatively recent introduction of tilapia fish into large numbers of water bodies throughout Madagascar. The tilapia are intended to supply a valuable source of easily won protein for the local inhabitants. This is good news for them and for the mainly fish-eating little grebe, but very bad news for the endemic Madagascar little grebe *Podiceps pelzelnii*, its populations seem to have declined in line with the increase in tilapia and the little grebes. This probably stems from the herbivorous tilapias' habit of rapidly depleting all the available waterweeds, thereby depriving dragonfly larvae, water beetles and other aquatic invertebrates of vital hiding places. As the Madagascar little grebe feeds mainly on these rather than fish, its numbers have suffered accordingly. Although thought still to be widespread, its status is now causing considerable worry, and conservation measures are being considered. Yet, unfortunately, the current plight of the Alaotra grebe *Podiceps rufolavatus* (also sometimes allocated to its own genus *Tachybaptus*, obviously erroneously, in view of the easy hybridization mentioned below) is very much worse. Seemingly always more or less confined to Lake Alaotra in north-east Madagascar, this species may be in terminal decline. This is partly because of human interference with the ecology of Lake Alaotra for rice growing and fish farming, and partly through hybridization with the ever more common little grebe. The survival of the Alaotra grebe in the wild now seems unlikely, and captive breeding would appear to be the only hope.

The outlook for the endemic Madagascar pochard *Aythya innonata* may not be much better. Once scattered on the lakes in the northern part of the Hauts Plateaux, this species may only ever have occurred in any numbers on Lake Alaotra, where hunting for the pot and habitat modification have led to a severe decline, such that recent searches have been unsuccessful. Total numbers are probably very low, and an urgent programme of captive breeding seems to be the only way of staving off extinction. The situation with the Madagascar teal *Anas bernieri* is better but still serious. This is one of the select band of Madagascan endemic birds in which the closest relatives are Asian rather than African. Always rather local, and found only on the west coast, usually on saline lakes and coastal marshes, this duck has also undergone a dramatic slump in recent years. Hunting, habitat destruction and a general lowering of the water table leading to a reduction in available habitat, have all contributed to the fall. This could be held in check by the creation of a suitable nature reserve for the species on a favoured lake, such as Lake Bemamba. Mellers' duck *Anas melleri* is similar to the European mallard and is the only endemic duck still widely found although it, too, has declined recently, probably from the same sad litany of causes.

Although widespread members of the Ardeidae, such as the night heron *Nycticorax nycticorax*, green-backed heron *Butorides striatus*, squacco heron *Ardeola ralloides* and grey heron *Ardea cinerea*, are all apparently holding their own in the island, Madagascar's two endemic herons sadly seem to be suffering the same fate as the endemic ducks and grebes. The Madagascar squacco heron *Ardeola idae* is present throughout the island, including in the capital Antananarivo, but a recent alarming decrease in pairs at its main breeding site does not appear to bode well for the future. The Madagascar heron *Ardea humbloti*, a large dark-plumaged bird, has probably always been rather localized, mainly in the west, but it, too, seems to have been on the wane rather drastically in recent years. It may still occur in some numbers in certain places, such as along the Betsiboka river and on Lakes Masama and Bemamba, but nesting sites seem to be very few and far between. Although it searches mainly for fish in the shallow water alongside rivers and lakes, on reefs, and in estuaries, it has also shown a willingness to venture into artificial wetlands, such as rice fields. Unless adequate protection is given soon, this species, too, may shortly approach the brink of oblivion.

Madagascar has eleven species of rails (Rallidae) of which six are endemic. Of these, the grey-throated rail *Mentocrex kioloides* is common in forests in the east, and is able to adjust to life in secondary forests and plantations. The white-throated rail *Dryolimnas cuvieri* is found throughout the eastern forests and in marshy places and streamsides on the Hauts Plateaux. The Sakalava rail *Amaurornis olivieri* is much rarer, known only from three widely separated localities in the west. These include Lakes Masama and Bemamba, already mentioned in connection with other rare endemics. This rail lives along streams or lakes bordered by dense stands of reeds *Phragmites communis* or slender reedmace *Typha angustifolia*, often tripping lightly across mats of floating vegetation, but retreating quickly into cover when disturbed. Because of its secretive habits, it may be somewhat under-recorded but, even so, it is undoubtedly rare. With its blue underside and contrasting bright-red crown, beak and legs, the Madagascar rail *Rallus madagascariensis* is the most beautiful member of the group. It is widely scattered in the east, north-east and Hauts Plateaux, being commoner at higher elevations, but is seldom seen.

Birds of prey

Madagascar has only 16 species of birds of prey; but eleven of these are endemic, so are of considerable interest for the ornithologist. Eagles, buzzards, hawks and kestrels are much less evident in Madagascar than in Africa where they are common everywhere. The Madagascar kestrel *Falco newtoni* is the commonest raptor on the island, however, and one of the few birds which seems quite at home on the Hauts Plateaux, probably because of its liking for open habitats rather than dense forest. It also does well in degraded forests and cultivated areas, so human interference has probably benefited the bird because the number of rodents increases where people live. This elegant little raptor also often nests on buildings, a habit shared with the European kestrel *Falco*

Top: **The Madagascar kestrel** Falco newtoni **is a small,
elegant, endemic raptor which probably benefits from
human destruction of the primary forests. It is the
commonest raptor on the island, being found in a variety of
habitats, including the uplands of the Hauts Plateaux.**

Above and right: **It is late December in Berenty Private Nature
Reserve and a male Madagascar kestrel** Falco newtoni
**returns from a successful hunt with the limp body of a
Chalaradon madagascariensis lizard hanging from his beak.
This small diurnal lizard is so abundant in this reserve that
it provided the bulk of the diet for the developing kestrel
family. Finally, the male kestrel hands over the lifeless body
of the lizard to his mate.**

The endemic banded kestrel **Falco zoniventris** *is a widespread but rather rare raptor which feeds exclusively on insects.*

tinnunculus. In the 'spiny desert', the Madagascar kestrel may feed its chicks exclusively on one or two species of lizards, particularly the very common *Chalaradon madagascariensis*. The male does all the hunting and announces his return from a productive foray with a series of high-pitched screams. A brief ceremony accompanies the handing-over of the limp body of a lizard, before it is torn apart by the female and fed to the young.

Fortunately, the Madagascar kestrel is not the only raptor which adapts well to degraded habitats. The Madagascar harrier-hawk *Polyboroides radiatus*, Frances's sparrowhawk *Accipiter francesii*, Madagascar buzzard *Buteo brachypterus* and banded kestrel *Falco zoniventris* are also found in such areas. The Madagascar cuckoo-falcon *Aviceda madagascariensis* is currently widely distributed in a variety of habitats. How much longer this situation will last is uncertain because adults and young are taken at the nest and head straight for the cooking pot. With the explosive growth in the human population currently taking place in Madagascar, such activities will inevitably place more and more pressure on bird numbers, especially because Madagascan boys virtually grow up with catapults in their hands, not with the aim of killing birds for fun, but to add some much-needed extra meat to the family menu.

The Madagascar fish-eagle *Haliaeetus vociferoides* is one of the rarest birds of prey in the world. This has not always been the case, but shooting of the adults, destruction of their nests and reduction of available wetland habitat through increases in rice growing, have led to such a catastrophic decline in the last 100 years that estimates indicate that there are now just 30 pairs left. The preferred habitats are estuaries and mangrove swamps, where fish are abundant and more easily spotted and caught in the shallow waters. In common with all large raptors, the rate of replacement of birds lost by hunting is slow because the birds do not start to breed until they are four or five years old, and even then, only a single chick is reared each year. Its chief remaining habitat seems to be on the coast north of Morondava, although there are some recent records from much further north, at Ankarana and near Diégo Suarez.

One of the greatest debates in Madagascan ornithology concerns the true status of the Madagascar

The small Madagascar Scops owl Otus rutilus *is widespread in the forests, and is also found on the Comoros.*

serpent eagle *Eutriorchis astur*. Until recently, the last definite sighting of this large eagle was more than 50 years ago. Then, in 1988, a party of British ornithologists surveying the birds of the Marojejy massif spotted one of these near-mythical creatures foraging beneath the canopy. The Madagascar serpent eagle was still with us! It seems always to have been rare although it is apparently very shy and considerable areas of the eastern rainforests, from where all the records have come, still remain relatively unexplored ornithologically. Although it undoubtedly eats reptiles, such as chameleons, there is no evidence

that it actually takes snakes, and the main prey is said to consist of mammals, including lemurs. If this is true, then the jumpy reactions exhibited by many lemurs to perceived threats from the sky, usually accompanied by a barrage of alarm calls, may indicate that this eagle was formerly very much more abundant than it is now because few, if any, of Madagascar's other birds of prey seem to pay much attention to lemurs.

Owls

Madagascar has six species of owls, four of which are endemic. The almost cosmopolitan barn owl *Tyto alba* is present while the marsh owl *Asio capensis* also ranges over a vast area of Africa. The much smaller Madagascar Scops owl *Otus rutilus* is widely distributed in primary and in degraded forest. The tediously repetitive, teeth-gritting screeching of the white-browed owl *Ninox superciliaris* is perfectly pitched to grate on the nerves of anyone sitting quietly in the forests near Morondava, patiently waiting for the distant rustle of a giant jumping rat returning to its burrow (I make this claim from bitter experience!). This owl is fairly common throughout these western forests although, strangely enough, there is also a single record from the rainforests of Marojejy.

The Madagascar long-eared owl *Asio madagascariensis* is similar to its relative the long-eared owl *Asio otus* of the northern temperate regions. The Madagascan species is a rather local rainforest bird, but it may be under-recorded. The Madagascar red owl *Tyto soumagnii* has been noted only once in the last 50 years, north of Périnet in 1973, although there are recent unconfirmed reports of its presence in the Masoala peninsula, a likely habitat. Little is known of its habits, although it is said to prey largely on frogs taken in clearings in the forest, a practice familiar in other tropical owls.

Game birds

With only nine species in all, the Madagascan fauna of ground-dwelling partridges, quails and sandgrouse is small indeed compared with any similar-sized African country. Nevertheless, those species which are present are often abundant and easily seen, and five of them are endemics. The Madagascar buttonquail *Turnix nigricollis* is widespread and common throughout much of the island, even on the Hauts Plateaux. It is found in some numbers in the open, savanna-like habitat around the Ankarana massif where, in company with the Madagascar sandgrouse *Pterocles personatus* (another endemic), it gathers in parties enjoying the shade cast by clumps of trees during the heat of the day. Although it favours such open habitats, the buttonquail is also found in woodland where it searches for seeds and insects among the dead leaves. Despite being hunted for food, it can be ridiculously trusting, running only a short distance ahead of an intruder, rather than taking flight.

The Madagascar pratincole *Glareola ocularis* is the

The endemic Madagascar buttonquail Turnix nigricollis *is usually seen skulking around in the forest understorey.*

sole representative of the Glareolidae, and the coursers so typical of the African savannas are absent. It is widely distributed and normally forages among rocks beside rivers and on the coast. During the dry season, the bird flies off to coastal areas of Kenya and Tanzania, so it is one of the few Madagascan endemics which is migratory. The Madagascar plover *Charadrius thoracicus* is a rare bird confined to coastal tracts in the south-western part of the island. The total population may now number less than 1000. Although it lives beside the sea, it does not appear to probe, wader-fashion, for food on mudflats, but searches instead for small insects in short coastal turf. The reasons for its rarity are little understood, but may stem from competition with the more recently arrived, non-endemic Kittlitz's plover *C. pecuarius*, from which the Madagascan species was distinguished only in 1896.

In the west, and to a lesser extent in the east, large flocks of the helmeted guineafowl *Numida meleagris* are as typical a feature of open grassy landscapes as they are in similar parts of Africa. The sight of a flock of these large, meaty birds flying across a road is sure to excite a chorus of yearning gasps from the passengers in a bus or bush taxi, for guineafowl meat is greatly savoured in Madagascar, as elsewhere. It is assiduously hunted and its tastily prepared flesh even finds its way on to plates in restaurants in western towns such as Morondava. This constant pressure seems to be reducing the numbers even of this adaptable species.

Although it is not strictly a game bird, the Madagascar crested ibis *Lophotibis cristata* is included here because of its terrestrial habits and appeal for the pot. Fortunately, it is still widespread in a variety of habitats, including degraded forest and plantations. It is an extremely impressive, large, dark-chestnut bird, usually found in pairs or flocks of 6 to 15. Even sizeable flocks can be amazingly inconspicuous in deep forest as they strut quietly around in the undergrowth, questing for insects and fruits on the forest floor. When disturbed, the bird's first reaction may be to run along in front of an approaching figure, but it will eventually take to the air if pressed, a most impressive spectacle as the broad dark wings are unfolded to reveal large, startlingly white patches. Fortunately, this imposing bird is present in several protected areas, reducing its chances of ending up on the local menu.

Miscellaneous non-passerines
The absence of woodpeckers (Picidae) from Madagascar has given rise to the theory that the niche normally occupied by these birds may have been taken by a mammal, the aye-aye. The Picidae is not the only major family which is not represented, however. With their bright plumage, the barbets (Capitonidae) are among the most conspicuous and typical of African birds; yet they have never managed to make it across to Madagascar. Nor have the hornbills (Bucerotidae) although, as already mentioned, the helmetbird has a rather hornbill-like

The long-tailed dove Oena capensis *is one of the commonest birds in Africa and in Madagascar although it is absent from the dense rainforests in the east of the island.*

beak. Alas, the Madagascan forests hold out no enticing prospects of seeing a breathtakingly gorgeous pitta (Pittidae) or resplendent trogon (Trogonidae), both of which are normally counted among the major jewels of the tropical avifauna.

Many familiar families do occur, however. Of the four members of the Columbidae, the most common species outside the rainforests is the long-tailed dove *Oena capensis*, a hugely successful bird which is also the most abundant dove over much of the less heavily forested parts of Africa. The green pigeon *Treron australis* is more suited to wooded areas, and is absent from the Hauts Plateaux. It, too, is common in Africa. Of the two endemics, the attractive Madagascar blue pigeon *Alectroenas madagascariensis* is a species of dense forests, particularly in the east and north, although it migrates westwards during the winter dry season. It is heavily hunted and is now the sole member of its genus for a second species, endemic to Mauritius, was exterminated in the early nineteenth century. The Madagascar turtle dove *Streptopelia picturata* is common throughout wherever there is cover, such as forest, scrubby areas or plantations. It is also found on the Comoros and on the islands of Aldabra and Chagos, and has been introduced into a number of islands, including Mauritius and the Seychelles.

All three species of parrots are endemic. They are born winners which thrive just about anywhere, to the extent that the lesser vasa parrot *Coracopsis nigra* has managed to earn a place on the Malagasy government's list of pest species. This and the greater

Left: **This Madagascar coucal Centropus toulou** *is searching a tree thoroughly for prey. Shortly afterwards it ate a small chameleon. Outside Madagascar, it is found on the islands of Mayotte and Aldabra.*

Opposite top: **The Madagascar malachite kingfisher Alcedo vintsioides** *is common in the eastern and in the western forests. It is often found near water but not necessarily so. This rock below a waterfall in the forests on the Montagne d'Ambre obviously serves regularly as a perch. This spectacular little bird is also found in the Comoros.*

Opposite bottom: **The endemic red and white kingfisher (also known as the forest kingfisher) Ipsidina madagascariensis** *is widely distributed apart from in the driest areas of the extreme south-west. Both this and the Madagascar Malachite kingfisher are usually amazingly confiding and show relatively little fear of humans.*

for a certain host, in this case the unwitting Madagascar cisticola *Cisticola cherina*. The cuckoo's relative, however, the Madagascar coucal *Centropus toulou,* makes its own nest and shuns the parasitic lifestyle. Like most coucals, it is a fairly large, robust, brown bird. It is greatly feared by smaller birds, which treat it much as they do other predators and mob it mercilessly. It is a patient and meticulous hunter, often devoting a considerable amount of time to combing a tree thoroughly for the nests of smaller birds, their eggs and nestlings suffering as a result. It is also a fearsome enemy of lizards, especially juvenile chameleons. The coucal makes a prolonged and painstaking search for these young reptiles. This coucal is common throughout much of Madagascar, although rare on the Hauts Plateaux, and also occurs on the islands of Mayotte and Aldabra.

Anyone suffering the strains of a lengthy taxi-brousse journey across Madagascar at night is almost certain to have the discomfort and monotony broken by a glimpse of a Madagascar nightjar *Caprimulgus madagascariensis*. Likely as not, it will be sitting plumb in the middle of the road, before spreading its hawk-like wings and ghosting off into the night. It is a widespread species which even manages to survive in Antananarivo. In some areas it seems to be extremely abundant. For example, one April on the road from Ankotrofotsy to Malaimbandy in the west, it turned up either singly or in pairs at intervals of about a mile (1-2 km) for a distance of about 19 miles (30 km). During the day, the bird rests hidden under a clump of trees in savanna or in open woodland, sitting tight and relying on its camouflage, only flying up at the last moment if a descending foot nearly steps on mottled brown feathers. The endemic collared nightjar *Caprimulgus enarratus* is rarer and confined mainly to forests in the east and the Sambirano.

Unfortunately, one of the glories of the African scene, the abundance of its kingfishers, has no parallel in Madagascar for only two species occur, although both of them are endemic. The Madagascar malachite kingfisher *Alcedo vintsioides* is, however, a living jewel of a bird, and allows its splendour to be appreciated in full because it is usually delightfully tame. It is not unusual to be able to approach one on foot to within 6 or 7 feet (2 m), when it will probably sit there unconcernedly preening its gorgeous plumage. Although it is not confined to water, it is most often

vasa parrot *Coracopsis vasa* are hardly likely to set the blood tingling as they are, unlike most of the world's parrots, a rather plain dark brown. Both are found elsewhere within the Malagasy subregion. The grey-headed lovebird *Agapornis cana* is quite another matter for, though small, it is a particularly brilliant shade of emerald green, and the sight of a noisily squawking party of these pert little birds winging their way through some drab, leafless, western forest and lining up to drink on a waterside log is one of the most rewarding ornithological experiences in the island. It is common all over, in a variety of habitats.

The Madagascar little cuckoo *Cuculus rochii* is another one of the handful of species which migrates to Africa from April to August, and from east to west in Madagascar during the rainy season. It thereby takes advantage of the explosion in nesting behaviour by the birds in the western dry forests when the rains arrive. It is found throughout most of the island, and rather resembles a small version of the common Eurasian cuckoo *C. canorus*. Unlike the latter, though, it calls at night as well as during the day, but does share the same habit of showing a distinct preference

seen near lakes and rivers. In Montagne d'Ambre one of these birds, which was perched on a rock below a waterfall, repeatedly flew straight into the spray at the base of the fall, each time returning with a tiny fish struggling in its beak. Presumably, the kingfisher's sharp eyes were able to spot the tiny silver slivers tumbling downwards in the curtain of water. They were then snapped out of the cauldron of spray with amazing agility and precision. Happily, this lovely bird is common enough to assure any visitor of a glimpse; it is also found in the Comoros.

The red and white kingfisher *Ipsidina madagascariensis* (also rather confusingly called the Madagascar hunting kingfisher and forest kingfisher) also enjoys a wide distribution within the island although it is commoner in the east than in the west. It, too, is often found far from water, and is frequently as tame as its relative. As in other kingfishers, the nest is placed at the end of a burrow in a vertical cliff of earth. The bird repeatedly throws itself against the cliff and tears off some earth in its powerful beak to get the hole started. Once a foothold is secured, the process can be speeded up considerably because the beak can be put to work on a more constant basis.

Although there is only a single species of bee-eater (Meropidae) in Madagascar, compared with eight in Zambia and eleven in Kenya, the Madagascan representative, the olive bee-eater *Merops superciliosus*, is seen regularly over most of the island. It is however rare on the barren Hauts Plateaux and in the densest rainforest. The Madagascan race is *M. s. superciliosus*, in which the top of the head is brownish, the back olive green, the throat dull brown and the cheeks conspicuously white. The *M. s. persicus*, the blue-cheeked bee-eater, found much further north in Africa and the Middle East is a much prettier bird, with the top of the head blue and green, the cheeks blue, and the throat bright brownish orange. The olive bee-eater has been well able to adapt to the alterations to the natural environment brought about by people, and is even very much a town bird in many areas. It is a welcome sight hawking exuberantly for flies, like some giant green swallow, over the unprepossessing rooftops of Morondava or Diégo Suarez, its liquid 'quilp' flight note constantly accompanying its fluent displays of aerial mastery. When perched on roofs or wires, these large graceful birds will also make short capture flights for insects (flies, bees, dragonflies, termites etc) much in the way of a flycatcher. This subspecies is not endemic, and also breeds in September and October in the coastal region of neighbouring Mozambique, possibly representing birds which have migrated across from Madagascar. The breeding pair excavates a hole in a bank, usually above a river where a sheer earthen cliff is more readily available; they are always accompanied by other pairs to form large colonies.

With its blushing pink plumage, boldly barred with black and white, and its black-tipped erectile crest, the hoopoe *Upupa epops* is one of the most conspicuous and characteristic birds of the dry forests of the west and the southern 'spiny desert'. The Madagascan bird is a distinctive subspecies, *U. e. marginata* which some authorities suggest should be regarded as a species in its own right. It differs from the African birds in a number of details of plumage, as well as in its greater size and weight and its different call. It spends a large part of its time on the ground, probing the soil with its long curved beak and rummaging among dead leaves for insects, which are swallowed with a toss of the head. It is particularly fond of ant-lion larvae, of which their diminutive sand pits are a common sight in the drier areas. It is a remarkably tame bird and seldom flies far when disturbed on the ground, often merely flapping into a nearby tree and eyeing the intruder, quickly returning to its feeding when the nuisance has passed.

Passerines

The majority of the Madagascan 'perching birds' are the classic 'little brown jobs', although there are a few notable exceptions. The Madagascar bush lark *Mirafra hova* is the sole representative of the Alaudidae, a family with many members in semi-desert areas of Africa. Despite the abundance of such habitat in the south and west, only this one species seems to have colonized Madagascar, where it is one of the few birds which can survive and even thrive in the degraded grasslands of the Hauts Plateaux. Even stranger, perhaps, is the presence of only a single member of the Motacillidae, usually highly mobile birds, yet with just the Madagascar wagtail *Motacilla flaviventris* having made it across the intervening gap. This

The endemic Madagascar magpie robin Copsychus albospecularis *is the tamest bird in Madagascar if not one of the tamest birds in the world. It is widespread over the whole island and often nests on buildings.*

*Left: **Benson's rockthrush** Monticola bensoni was recognized as a separate species only in recent years. In a highly typical pose, it perches on the lichen-spattered cliffs of the Isalo mountains; it is endemic to this region.*

*Above: **Benson's rockthrushes** Monticola bensoni often descend from the rocky escarpment of the Isalo mountains to forage on the burned-over pasture lands near the town of Ranohira.*

unmistakable bird, with its prominent black chest band and tail-flicking mannerisms, seems actually to favour the barren uplands of the Hauts Plateaux where it is commonly found in and around villages, often nesting on buildings.

There are six endemic members of the Pycnonotidae, all undistinguished little birds, much like their relatives in Africa and Asia. The Madagascar bulbul *Hypsipetes madagascariensis* is one of the commonest birds in the island, and is found in every kind of habitat. Its origin lies far away in Asia rather than in nearby Africa, and it is closely related to certain Indian bulbuls. The other five are all of African ancestry, although three of these are rare and confined to a few spots in the eastern rainforests.

The family Turdidae (thrushes etc) contains the tamest bird on the island (possibly even one of the most naturally tame birds in the world), the Madagascar magpie robin *Copsychus albospecularis*, another species of Asian, rather than African, origin. The strange thing about this little black-and-white bird's fearlessness is its constancy. Although nests are sometimes placed on or near buildings, giving the builders plenty of chance to get used to people, a magpie robin encountered in some remote forest seems to be just as tame as one which lives near a village. The males have the strange habit of frequently breaking into their sweet-toned song when a human comes near. In fact, the mere sight of a person seems actually to attract these birds to come to have a closer look. This audacity can reach quite ridiculous heights

for, when I was busy photographing a wasps' nest in a western forest, it was necessary to keep a constant watch to avoid stepping on a female magpie robin perched on a fist-sized stump just below the nest. Despite the fact that I was looming directly above her, she was not in the least inclined to move, even with a pair of large boots stomping around at less than arm's length of her position.

Two endemic rock-thrushes of the dry south-west closely resemble such African species as the sentinel rock-thrush *Monticola explorator* and Angolan rock-thrush *M. angolensis*. One, the endemic littoral rock-thrush *Monticola imerina*, is a local bird of coastal dunes and arid grasslands studded with stands of *Didierea* and coralliform euphorbias. Although dry, this is a rather unusual habitat for a rock-thrush because, in Africa and southern Europe, these birds usually prefer open, rocky hillsides. It is hardly surprising, then, that a second Madagascan endemic, Benson's rock-thrush *Monticola bensoni*, should thrive in such a typical habitat as the sun-baked, boulder-strewn, craggy terrain of the Isalo massif. In this desolate landscape, these little grey and rust-red birds perch high up on the eroded, lichen-spattered cliffs. The males utilize the highest pinnacles as springboards for launching their display flights during which the clear, melodious song rings out across the barren landscape. It is surprising, perhaps, that this bird was described only in 1971, from two old skins collected at an untraceable locality. The living animal was rediscovered in 1962 in the region near the Mangoky

Dense rainforest is an unusual haunt for a rockthrush, yet this is the preferred habitat for the endemic forest rockthrush Monticola sharpei erythronotus *photographed in the Montagne d'Ambre National Park.*

forest rock-thrush *Monticola sharpei*, is found in a most unusual habitat, confined mainly to areas of dense cover in the eastern and northern rainforests, in each of which it is present as a distinct subspecies.

The elegant, streamer-tailed males and rather more dowdy shorter-tailed females of the Madagascar paradise flycatcher *Terpsiphone mutata* are perhaps the most commonly seen birds in any of the island's forests. They often hawk for insects from a twig by a forest path and, like a surprising number of Madagascan birds, they are very tame. A combination of keen eyesight and superlative aerobatic prowess makes this species a formidable hunter of airborne insects — a female's wings almost brushed my face as she took a butterfly zig-zagging rapidly past. The bird is found in wooded areas throughout the island as well as in the Comoros, Seychelles, Mascarenes and Réunion. It belongs to a genus of similar-looking birds also found in Africa and Asia. Ward's flycatcher *Pseudobias wardi*, in which the sexes are similar, belongs to an endemic genus and is much rarer, only occurring in the eastern rainforests from Ivohibe to Tsaratanana.

Throughout Africa and Asia, brilliant metallic sunbirds (Nectariniidae) are a regular feature in gardens, even in large cities, where they are attracted

river and the Isalo massif. Remarkably, bearing in mind this late rediscovery, the bird seems to be quite common in parts of this area, so just how it went unnoticed or unrecognized for so long is a mystery. Despite its status as a National Park, however, Isalo suffers from considerable illegal poaching, mainly by youths armed with catapults, who enter the area almost daily to kill birds for food. A third species, the

The elegant streamer-tailed males of the Madagascar paradise flycatcher Terpsiphone mutata *occur in two different forms, one white breasted* (below left), *the other rufous breasted* (below right). *This is one of the most characteristic birds of forests throughout the island. It is also found on the Comoros, Seychelles, Mascarenes and Réunion.*

to the wide variety of cultivated flowers on offer. Unfortunately, Madagascar has only two sunbirds, neither of which is common in gardens. The Madagascar green sunbird *Nectarinia notata* has African affinities; it is a dark, metallic-green bird with a long, curved beak suited for probing into flowers. It is found virtually throughout, including in parts of the Hauts Plateaux, but it is rarer in the dry south-west; it is also found in the Comoros. The Souimanga sunbird *Nectarinia souimanga* is probably of Asian origin; it is a smaller, prettier bird with a shorter beak. It, too, is widespread and, like most sunbirds, relatively tame and approachable. It is also found on Aldabra, reinforcing the idea that it is probably hails from Asia.

With only four species present, the weavers (Ploceidae) are poorly represented in Madagascar, and a tree decorated with their rotund nests is not an everyday part of the Madagascan scene as it is over most of Africa. In fact, only two of the Madagascan species actually build conspicuous, beautifully crafted hanging nests of the African type. The finest handiwork is achieved by the Nelicourvi weaver *Ploceus nelicourvi*; its end product resembles an inverted water bottle, with a very elongated 'spout' forming the downward-pointing entrance. It is reasonably common in the east and north-east (Sambirano) in primary and in disturbed forest.

The attractive brown and yellow Sakalava weaver *Foudia sakalava* belongs to a genus otherwise known only from a few small islands in the western part of the Indian Ocean. Like many African weavers, it prefers to place its colonies near human habitations, often suspending its nest from remarkably low twigs hanging within easy reach of the ground. As in other weavers, it is the males that slave away at the complex task of piecing together thousands of individual strands to form a robust enclosed structure, able to withstand the violent thunderstorms which batter the forests during the breeding season. The Sakalava weaver is very localized, and is absent from many apparently suitable areas, a puzzling feature because weaver birds are generally noted for their adaptability. Its range comprises: the south-west, for example, around Morondava; the north centre, especially in the dry forests to the south of Mahajanga; and the north-east near Diégo Suarez. Although typical of dry forests, it also breeds in considerable numbers in mangrove swamps on the coast.

When in the full scarlet splendour of their breeding dress, the males of the red fody *Foudia madagascariensis* are perhaps the showiest birds on the island. As a result, they are among the few that can be spotted easily from a speeding car as they perch on telephone wires along the roadsides. In some areas, they gather in considerable numbers such that, on the winding dirt road from Anivorano to Matsaborimanga in the north-east (heading for Ankarana Special Reserve) in early June, a gaudy fody male was posed prominently on a wire every 1-200 yards (90-180 m) in the savanna-like landscape; while flashes of scarlet among the bleached grasses indicated the presence of many more birds lower down. Even

The endemic Sakalava weaver **Foudia sakalava** *has a scattered distribution but is locally very common. The male builds the nest which is often placed near human habitations.*

when it is not immediately obvious, the male can be located easily by his incessant, twittering little call, which he usually gives from some favourite perch, returning regularly to the same spot after short sorties into the surrounding trees to feed. He will also desert his post to chase off a rival male or to mob furiously an intruding coucal. The red fody is one of the few Madagascan animals which has gained from human destruction of the primary forests, apparently being more abundant in open bushy places and degraded forests. It also manages to make a good living in plantations of alien trees. In the Ampijeroa forest reserve, the territories of at least two males were seen to consist primarily of stands of alien teak trees *Tectonia grandis*. This is an Asian native, the leaves of

The male Red fody **Foudia madagascariensis** *is one of the most flamboyantly plumaged birds on the island. It is becoming increasingly common as the area of degraded vegetation continues its inexorable increase.*

brilliantly plumaged starlings of nearby Africa. It is fairly common in the east, west and north, living in a wide variety of habitats, although it is more abundant on the flat coastal plain than in higher areas inland.

With its coal-black plumage, strongly forked tail and twin-plumed adornments on its head, the crested drongo *Dicrurus forficatus* is perhaps the most easily recognized bird in Madagascar, and it is unmistakable, even in silhouette. It is closely related to the fork-tailed drongo *D. adsimilis* of Africa, although the latter lacks the plumes. Both birds have the habit of sitting in conspicuous places in trees and have little fear of humans. Although it is common enough in wooded areas and degraded forests over most of the island, the crested drongo is absent from the open grasslands of the Hauts Plateaux. In some localities, its well-known air of confidence in the presence of humans is well founded, for there is sometimes a local *fady* against killing it. There is such a taboo near Maroansetra on the north-east coast which has arisen, apparently, because of a real event. Hundreds of years ago pirate bands landed regularly to pillage villages on the eastern seaboard. The news of approaching pirates would send the villagers dashing for safety into the nearby forest. This strategy failed one day in Ambinanetelo when the women, slowed down by their young children, lagged behind the main party and were forced to stay where they were, hoping to

which have been successfully colonized by a number of local insects, yielding a supply of food for the resident fodies. The red fody also feeds on rice, and its inroads into this staple crop have earned it a place on the government's list of harmful species.

The burgeoning success of the red fody in response to the retreat of the primary forests has meant increasing problems for the red forest fody *Foudia omissa*. Originally, the red fody was probably confined to the western savannas and dry forests, but the increase in degraded areas in the rainforests has enabled it to colonize the east, and now brings it into increasing contact with its relative. Unfortunately, the two birds are so closely related that hybridization is simple, so that, in long term, the forest fody's stock may be diluted to the point that it ceases to exist in a pure form.

The Madagascar starling *Saroglossa aurata* is a rather drab bird, suggesting an Asian ancestry, rather than any close relationship to the numerous species of

remain undetected in a small stand of trees. Their presence was betrayed, however, when a baby suddenly cried out, just as the pirates were walking by. Alerted by the cry, the pirates headed for the group's hideout, but stopped in their tracks when they heard the cry again, coming not from a baby, but from a drongo perched prominently on a nearby tree. Convinced that all they were chasing was a useless bird, the pirates gave up and went back to their craft. Since then, this accomplished mimic has been honoured in the valley, where it is forbidden to do any harm to this saviour of the people.

Seabirds and shorebirds

The Madagascan shoreline has its share of seabirds and wading birds, many of which are far-ranging wanderers with an almost cosmopolitan distribution. Thus, turnstones *Arenaria interpres* are as likely to be seen pottering busily around on the warm gleaming mud among the mangroves at hot tropical Morondava, as on the cold windswept mudflats of England's east coast saltmarshes. A variety of other familiar Eurasian waders are rare-to-common visitors to Madagascar during the northern winter, as they are to the neighbouring coast of Africa. Many of the seabirds are widespread throughout the tropical regions although a few breed in or near Madagascar. These include fourteen species of terns. The swift or crested tern *Sterna bergii* is common on all coasts save the east, and breeds on a number of off-shore islands. The lesser crested tern *Sterna bengalensis* is the commonest tern in Madagascar and probably breeds in some hitherto unlocated spot. Both these terns are wide ranging and found as far away as the east coast of Australia where they nest together on islands on the Great Barrier Reef.

The pan-tropical brown noddy *Anous stolidus* is common around the coasts of Madagascar, establishing nesting colonies south of Tamatave. The sooty tern *Sterna fuscata* is another pan-tropical species which breeds near Tamatave and Tulear, as does the roseate tern *Sterna dougalii*. Among the other seabirds, the wedge-tailed shearwater *Puffinus pacificus* breeds in small numbers on islands near Morombe, while the white-tailed tropicbird *Phaethon lepturus* does likewise near Diégo Suarez.

Opposite: **The African darter** Anhinga rufa **is found near lakes over most of Madagascar. It also enjoys a huge distribution over the African continent.**

Top right: **The three-banded sandplover** Charadrius tricollaris **is common throughout the whole island, as it is over much of Africa.**

Above right: **Only the mangrove seedlings protruding from the shining mud betray the fact that these turnstones** Arenaria interpres, **among the most familiar of our north-temperate shorebirds, are actually foraging on Madagascar's tropical mudflats. This is a common migrant from September to May, with some birds remaining in the island throughout the year.**

Right: **The crested or swift tern** Sterna bergii **is common around all the coasts except for the east. Breeding colonies of this pan-tropical species are known from a few coastal islands.**

Chapter 6
Mammals other than Lemurs

Relatively few species of mammals managed to find their way across the seas to Madagascar as the gulf separating the island from the African mainland gradually widened. Thus, there is a very restricted mammal fauna but, of these, so many are endemic that Madagascar is fascinating for anyone interested in mammalian evolution. In some ways, Madagascar is almost as interesting for what is not there as for what is. There are many familiar African mammals which failed to make it across. These absentees include such major groups as: the cats; dogs; lagomorphs (rabbits and hares); ruminants, such as the antelope which grace the African scene in countless numbers; elephants; and those striped wild horses of the wide savannas, the zebras. Even among groups which did arrive, there are notable omissions: squirrels, porcupines and gerbils among the rodents; and monkeys and apes among the primates which, in Madagascar, are represented by the lemurs, the most abundant and successful living representatives of the most primitive of primates, the prosimians.

Thus, Madagascar's lack of mammalian diversity is caused by its history, the same factor which has influenced the high degree of accompanying endemism. Those mammals which did manage to make the trip found a clean ecological slate on which they could write freely their own evolutionary progress. They radiated into a multiplicity of species suited to the variety of free niches available on the island. In so doing, they became quite different from their relatives on the African mainland. Some of their number have almost certainly enjoyed a more recent assisted passage, having probably arrived by boat, together with colonizing humans, from the African mainland. This probably accounts for the presence of the African bush pig *Potamochoerus porcus* and the African shrews *Suncus etruscus* and *S. murinus* on Madagascar. The former has become a widely established nuisance, rooting up the soil in search of tubers, insects and worms, and destroying precious crops. In some regions, it is hunted for its meat, but in the Muslim areas it remains an unmitigated pest and is probably partly responsible for the increasing rarity of the Angonoka tortoise in its restricted home in the north-west.

Chiroptera: the bats

Although richer than the other groups of mammals, the Madagascan bat fauna, with its 28 species, is still relatively impoverished. Not surprisingly in such accomplished aeronauts, the rate of endemism is much lower than in the ground-living mammals, and only nine of the above total are endemic to the island. This is a rate of just 32 per cent compared with 90 per cent or so for most of the other groups.

The largest species is the flying fox *Pteropus rufus* which often assembles in dense roosts in tall trees or in caves. It is a member of the group of bats (Megachiroptera) which feed on fruits. Many visitors to the reserve at Berenty are shown groups of this bat roosting in the large tamarind trees, although such close human intrusion appears to cause them some distress and may account for the apparent reduction in numbers at this site. Its future in this protected area, however, is perhaps more secure than elsewhere, for human taste for its fatty meat leads to its destruction in some numbers at the hands of local hunters. *Pteropus rufus* is endemic to Madagascar and, in some ways, it is surprising to find it here, for it is quite unrelated to any African bats. Instead, it is one of the most westerly representatives of a widespread Asian genus. It is found mainly near the coast and is widespread though local. When roosts are situated on offshore islands, they enjoy some measure of protection from hunting, especially when making a landing from a small boat is difficult or dangerous, as is the case on one roosting island in the Bay of Antongil. Unfortunately, the more accessible roosts of this large attractive bat are probably doomed.

A smaller fruit-bat, *Rousettus madagascariensis*, is now known to be endemic although, formerly, it was included in the widespread African species *Rousettus lanosus*. A third species, *Eidolon helvum*, is widespread in tropical Africa and in Madagascar. Among the bats which feed on insects or nectar (Microchiroptera) there are numerous non-endemics while a number, which are classed as endemics, are close relatives of widespread African species.

The most interesting Madagascan bat is not only an endemic species but belongs to an endemic family, the Myzopodidae. *Myzopoda aurita* is a little-known animal from widely scattered localities in the eastern rainforests. Most of the specimens were collected before 1900 and it is not known how severely human interference since then has affected this unique species.

Insectivores
FAMILY TENRECIDAE — THE TENRECS

There are no native moles, shrews or hedgehogs on Madagascar; there are, however, animals which not only fill the niches usually occupied by these creatures, but even resemble them in a number of ways. To add to this, they have also succeeded in occupying other niches left vacant in Madagascar. These versatile beasts are the tenrecs, usually considered to be among the most primitive of living mammals because of their very conservative body plan which differs little from what is thought to be that of the very first mammals. Tenrecs are probably the first mammals to have arrived on the island. Finding every niche up for grabs they radiated into an amazing variety of species, varying in size from small and mouse-like to about the size of a small domestic cat, eventually colonizing a wide variety of habitats in their isolated home.

The group is divided into two subfamilies. The Oryzoryctinae contains 25 species in four Madagascan genera; and the Tenrecinae five species in four Madagascan genera (formerly six species in five genera but now excluding *Dasogale fontoynonti*, known to be an aberrant *Setifer setosus*). Members of the Oryzoryctinae are characteristically soft-furred animals with reasonably prominent tails. The largest genus is *Microgale* with around 20 named species, all of which possess conspicuously long tails giving rise to the name of long-tailed tenrecs. They include the smallest of all tenrecs *Microgale cowani* which, at just over 2 inches (6 cm) in length, is very shrew-like with its pointed nose and low, rather elongated body shape, characters which it shares to a greater or lesser degree with many other members of the genus.

The largest species, *Microgale talazaci*, reaches a length of 6 inches (15 cm) excluding its tail. It seems equally at home snuffling busily on the ground or climbing around in a tree in the rainforests of the eastern escarpment, the favoured habitat for most of this group. The dumpy bodied *Microgale dobsoni* is particularly interesting, because it has the ability to store fat in the tail during times of food shortage in the dry season. It inhabits the Hauts Plateaux where the leaf-litter insects which comprise its main food decrease greatly in numbers during the long dry season. The tenrecs of the wetter eastern forests, where insect densities do not vary so alarmingly from season to season, do not have so much of a problem. While grubbing around in its search for food, *M. dobsoni* is thought to use echolocation to improve its chances of discovering an insect hidden away among the confusing clutter of debris on the forest floor.

Members of the genus *Geogale* also have long tails but they are usually called large-eared tenrecs for obvious reasons. *Geogale aurita* inhabits the dry western forests, unlike the wetter eastern forests preferred by *Microgale*. It uses its flap-like ears to locate termites from the faint sounds they make. Thus, it occupies the niche which, in Africa, is taken by elephant shrews, such as species of *Elephantulus*, which apply their similarly large ears to the same problem. *G. aurita* spends much of its time scrambling around inside rotting trees, where one would have thought its projecting ears could get in the way. To prevent this, the ears are neatly folded down against the body when not in use. Like most members of the

Oryzoryctinae, the natural habits of this tenrec are poorly known, because it is difficult to observe the animal in the wild.

The three species of *Oryzorictes* rice-tenrecs rather resemble moles, as the scientific name of one of them, *O. talpoides*, indicates (*Talpa* is the generic name for various moles). The pronounced snout, with its pink elongated nose, very soft, close-knit velvety fur, tiny beady eyes, small ears flattened down to the body and quite well-developed front feet, amply provided with long, earth-moving claws, are all mole-like. The rice-tenrecs' burrowing habits also fit the part, although their small size, less than 4 inches (10 cm) long, perhaps places them more in parallel with the North American mole-shrews which also share these characteristics.

The most impressive member of the Oryzorictinae is the aquatic tenrec *Limnogale mergulus* which, with a body length of 8 inches (20 cm) excluding the tail, looks something like a cross between a large shrew and an extremely small otter. Its smooth, dense fur enables it to slide easily through the water, propelled efficiently by its webbed back feet and steered by its long tail, which is rather flattened laterally for its role as rudder. It inhabits the fast-flowing streams typical of the Hauts Plateaux, where it dives and searches for the small fish, crayfish and freshwater shrimps that make up the bulk of its diet. It seems likely that the long hairs on the tenrec's snout vibrate in response to any small underwater movements and, in this way, the prey is detected. Although obviously thoroughly at home in the water, *Limnogale* also seems to spend a considerable amount of time on the bank, judging by the abundance of its droppings on stream-side rocks. Its nocturnal habits do ensure, however, that the animal itself is rarely, if ever, seen in the wild, even by the local people, whose only encounter with this rare beast is when one turns up in a fisherman's net.

Madagascar's upland streams are greatly threatened because of the smothering burden of silt they are forced to carry when torrential rain scours the vulnerable red lateritic earth from the deforested hillsides. Too much silt kills the lace plant *Aponogeton fenestralis* and other water plants with which the aquatic tenrec always seems to live. This association may be based on the way in which the prolifically ramifying fronds of these plants provide numerous hiding places, thereby encouraging high densities in the tenrec's invertebrate prey. Because of its apparent rarity, there are plans for an intensive survey of likely localities, to establish its true status. Investigations into its lifestyle and ecological requirements should provide the basis for the possible establishment of a captive-breeding programme. At present, the only rivers where the species is now thought to occur in reasonable numbers are: north-east of the Andringitra Strict Natural Reserve; 22 miles (35 km) south of Antsirabe; and near Ranomafana, an area already renowned for the richness of its mammalian fauna. In the latter area, this elusive animal finally appeared in the flesh during 1990 when Dr David Stone of the World Wide Fund for Nature (WWF) managed to lure

A Japanese-built hydro-electric plant at Ranomafana is a vital part of the economy of south-central Madagascar because it is the sole source of electricity for several important towns in the area. At present, a relatively constant and silt-free flow of water is reliably available from the River Namorona, thanks to its running for much of its distance through rainforest. If the forest disappears, the future of the electricity supply for such towns as Fianarantsoa will be in doubt, as silt and fluctuating water flows reduce the power output. This is a perfect example of how it is not just the native animals — such as the 12 species of lemurs in these forests — which suffer if the forest is destroyed. Humans suffer, too, underlining the principle that conservation is not just for wildlife.

a specimen into a live trap, of a type similar to those he had used previously while studying the Pyrenean desman *Galemys pyrenaicus*. This became the first aquatic tenrec to be caught alive for 25 years. Capitalizing on this success, the same techniques were used to capture four more specimens from the same area, one of which was taken back to Antananrivo for three weeks for study purposes, before being returned safely to the river at Ranomafana. Here the River Namorona runs through relatively untouched rainforest, much of which is proposed for inclusion in a new National Park. There is an economically vital hydro-electric generating station not far below the tenrec's habitat. Hydro-electric stations need a reliable, and almost silt-free flow of water down the river so this is an additional reason why it would be foolish to encourage increased erosion of the catchment area through uncontrolled deforestation.

Members of the Oryzorictinae have one more feature in common; they are highly unlikely to be seen by most visitors to the island, because they are nocturnal, often burrowing, very retiring and sometimes quite rare. For this reason, there have been few observations of their normal activities in the wild, and much inference has to be drawn from dietary preferences in captivity. Contrast this with the Tenrecinae, some of which are common enough to be seen by anyone spending a few nights in a forested area. Several species show a tendency to come sniffing around houses and campsites in search of garbage, and this greatly increases both their success and the chances of an encounter with an interested observer. In appearance, members of this subfamily are quite different from the soft-furred, long-tailed, shrew-like forms characteristic of the Oryzorictinae. The six members of the Tenrecinae are generally rather stout-bodied animals, having no obviously visible tail and, in several cases, furnished with a bristling armament of defensive spines. Their habits are not so strictly nocturnal as in the previous group, and two species can even be seen regularly in daytime.

The biggest species, indeed the biggest of all living insectivores, is the common tenrec *Tenrec ecaudatus* which may attain weights of 3.3 pounds (1.5 kg). It is an extraordinarily prolific breeder. The size of its litters ranks among the largest known in any mammal, with up to 32 offspring being recorded! These legions of hungry youngsters are supplied with nourishment via any one of as many as 29 nipples. In shape, the common tenrec rather resembles a large, brown, furry hedgehog although, in the adult tenrec, the spines are restricted to a rearward-facing tuft on the crown of the head. These can be flexed forwards and driven into the body of an adversary when the tenrec is cornered, like some multipronged battering ram. This initial head-butting assault is backed up by an open-mouthed display of slashing teeth, which include prominent canines capable of inflicting severe gashes. At first glimpse, the juveniles could be taken for a completely separate species, for they sport a striped, black-and-white coat densely studded with sharp detachable spines set in longitudinal lines. Such a marked difference between adult and juvenile coloration might seem puzzling, but the pressures involved in feeding such a large family force the female and her entourage of infants — by this time usually reduced somewhat by losses to between 10 and 20 — to extend their foraging into the perilous hours of daylight. Small diurnal rodents tend to exhibit a camouflaged pattern of dark and light stripes, which helps to break up their outline in the dappled light among vegetation. The African *Rhabdomys* striped mice are typical examples. Mouse-sized juvenile

common tenrecs have merely evolved the same answer to the same problem. During the course of their very rapid growth, these infants gradually lose their spines until only the tuft on the nape remains. At the same time, the stripes are replaced by the dark-brown coloration of the adult.

The common tenrec occurs over almost the whole of Madagascar and must be counted as one of its most adaptable and successful native mammals. This success continues despite the changes wrought on the natural landscape by people and despite pressure from hunting. Its flesh has long been considered a delicacy in Madagascar, where it is a welcome addition to a diet generally deficient in protein. In some ways, the common tenrec actually takes advantage of human presence, for it is commonly seen rooting around in rubbish bins, where its omnivorous tendencies serve it well.

Waste food scraps also attract the greater hedgehog tenrec *Setifer setosus* which often raids the rubbish pits on research campsites in the nature reserves. It is common over much of the island and even survives in the midst of the teeming multitudes of people in Antananarivo, where it makes a good living from the malodorous contents of rubbish bins. As its name implies, this creature bears such a close resemblance to the familiar Eurasian hedgehog that few people would notice the difference. Even the defensive behaviour is similar, the tenrec rolling itself tightly into a ball and tucking its nose firmly into its stomach, to leave nought exposed save an unbroken thicket of spines. With their short legs, hedgehog tenrecs also walk with that slightly waddling motion typical of their namesakes. They even fill the same ecological niche, feeding as opportunists mainly on a diet of soft-bodied plant and animal material, including fruit as well as worms and a variety of insects.

The superficially similar, but rather smaller, lesser hedgehog tenrec *Echinops telfairi* differs by leading an arboreal existence in the dry forests of the south and west. For such a corpulent and ungainly looking creature, it is surprisingly nimble footed while performing its high-wire feats along a slim branch, its gymnastic skills greatly assisted by sharp toenails. In common with a number of other mammals from the seasonally productive forests of the south-west, *Echinops* bypasses the dry season's food shortages by falling into a prolonged torpor. It chooses a secure retreat in a hollow log or tree, which often plays host to several individuals having a communal 'sleep-in'.

Undoubtedly, the most bizarre of all tenrecs, in appearance and in behaviour, are the two species of streaked tenrec *Hemicentetes semispinosus* and *H. nigriceps*. The former is the only tenrec which is regularly active during the day, trotting busily around in the lower regions of the eastern rainforests which are its preferred habitat. Its basic colour is black, overlain by a dense armament of detachable barbed quills, some of which are yellow and form an arrangement of longitudinal stripes. The crown is decorated with a fan of backward-facing yellow spines which can be tilted forwards to form a spiky stockade.

This greater hedgehog tenrec Setifer setosus scurrying across the rainforest floor at night was a regular visitor to the garbage pit on Nosy Mangaby. This highly successful species is widespread in wet and in dry forests.

When fully at defensive action-stations, for such a small animal, *H. semispinosus* can present quite a formidable sight. With its fringe of spines bristling over its long, tapering nose, it bucks its head repeatedly, trying to impale the tender snout or hands of its adversary. It reinforces its fierce image by striking up an intimidating rattling sound, backed up by bursts of defiant hissing. This sabre-rattling performance is produced by a clump of specialized quills set in the middle of the back. These quills can be vibrated rapidly to produce a very wide range of sounds including high-frequency emissions unheard by the human ear, as well as the clearly audible rattling sounds which seem so impressive coming from such a diminutive animal. In addition to their defensive uses, these stridulations form part of the tenrec's sophisticated communications system, designed to maintain contact within a family group when out foraging together. These family groups may be very complex, consisting of more than one overlapping generation. Tenrecs mature very quickly and are capable of reproducing after only five weeks.

H. semispinosus is quite common in the eastern forests and is one of the tenrecs most often seen by visitors. It is, for example, often encountered rooting around under leaves on the roadside between Périnet railway station and the reserve, probing in the damp earth for its specialized diet of earthworms. These are easily subdued prey which also figure largely in the

diet of *H. nigriceps*, a similar-looking but less spiny tenrec which lives in forests at a higher altitude than its prickly relative.

Although remarkably diverse in their feeding, defensive and ecological adaptations, tenrecs are more conservative in other ways. Their breeding habits are unconventional in a number of characteristics. The males are unusual among mammals in retaining the testes within the body cavity. They lack a scrotum, therefore, the means used by other male mammals to keep the temperature-sensitive spermatozoans cool. To make up for this, the male tenrec reduces the temperature of its whole body by about 0.9 °F (0.5 °C) during the breeding season, when healthy sperm are required. This lowering of body temperature is not unusual among tenrecs of both sexes. The large-eared tenrec and all members of the Tenrecinae are capable of entering a period of torpor to carry them through unfavourable times of the year. The thermoregulation is flexible enough in operation to allow it to be used from short, opportunistic bursts when conditions demand to protracted spells lasting as long as six months. Even on a daily basis, most, if not all, tenrecs save energy when not foraging by temporarily allowing the body temperature to fall roughly to ambient. This 'stop-go-stop' method of fluctuating energy conservation is continued even during pregnancy, and probably results in considerable variations in the period needed for complete fetal development.

Courtship in tenrecs involves an idiosyncrasy also noticeable during normal daily activities — noisy sniffing. The male streaked tenrec *Hemicentetes*

semispinosus waddles towards the female to the accompaniment of loud hissing, his long, pointed, flexible snout arched upwards, ready to delve wetly into the female's ears, cheeks and even the quills on her body. If this combination of noisy hissing and enthusiastic ear probing proves sufficiently seductive, she flattens her spines, much in the way of a female hedgehog, allowing him to climb on board without too much risk of impalement.

Communication in tenrecs is interesting enough to be one facet of their behaviour to be reasonably well studied. Many tenrecs can emit tongue-clicks, each lasting only a fraction of a second and covering a wide band of frequencies. Their precise function is yet to be convincingly demonstrated, although their similarity to devices used in such other nocturnal foragers as bats suggests that they are used for echolocation. Apart from the stridulations produced by the streaked tenrec *H. semispinosus*, the main method of communication between tenrecs is scent. The ano-genital region may be dragged over the ground to leave an odour trail clearly identifying the individual. A highly unusual method is used by the hedgehog tenrecs and by two species of *Microgale*. Glands situated on the eyelids yield a white secretion which is smeared against vertical objects in the vicinity. The exact reason for this strange behaviour is the subject of some speculation, varying from a straightforward territorial 'odour flag' to the deposition of sexual pheromones designed to stimulate ovulation. An even more puzzling and bizarre practice is self-anointing. If a tenrec wandering through the forest stumbles across the urine of another of the same species, it may sniff

The yellow-streaked tenrec Hemicentetes semispinosus *can often be seen foraging for food at dusk in the eastern rainforests.*

at the urine with obvious interest and then start to lap it up. This seems to act as a stimulant, causing the tenrec itself to urinate and then salivate quite profusely. After mixing a kind of urine-saliva cocktail, it uses its forepaws to anoint its flanks and face with this strange concoction. So far, no one has proposed a credible theory to explain this strange behaviour.

Tenrecs vary greatly in their vulnerability to habitat changes brought about by people. Some of the Oryzorictinae, such as many species of *Microgale*, have relatively small numbers of offspring. These mature rather slowly into adults which are usually destined to enjoy fairly long lives. This reproductive strategy works well in the stable rainforest environment where most of these species live, but it makes them very sensitive to rapid changes in habitat caused by deforestation. Members of the Tenrecinae, with their large litter sizes and rapid maturation, are far better suited to move with the times and survive in the face of adversity. Indeed, many of them actually thrive alongside humans and live almost as commensals around their habitations.

The rodents

Madagascar is astonishingly poor in rodents. The fourth largest island in the world, Madagascar has only some 11 species of rodents, a total easily exceeded in a single locality in parts of the south-west United States or certain areas in Africa. The reasons for this are unclear, although the absence of such animals as squirrels, flying squirrels and ground squirrels characteristic of the Old World tropical forests, obviously contributes to the paucity of numbers. Yet the rodents which do occur are a very diverse assemblage, varying greatly in dentition, anatomy and ecology. They all belong to a single subfamily, the Nesomyinae within the Cricetidae, which, these days, is endemic to Madagascar although remains of a nesomyine rodent have recently been found in Miocene deposits in Kenya.

In the absence of any conspicuous day-active animals such as the squirrels, the visitor to Madagascar is unlikely to glimpse any native rodents at all. The single exception may be the diurnal red forest rat *Nesomys rufus* (perhaps actually comprising two species *N. rufus* and *N. auduberti* distinguished mainly by the presence or absence of a white tip to the tail) which is often encountered by lemur-adoring tourists as it dashes swiftly across a path in some shady forest. This attractive and highly personable rat is widely distributed in the eastern rainforests. It may become extremely common in certain areas, such as at Ranomafana. Fortunately, perhaps, researchers and tourists seem to look favourably on this confiding animal because it is incurably curious. Even noisily chatting biologists, sitting around waiting for a group of lemurs to snap out of their midday lethargy and move on, will often be visited by a red forest rat, rolling up for a close inspection of who is trespassing on its territory. Its natural food probably consists mainly of fallen fruits and seeds, although it shows its adaptability by paying regular visits to the rubbish dumps attached to permanent encampments in the forest.

Far less likely to be seen, even by researchers looking for lemurs, are the nocturnal rodents. The most widespread is *Eliurus myoxinus* which inhabits forests throughout most of the island; *E. minor*, on the other hand, is restricted to the eastern rainforests. *Eliurus* is a complex genus and further research may lead to the recognition of more than just these two species in Madagascar.

Macrotarsomys bastardi is a small, nocturnal rodent which inhabits the dry forests of the west. It is quite abundant, for example, in certain parts of the Kirindy forest north of Morondava. In size, appearance, behaviour and ecology, it is perhaps the Madagascan equivalent of some of the African gerbils, such as *Tatera* and *Gerbillurus*, and shares their rapid scurrying-hopping locomotion across stretches of bare open ground. It probably feeds mainly on fallen seeds which it holds in its front paws while it nibbles away. Its ears are prominent, and it would be interesting to know whether its hearing is as acute as that of certain African *Gerbillurus* which can hear the flight of an owl swooping in for the kill. A second species, *Macrotarsomys ingens*, is much rarer, occurring only in the forests of Ankarafantsika in the north-west of the island.

The two largest species of Madagascan rodents are by far the most interesting. *Brachytarsomys albicauda* is restricted to the eastern rainforests. It is strictly

arboreal and spends the day in a hole in a tree, emerging after dark to run around surefootedly even on slender lianas and vines. Little is known of its habits but, because it is arboreal, presumably it competes for food resources with certain small nocturnal lemurs. The head is large and the eyes bulbous; in fact, in some ways, *Brachytarsomys* even resembles a small nocturnal lemur.

The largest Madagascan rodent is the giant jumping rat *Hypogeomys antimena*. About the size of a rabbit and weighing on average 2 pounds 10 ounces (1.2 kg), it is found only in a small area of western deciduous forest to the north of Morondava, not far from the coast. Its total geographical range is believed to cover no more than about 39 square miles (100 sq km). Cutting and burning have continued to make inroads into the rat's forest home, and it is in dire need of some form of real, on-the-ground protection. Giant jumping rats live in long, deep burrows, usually in close juxtaposition so that several animals inhabit a system with several holes — up to six — emerging closely together at the surface. In the Kirindy forest these burrows seem to be restricted to areas of easily dug, sandy or lateritic soils; localities with stony, difficult-to-work soils seem to lack burrows and rats.

The burrow systems are fairly easy to spot in the gloom beneath the canopy. They are betrayed by the mounds of pale-coloured earth heaped up around the entrances. The holes are amazingly broad, with an average diameter of about 18 inches (45 cm), and are provided with a 'front door' in the form of an earth barrier a little distance inside the entrance. This is dug away and rebuilt each time the occupant enters and leaves its home. Animals from the same burrow system — usually consisting of one adult male, one adult female and a third individual of either sex, often a juvenile — forage within more or less the same area of forest. Each individual home-range strikes out on its own to establish a 'sole-occupancy' belt around part of its periphery, but all the home ranges overlap to a large extent over much of the core area. In contrast, each rat is probably territorial towards its neighbours from other systems and there is virtually no overlap between the foraging ranges. Thus, it seems that *H. antimena* lives in family groups consisting of a pair accompanied by their offspring, occupying a territory which may abut closely upon, but does not overlap, the territory of adjacent family groups. Each group regularly uses latrines within its territory but, whether these also function as territorial odour signals or are exclusively for hygiene is unknown. Each family occupies a territory of about 13.5 acres (5.5 ha) giving a population density of about 124-140 animals per square mile (48-54 animals per sq km) at least in favourable forest where there are few limitations on the ability to dig burrows. The population for the whole Kirindy forest may thus be less than 3000 individuals, although it is impossible to use this

Opposite: **The attractive red forest rat** Nesomys rufus **is particularly common in the rainforest at Ranomafana. Being diurnally active, it is easily seen and frequently comes up to investigate humans within its territory.**

The charming little Macrotarsomys bastardi is found over a wide area of the dry western forests although, because it is nocturnal, it is seldom noticed.

information to estimate total population size, in view of our current lack of knowledge of soil types and the state of the forest cover in other parts of the rat's presumed range.

The giant jumping rat is not particularly wary of artificial lights and can be watched at night without too much difficulty. Although it probably breaks into a hopping, kangaroo-like form of locomotion when severely pressed by a predator such as a fossa, its normal method of travel is on all fours, a habit also shared with kangaroos. Each animal usually visits several of the burrow systems within its territory each night. By sitting and waiting quietly by one of these, the patient observer can witness enjoyably close encounters with this remarkable beast. Its approach is usually announced by the noise it makes as it scuffles across the carpet of dry leaves typical of these forests. If a rat senses someone nearby, it may utter a burst of strange, low-pitched, almost warbling calls. This an unexpected sound from a rodent and, when heard for the first time in the forest at night, it can be most unsettling.

The main food seems to consist of fallen fruits and seeds which the rat picks up off the ground in its short front legs and eats while sitting semi-upright on its ample haunches. The tender young bark of saplings is peeled away using the teeth; the rat may then stand up on its long hind legs to reach as much bark as possible.

Brachyuromys betsiloensis and *B. ramirohitra* are small, rather rare, vole-like rodents recorded from the Betsileo region and the Andringitra massif. Their similarity to voles extends to the nature of their dentition and to the marked extent of their adaptation for feeding on grass. They inhabit damp grasslands and rank marshy places, where the casual observer could easily mistake them for a Eurasian water vole.

Unfortunately, the brown rat *Rattus rattus* is well established on Madagascar and has also invaded such offshore islands as Nosy Mangabe. It has even managed to penetrate into the rainforests, and may make a nuisance of itself raiding foodstores in research campsites. When I was camped out in a small wooden hut in the forest, I was often kept awake by the resident rats crawling around and over me. Strangely enough, they also had a taste for a bar of laundry soap (strong stuff!) which was virtually gnawed away over a period of three days. The effect of this destructive pest on species of native rodents is unclear, but there does seem to be circumstantial evidence that the presence of the brown rat adversely effects *Gymnuromys roberti*, an endemic rainforest rat.

The carnivores

Madagascar has nothing to compare with the hosts of carnivorous mammals to be found in Africa. Those which do occur all belong to the same family, the Viverridae, a nearly cosmopolitan family containing such familiar tropical animals as civets, genets and mongooses. Although the eight endemic Madagascan species are shared among three subfamilies, namely Fossinae, Galidiinae and Cryptoproctinae, there are enough similarities in anatomy to hint that all may be derived from a common ancestor, which somehow made its way across the Mozambique channel and subsequently speciated within Madagascar.

The Fossinae contains two species, the striped civet *Fossa fossana* and the small-toothed mongoose or fanaloka *Eupleres gaudoti*. The striped civet (not to be confused with the fossa *Cryptoprocta ferox*) is a rather heavy bodied animal with quite a large, long-muzzled head, prominent ears and an attractive greyish-brown coat decorated longitudinally with rows of black spots which, in places, coalesce to form stripes. The tail is fairly short and noticeably bushy, and is used during the winter for the storage of fat deposits. Fat is also stored in the body, and the total combined weight of these accumulations may reach a quarter of the total body weight. This civet is widely distributed throughout the eastern rainforests, usually along or near rivers but, because it is nocturnal, it is seldom seen. Family groups bed down together during the day, hidden away in hollow logs or in a snug, dry hole among rocks. They emerge at night to forage over a wide area encompassing hundreds of acres. They are usually seen hunting singly, although the second animal of a pair may often be present in the same general vicinity. The boundary of the territory is delineated by scent marking on prominent objects, using secretions from glands in the anal region and on the head.

With its rather long legs, the striped civet can reach respectable speeds, which probably enable it to catch small prey such as rodents. It is an opportunistic predator which will catch and eat most kinds of prey including frogs, insects, earthworms, crustaceans and the occasional bird. Much of its food is probably taken in or near water, from which fish, crabs and crayfish will be grabbed in the powerful jaws. This is in direct contrast to certain other viverrids which give a swipe with their paws, designed to flip the prey on to the bank first. When permanent campsites are established in the forest, as at Ranomafana, the striped civet soon shows its adaptability by becoming tame remarkably quickly, entering the camp at night to scavenge on rubbish. It seems to be particularly fond of cheese rinds and any scraps of meat or fish left inside opened cans. Its sense of smell is acute, and it will easily track down single tiny crumbs of cheese hidden among grass. In summer, during November and December in the southern hemisphere, the female, secure in her den, gives birth to the single offspring. For a carnivore, the infant is extremely well developed at birth, with fully open eyes and a complete coat of fur. Despite this precocious start, the baby develops

The striped civet **Fossa fossana** *is the sole nocturnal viverrid which is liable to be seen with any consistency, as it often comes looking for food around forest camps. It is found only in forests in the east.*

relatively slowly and will not completely forsake its mother's milk until it is about 10 weeks old. It is not fully independent of its parent until it is at least a year old.

Fortunate indeed is the visitor to Madagascar who sees the other member of the Fossinae *Eupleres gaudoti*. The local people probably see it more often, mainly because they set traps for it, its meat being greatly relished. Unfortunately, this is leading to the increasing rarity of an animal which has probably never been particularly abundant anyway. It is widely, though locally, distributed in the eastern rainforests and in the Sambirano region of the north-west, usually inhabiting marshes with rank vegetation. It is a heavy bodied, grey-brown animal, but the head is much smaller in relation to the body than it is in *Fossa fossana*, and the snout is very slim and pointed. The teeth are tiny and quite unsuited for tearing up the tough-bodied prey often seized and crushed by other viverrids. They are adapted solely for dealing with the soft-bodied earthworms which probably constitute the bulk of the fanaloka's diet. These are dug out with the aid of long capable claws on the forepaws, which also have the potential to inflict a severe gash if used defensively. Territorial behaviour and reproduction are much as in the striped civet.

Although four out of the five Galidiinae are diurnal, there is only one which is commonly seen. This least elusive of the Madagascan viverrids is the ring-tailed mongoose *Galidia elegans*, a handsome rusty red animal measuring about 20 inches (50 cm) long. Nearly half of this is taken up by the tail, which always sports five prominent dark-brown rings. Three subspecies are recognized including *Galidia elegans elegans*, a deep reddish-chestnut animal with an even darker underside studded with grey hairs and noted for the black tips to the limbs. This subspecies is common throughout the eastern rainforests. *G. e. dambrensis* has a local distribution in the north, in the mountain massifs between Diégo Suarez and Ambilobe. The whole body is a handsome light foxy red which glows a fiery auburn in the sun's rays. This beautiful creature is easy to see at very close quarters in Ankarana Special Reserve, where a family group quickly homes in on an occupied campsite. Here, they are almost too tame, running around among the campers' feet, generally getting in the way and cutting short their welcome by poking their noses into any food left unattended. For carnivores they have an unexpected liking for jam, any flavour, and will lick out an empty can of jam with the same devotion and thoroughness normally reserved for discarded cans of sardines or corned beef. The third subspecies, *G. e.*

occidentalis, is distributed in certain forests in the west. Like that of *G. e. dambrensis*, the fur is light reddish but, in *G. e. occidentalis*, this contrasts with a black underside, paws and flanks.

The ring-tailed mongoose is strictly diurnal, usually sheltering during the night in burrows which it excavates itself although, like the striped civet, it also takes advantage of natural hiding places such as hollow logs or rock clefts. Because it is an agile climber, it can also hide in tree holes at some distance from the ground. It lives in small family units comprising three or four individuals, although groups of five or six are not uncommon. The nucleus of the group is a male and female that pair for life, accompanied by their latest young and sometimes by their previous set of offspring. Relationships within the group are generally good and the members devote a lot of time to prolonged rough-and-tumble play sessions on the ground, often terminated suddenly when the participants snuggle down close together for a quick snooze. By contrast, encounters between animals from neighbouring territories may be quite violent, and are manifested by such a prolonged barrage of shrill screams that it sounds as though one is being slaughtered by the other. Yet, despite the stridency of the protest, actual wounds seem rather rare from such meetings. This screaming is, in fact, part of a vocal repertoire which is distinctly wider than in the mainly silent members of the Fossinae. It also includes a shrill bird-like whistle, which seems to function as a contact call between foraging members of the same band.

Galidia will eat just about anything, including insects, worms, molluscs, the eggs and nestlings of birds, particularly ground-nesting species, lizards and snakes. The latter can be detected by scent even through a muslin bag, so herpetologists collecting live specimens need to be careful where they put them. When eggs and large snails are found, they are dealt with in the same way; using the hind feet, the animal hurls them backwards against a tree or stone. *Galidia* is also thought to take small lemurs, although a group

*Opposite: **Thanks to its diurnal habits and confiding nature, the ring-tailed mongoose** Galidia elegans **is the most frequently seen viverrid on the island. It climbs well and takes a wide variety of animal food. This is the dark-russet** G. e. elegans **from the eastern rainforests.***

*Right: **The subspecies** G. e. dambrensis **of the ring-tailed mongoose is restricted to an area around Diégo Suarez in the north. This beautiful animal, with its light russet fur, is particularly easy to see in the Ankarana Special Reserve.***

of crowned lemurs *Lemur coronatus* sitting on the ground close to a foraging party of ring-tailed mongooses did not react either with outright panic or pronounced hostility. When a *Galidia* ran suddenly towards a lemur, however, the lemur retreated rapidly into a tree to the accompaniment of much grunting. The ring-tailed mongoose's liking for jam suggests that it may also take fallen fruit when this is available; and, like the striped civet, it will enter water to catch frogs and fish. It also frequently captures rodents, and can dig them out of their burrows. When foraging in the forest, *Galidia* pokes its nose into every nook and cranny, particularly holes in dead trees and stumps, presumably turning up a broad spectrum of meals.

The female ring-tailed mongoose gives birth to just a single offspring in the safety of a den from which the newborn's father is firmly excluded. His status as unwelcome guest in the close vicinity of his offspring continues for more than a month, before the female finally condescends to allow him to touch the youngster.

Although rarer than *Galidia*, a glimpse of the narrow-striped mongoose *Mungotictis decemlineata* is, nevertheless, at least a possibility for anyone visiting the tropical deciduous forests of western Madagascar. This applies especially to the area around Morondava, where *M. d. decemlineata* occurs. A second subspecies, *M. d. lineata*, is highly unlikely to be seen because it is one of the rarest animals in Madagascar, known from only a handful of specimens from around Tulear and the reserve of Lake Tsimanampetsotsa. The commoner of the two subspecies is a greyish-beige animal with from eight to ten very fine, rusty red stripes on its back and sides. The tail is an impressive adornment, nearly as long as the body and prolifically furnished with long spreading hairs, which can be bristled in a threatening manner when the animal feels endangered. During the June-to-October dry season, a *Mungotictis* family takes up residence in a single-entranced burrow excavated communally. With the coming of the rains in November, they move house and settle into lodgings less prone to flooding, usually a hollow tree. Their prowess in climbing enables them to adopt an apartment more than 30 feet (10 m) above the ground.

As in most Madagascan viverrids, the diet is very varied and most forms of animal life are taken. During the long, cool, dry season, however, the variety of available food is greatly reduced, and then *Mungotictis* relies more on insect larvae which are passing the winter period in the soil or in the slowly mouldering logs which litter the western forests. The rains bring a flush of life, offering broader scope for the diet with the increasing availability of large numbers of juvenile lizards and rodents, the eggs and nestlings of birds, and a multitude of different invertebrates from beetles to cockroaches. At this time of plenty, the mongooses are very sociable, forming groups of 10 to 12 animals which forage over a home range of around 370 acres (150 ha). When the lean times return in June, these large units break down into two or three groups with more restricted ranges in the original general area.

The plain mongoose *Salanoia concolor* is one of the least-known mammals in the fauna. It inhabits the eastern rainforests where its apparent rarity makes encounters so few that virtually nothing is known of its day-to-day life. As its name suggests, it is a slim-bodied, plain brown mongoose which is rather like *Galidia* but it has a noticeably shorter tail which does not have the rings.

The handsome, but strictly nocturnal, broad-striped mongoose *Galidictis fasciata* is also a little-known animal with a local and scattered distribution in the eastern rainforests. It has been implicated in poultry raiding, although not much is known about its diet in the wild. In 1986 a second species of *Galidictis* was described from a specimen collected in the 1930s from the area around Lake Tsimanampetsotsa, in the 'spiny desert' to the south of Tulear. *G. grandidiensis* is known from only two specimens, which probably makes it the rarest of the world's known viverrids. It is the largest member of the Galidiinae and there are plans to census the population around the lake and possibly establish a captive-breeding programme for this dangerously scarce animal.

The largest of all Madagascan viverrids and indeed the island's largest predator belongs to the subfamily Cryptoproctinae. Known locally as the fossa (not to be confused with the striped civet *Fossa fossana*). It is a very successful animal and still occurs widely, although it is rare or absent over much of the Hauts Plateaux. In appearance, it rather resembles a cross between a dog and a cat, with features of both. The short, reddish-brown fur covers a low-slung body carried on powerful legs. The tail is nearly as long as the body and works as a counterbalance during the fossa's frequent forays through the forest canopy. The muzzle is noticeably blunt and dog-like, and the eyes are large, as befits an animal which hunts mainly at dusk and after dark. It shows remarkable agility in tree climbing, and this scourge of the lemurs is greatly assisted in its arboreal depredations by its tail and by the soles of its paws, which are provided with smooth, shiny, raised pads. The large powerful front paws are used to grab a victim, which is quickly despatched with a bite to the back of the head. The prey consists mainly of reptiles, birds and mammals including the smaller civets and mongooses, as well as lemurs. Groups of lemurs display extreme and highly vocal signs of alarm when a fossa is detected, and they make quickly for the highest and least accessible tips of the branches. The fossa's ability to climb even quite large tree trunks probably brings it into frequent contact with bark-living geckoes, and the absence of this efficient predator from Nosy Mangabe may be a significant factor permitting the exceptional abundance of leaf-tailed geckos *Uroplatus fimbriatus* on that island. Contrary to practice in the other endemic viverrids, the fossa gives birth to a litter of from two to four young. The babies develop extremely slowly and are probably not fully adult until they are about three years old. Fossas are generally solitary hunters although groups of two to three animals are sometimes seen.

Chapter 7
The Lemurs

When most people think of Madagascar they think of lemurs. Not surprisingly, many tourists coming to the island, regardless of the main purpose of their visit, will take the trouble to see at least one or two kinds during their stay, bewitched by the cuddly appearance and wide-eyed charm so amply demonstrated by most species. But lemurs are not just cute and entertaining. They are also of absorbing interest to zoologists because of their unique place in primate evolution. They are, for example, the only prosimians with a social organization.

The lemur story begins many millions of years ago in the Eocene period, when lemur-like animals in the family Adapidae roamed the Earth. They viewed their world from a face sporting a snout which was even more pronounced than the prominent structure typical of modern lemurs; they also had smaller brains. Even now, lemurs are not regarded as the most intelligent of primates and, although they can perform certain tests as well as some kinds of monkeys, it seems that, in general, monkeys unquestionably have the critical edge in brain power. But, well before the true monkeys arrived on the evolutionary scene, the ancestral lemurs had somehow managed to make their way across the sea to the island of Madagascar. At this date, still millions of years ago, the intervening waterway now known as the Mozambique channel was relatively narrow because Madagascar had only recently broken away from the main African landmass. Quite how the crossing was made is unknown. It has been suggested that they sailed intrepidly across on logs, or matted rafts of tangled vegetation, like some furry early Thor Heyerdahls. Their presumed accomplishments at clinging to trees would, it is suggested, have served them well during such a journey across wave-tossed seas. This theory does, however, beg the question of why the boundaries between the subspecies of certain lemurs are apparently formed by relatively narrow, shallow rivers which must have been easier to cross than even an embryonic Mozambique channel. What seems more plausible is that these early migrants were able to keep their feet dry by crossing a series of islands and ridges connected during a period of lowered sea levels (during glaciations, for example). Whichever method was used, we now have no way of knowing whether just a few lemurs managed the trip on a single fortunate occasion, or whether successive waves of colonization took place.

These early lemur-like pioneers were safely established on their island by the time the true

monkeys arrived on the scene back in Africa, in the Oligocene around 30 million years ago. But, by then, any possibility of these intellectual upstarts quickly adding Madagascar to their range at the expense of the resident lemurs had long gone, for the Mozambique channel had widened enough to be impassable to animals as large as monkeys. Would the monkeys have supplanted the lemurs had the voyage proved possible? The answer is probably yes. Many monkeys boast in abundance all the qualities necessary to ensure upward mobility in the competitive world of primates — cunning, aggression, guile, a brash effectiveness, a willingness to use deception to attain their ends, and a viciousness backed up by the necessary hardware, such as powerful canines, which enables them to take what they want by force if there is no easier way. It is difficult to imagine the easy going lemurs standing up to an assault by such well-equipped invaders, and territory would surely have been yielded until there was nowhere left to go; then the monkeys would have reigned supreme.

But the monkeys did not arrive; and the lemurs made a remarkably thorough job of adapting to conditions in their island refuge. In Africa and Asia, the remaining prosimians (such as bushbabies, pottos, lorises and tarsiers) remained small, solitary and nocturnal, leading cryptic retiring lives designed to avoid contact and competition with the diurnal monkeys. In Madagascar alone did the prosimian line still flourish and expand, as the lemurs took advantage of the numerous vacant niches available for colonization. In so doing they evolved a wide variety of life-styles which elsewhere are filled by monkeys, squirrels, woodpeckers and even large grazing ungulates. They also developed varying degrees of social organization, a sophistication which did not arise among the few remaining prosimians on the mainland. There is still one 'primitive' feature shared by all today's prosimians, however. This is their heavy reliance on the sense of smell as a method of communicating information, among individuals and between groups. The projecting muzzle of a ring-tailed lemur *Lemur catta* is a sure indication of the importance of scent in its daily life for, in lemurs, as in their primitive ancestors, the nose is placed well up on a conical snout, where it is perfectly positioned for sifting olfactory messages from the environment. With their flatter, more human-like faces, monkeys have virtually dispensed with scent as a means of communication, and rely upon sight and hearing.

Left: The ring-tailed lemur Lemur catta *is often found in the 'spiny desert' of the south. This ring-tail is happily climbing around in a large specimen of the octopus tree* Alluaudia procera *while taking little heed of the plant's abundance of spines.*

Opposite and overleaf: Ring-tailed lemurs Lemur catta *often adopt some fetching postures while relaxing in the mid-day heat.*

fact, we may have missed witnessing some of these giant species by a mere whisker of time, for at least one large lemur managed to hold out until the arrival of the first European settlers. In the 1650s, travellers returned to Europe with tales of a lemur the size of a two year-old calf, its head rounded and its face and ears uncannily like a human's. The *tratratratra*, as this beast was known, succumbed shortly after this, although it was perhaps even then no more than a persistent legend, and had already long ago gone the way of so many of its relatives. The presence of skeletal remains of many of these creatures alongside cooking utensils suggests one possible cause of their extinction. Large, slow-moving animals are, after all, much easier to hunt than small, agile ones, and the hunter gains a much bigger meal for less effort. Major changes to the environment caused by people, especially the rapid conversion of forest into open, sunbaked, sterile grassland (which quickly overtook much of the tree-covered Hauts Plateaux and lowland coastal forests) would also have sealed the fate of any large, less adaptable lemurs. This one-way process still continues. In the long term, will the surviving lemurs be any more successful than their extinct relatives?

Today there remain 23 species of lemurs, most of which are divided into a series of subspecies based on mutually isolated geographical ranges. Some of these subspecies differ so markedly in appearance — for example, the brown lemur *Lemur fulvus* — that they may once have been considered to be separate species; further studies may well re-establish this view, at least in part. Other subspecies, of *Lepilemur*, for example, resemble one another superficially but differ in detail as well as genetically. This has provided certain authorities with the basis for increasing the number of species in the genus from just one to a total of seven. For the present, I shall consider there to be the 23 species described below.

Family Lemuridae — the true lemurs
GENUS *LEMUR*

Although they look much larger when sitting in a tree, the members of the genus *Lemur* are all about the size of a domestic cat, and it is the long tail and prominent muzzle which probably make them look bigger. The genus contains perhaps the best-known and certainly the most behaviourally interesting of all the lemurs, the ring-tailed lemur *Lemur catta*. This animal breeds very successfully in zoos far from its Madagascan homeland so that many people will have seen live specimens. There is nothing to compare with seeing an animal in its natural environment, however.

The ring-tailed lemur inhabits the dry southern part of the island. Here, the preferred habitat is the tall,

There are variations but, to a greater or lesser extent, lemurs still scent mark and sniff their surroundings in the way that the earliest prosimians did. Although they have keen eyesight and an often broad vocal repertoire, for lemurs, scent remains the most important method of communication in most cases.

The final result of the lemurs' long isolation in Madagascar was the evolution of about 38 to 40 distinct species occupying a wide variety of niches. Alas, we will never be in a position to watch a gorilla-sized giant *Megaladapis* clinging to some forest tree like an overgrown koala. For the lemurs are already well past their peak. Twelve or so species are now extinct and many more are set to follow within quite a short period if present conservation efforts fail to halt the destruction of their habitat. As is often the case with extinct animals, the lemurs which have disappeared were all bigger, sometimes much bigger, than their extant relatives. Large size seems to have been an increasing handicap over the last few million years. In the case of the lemurs, however, it is only quite recently, during the last one or two thousand years, that the extinctions seem to have taken place. In

resource-rich gallery forest which fringes major rivers, although *Lemur catta* is also found in brush and scrubby forests and even in the 'spiny forest' dominated by members of the Didiereaceae. Throughout this area there is a marked dry season lasting seven to eight months, and annual rainfall does not normally exceed about 40 inches (100 cm). In particularly favourable areas with abundant food supplies, such as in gallery forest, the ring-tailed lemur may live in populations as dense as 900 animals per square mile (350 per sq km) although, in drier areas of scrubby bush, this may drop to around 390 per square mile (150 per sq km).

The ring-tailed lemur shows little change in appearance across its range and there are no subspecies. Whereas most other *Lemur* are proving to be intermittently active throughout a 24-hour period, (*cathemeral* activity pattern), *Lemur catta* is active mostly during the day. This lemur is also the most terrestrial member of its kind, spending a much greater proportion of the day on the ground than is typical of any other species. Indeed, ring-tails seldom seem more at home than when strutting confidently down some forest path with their ornate tails cocked over their backs in an elegant curve and their rumps stuck out and up, the consequence of having front legs shorter than those at the rear. Although they are obviously relaxed when on the ground, 70 per cent of a lemur's time is spent in the canopy, where most feeding is carried out. When lemurs patrol their territories, however, 70 per cent of their travel is on the ground. Their fondness for the forest floor increases on particularly hot summer days when many members of the group forsake the over heated canopy and flop out for a midday siesta on the carpet of leaves in the gloomiest part of the forest. Other members of the group may loll around in the lowermost branches of their favourite rest tree, head sunk in hands as they snooze away the heat of the day. The rest period usually lasts from about midday until roughly 2.30 pm but, in very hot weather, it may begin as early as 10.30 in the morning. As the afternoon wears on and the forest cools down, the glassy eyed lemurs gradually shake off their lethargy and resume their activities. A lengthy session of mutual grooming usually forms the preamble to setting off again, often on foot, gradually forming a strung-out column of self-assured animals.

Groups of *L. catta* seem to like using humans' paths and roads as easy ways to patrol their territory. This makes them particularly easy to locate and to follow in areas such as the well-known private reserve at Berenty. Groups usually contain from 12 to 25 members, with equal numbers of males and females. At the core of each group is a number of females, together with their infants and juveniles which have not yet reached sexual maturity. In ring-tailed lemur groups, as in several other (possibly most) lemur societies, it is the females that lead the group and are its dominant members. It is important to bear this in mind whenever lemur social behaviour is being considered. Many people find it hard to grasp this

Below and bottom: **The ring-tailed lemur's long, banner-like tail receives a considerable amount of attention during self-grooming sessions.**

Opposite, above, and above right: **Ring-tailed lemurs are the most sociable of their kind and devote a great deal of each day to enjoyable sessions of mutual-grooming. When several animals join in, it can be difficult to decide which is doing what to which, although it is important to note that status does not dictate the degree of participation in this pleasurable activity.**

Below and below right: **The fur of ring-tailed lemur infants comes in for a good deal of vigorous licking by their own mothers and by other eager members of the group, for the babies are very much a focus of attention.**

concept of a matriarchal society in which the males generally follow meekly behind in the females' footsteps, obediently yielding to them in numerous matters. It is perhaps indicative of our deeply ingrained sexual attitudes when a western tourist points at some subservient male lemur and auto-matically credits him with being 'the boss'. In *L. catta* (and in many other species) it is the females that take priority in matters such as access to the choicest items of food, choosing a spot for a snooze and in defence

of territory or against enemies. The females remain with the same group throughout their lives, but the males are more footloose and may transfer to another group during November. This shuffling of the sexual pack ensures a regular exchange of genes from one group to another, especially as the itinerant males may change their allegiances more than once.

Although relationships within the group seldom involve outright aggression, there does tend to be a surprising amount of generally ill-tempered behaviour. Chasing and cuffing are common, usually between females settling a dispute over which one owns a particularly enticing tamarind pod. Despite such tetchy encounters, the members of the group constantly solicit close bodily contact with one another, often leading to the formation of snoozing-huddles in which several animals form a complicated embrace from which tails and feet stick out in all directions. Social grooming with the teeth can take up as much as 10 per cent of the day; females in particular spend a good deal of time grooming each other and one another's

Left: **With her baby clinging firmly to her back, a female ring-tailed lemur performs a handstand and scent marks a sapling on the boundary of her group's territory. One after another, virtually the whole group proceeded to mark this same tree, including the males which used their wrist spurs for the purpose.**

Above and opposite: **Female ring-tailed lemurs carry their offspring until they become heavy burdens, although the youngsters spend quite a time away from their mothers in play-groups formed of their contemporaries.**

babies. The idea that grooming has important social implications, and is not merely designed to reach the inaccessible bits which defy the efforts of the solo groomer, is evident from the way in which all parts of the body habitually receive attention. A pair of enthusiastic groomers may be joined by a third or even fourth animal, so that grooming pods are formed in which it is difficult to decide exactly which animal is doing what to which.

Contact with the infants is always greatly coveted by other members of the group, and they take every opportunity to sneak in and groom them if the mother allows. When this involves rapid and energetic licking of the infant's face, it seems not to be appreciated by the recipient which, like-as-not, makes strenuous efforts to escape these unwanted attentions. Grooming is one activity which is status-free so that even the dominant female group leader can be freely approached by any other female and will full-heartedly reciprocate in a bout of impartial mutual grooming. Hierarchy and rank are simply not allowed to stand in the way of this important and enjoyable method of amicable social intercourse.

Scent plays an important role in the daily round of ring-tailed lemurs. They use it to define their territorial boundaries, although these may not be exclusive to one group, so special attention is devoted to marking areas where there is a territorial overlap with some unwelcome neighbours. As they move around their territory, the females stop at regular intervals and perform a peculiar kind of handstand against a tree, usually a smooth-trunked sapling. The animal's rear end is rubbed against the bark which is smeared with vulval secretions. As each animal in turn passes the spot, it will usually stop, sniff delicately and then perform the same ritual, adding its own mark to reinforce the effect of the first. Males also perform handstands but, after sniffing at the fresh female deposits, they are more likely to grasp the stem in all fours in an upright position and force their scent into the wood by gouging it vigorously with a horny spur situated within a large glandular patch on each wrist. This is accomplished in a jerky fashion, with the lemur swinging from side to side on the sapling, and it actually tears the bark and exposes the inner tissue.

Within an area of territorial overlap, there is always a potential for dispute, so establishing their right to be there is particularly significant. Under these special circumstances, they may actually stand in line, each waiting its turn to add its odorous calling card to a tree which has previously been marked by members of a neighbouring group. When a neighbour's mark is on the very edge of a territory, however, it is merely sniffed at, noted and then left, without a competing mark being added. This lack of reaction is apparently an acknowledgement that the mark has every right to be in that particular spot, and that the territorial boundaries are in the mutually acceptable 'correct' place. Neighbouring groups seldom come into actual contact, because they tend to arrange their day in a manner which avoids this but, when they do, it is the females that respond first by jumping and running full tilt at their opposite numbers, bolstered by the hurried application of generous amounts of scent to the nearby saplings. The males tend to be more reserved in these encounters, leaving the females to get on with the physical stuff, preferring to rely on their traditional, and less risky, scent marking to establish ownership in that particular piece of forest.

The males can 'out-gun' the females by using an additional 'long-range' odour weapon, although its use is restricted to encounters with other males. After drawing his tail between his wrists, so as to anoint it thoroughly with his personal scent, he propels a kind of scent bomb at a rival male by jerking his tail

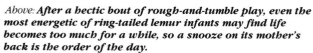

*Above: **After a hectic bout of rough-and-tumble play, even the most energetic of ring-tailed lemur infants may find life becomes too much for a while, so a snooze on its mother's back is the order of the day.***

*Top right and right: **Even well-grown ring-tailed lemur infants still spend a considerable amount of time being suckled.***

forwards over his head and quivering it violently like some smelly banded ballista. This sophisticated synthesis of visual and olfactory signals provides an effective way of telling a rival in no uncertain terms to 'get lost'. These so-called 'stink fights' can take place at any time, but build up to a crescendo during the mating period in April. At this time, male rivalry escalates rapidly to reach a climax when the strict hierarchy, which more-or-less serves to keep the peace throughout the year, collapses in a tumult of 'anything-goes' sexual gamesmanship. Thoroughly belligerent shouting matches and frequent 'stink fights' are now scarcely sufficient to settle the score, and real fighting takes place. This is conducted in deadly earnest, with each contestant cavorting around the other in a kind of bobbing dance. The dance is designed to gain just enough height advantage to allow a downward slash against the opponent with the long, vicious canines. Blood may flow.

In this sexual free-for-all, a male's previous status becomes irrelevant and, in the mad scramble of the mating game, any individual may win. Even a rank outsider, such as a recently mature juvenile, is not excluded and he may slip in quietly to claim the prize while his elders and betters are otherwise occupied in fighting over who should win a female. This frenzy of male competitiveness is stimulated when the females come into oestrus over a two-week period in April. As each female becomes sexually receptive for less than a day, there is obviously a powerful incentive to secure a place at the head of the queue. With the ending of this brief orgy of sexual activity, however, life soon returns to peace and harmony although the in-fighting may have modified the social structure of the group. Triumphant males are not only winners in the sexual stakes, they may also gain promotion in their social rank, while formerly high-ranking losers suffer demotion.

The females give birth in early September with the coming of springtime in the southern hemisphere. The single infant (occasionally twins) clings head-foremost beneath its mother's underside, unlike most lemurs whereby the infant clings across its mother's belly. *L. catta* babies are noticeably precocious, however, and within the first week, this low-slung anchorage is discarded for a 'seat-with-a-view' on the mother's back. As it grows, the infant rides well forward on its maternal mount, its head resting between its mother's ears, so that two piebald, amber-eyed faces turn as one to view the world. The infants dismount frequently to join their peers in bouts of mad-cap gambolling on the ground or acrobatics in the trees, soon forming established play groups, which take the growing infants more and more away from their mothers, and increasingly into association with other juveniles. But, when danger threatens, they immediately seek refuge with their mothers, often chasing after her retreating rear end and leaping on, like some Wild West hero.

Suckling often takes place while the females are resting on the ground but, within three months, the infants are eating solid food, although they will not reach sexual maturity until they are about two-and-a-half years old. When twins are born, one of the pair may be 'adopted' by a non-pregnant female, and she may also begin to produce milk in response to her surrogate role. This behaviour has been observed in many other species of primates, including humans. 'Baby-swapping' sessions seem to be socially acceptable among *L. catta*, and a female will often show an amazing indifference about exactly which baby she is suckling.

In the private reserve at Berenty, some of the ring-tailed lemurs seem to have become addicted to the bananas brought in by tourists. Their craving for this alien fruit is such that it is better not to carry bananas for food during a day's observations in the forest, especially if you are likely to be near ring-tails. No matter how surreptitiously the banana is produced and the skin peeled back, some unnoticed ring-tail will spot the treasured object and, within seconds, you are buried under a horde of slavering, craving-eyed bandits all desperate to be the first to grab and run. After this had happened to me twice, I decided that the only way to get a meal in peace was to steal silently away from the group under observation and hide cravenly behind a large tree, hoping that no more ring-tails were watching unseen from the canopy. Although this artificial feeding has been much criticized in some quarters, it does allow a tourist with little time to spare to come into close contact with the ring-tails, surely the most charming and entertaining of all the island's lemurs.

When not gorging themselves on bananas, the ring-tails forage normally in the forest, gleaning a diet of fruit and, to a certain extent, young leaves. They also relish certain insects, and one individual was seen to spend a good deal of time trying to eat the moulted skins of a colonial caterpillar. These shrivelled tatters were firmly stuck to the pad of silk on which the caterpillars had left them, and the lemur had to make repeated efforts merely to tear off a modicum of edible material with its front teeth.

Even a large group of animals as conspicuously marked as *L. catta* can be surprisingly difficult to locate in the depths of the gallery forest. In these circumstances, it is their vocal repertoire which may come to the rescue, particularly the soft mewing contact calls often given between group members. The sudden eruption from close quarters of a synchronized 'bark-howl' may also betray a previously unnoticed group, as the males give voice to a penetrating proclamation which can be heard more than half-a-

A ring-tailed lemur **Lemur catta** *feeding on berries in gallery forest. See also overleaf left, top, and bottom.*

mile (up to 1 km) away and is probably aimed at keeping the groups spaced out.

In its variability, the brown lemur *Lemur fulvus*, contrasts strongly with the ring-tailed lemur's uniformity, and it can be split up into a series of easily recognized subspecies forming a ring around the island. In some of these subspecies, the females may resemble one another, but the males are always strikingly different, not only from the males in the other subspecies but, in many cases, from their own females as well. These were all once treated as subspecies of the black lemur *Lemur macaco* but, since populations of the two have been discovered living in the same forest without interbreeding, they are now regarded as forming two separate species. Genetic differences have confirmed the validity of this view. Only in the brown lemur *Lemur fulvus fulvus* are the males and females difficult to distinguish on sight, because the only obvious difference is the male's beard, which is slightly whiter than that of the female. This is probably the least attractive subspecies, and is

Below: **This ring-tailed lemur went to considerable trouble to tear the tattered remnants of some moulted caterpillar skins off the tough silken pad on which they lay.**

Opposite: **With its all-black face, the L. f. fulvus *race of the brown lemur* Lemur fulvus *is the least attractive of the various subspecies around the island. In addition, it is in only this subspecies that the sexes are virtually identical. This group is relaxing in the dry forest of the Ampijeroa Forest Reserve, by far the best place to see this form in Madagascar.***

Above: A female red-fronted lemur **Lemur fulvus rufus** *in rainforest at Ranomafana. Her group inhabits one of the higher areas of forest where the trees are thickly festooned with mosses and lichens. This is the commonest member of the* **L. fulvus** *complex and can be seen with ease at Périnet and Berenty as well as at Ranomafana. Although the sexes can be easily distinguished, they are not as radically different as in some of the other subspecies.*

Left: A male **Lemur fulvus rufus** *(note his ginger cap and paler fur) in dense, moss-festooned forest at Ranomafana. This subspecies has been well studied at this site by Deborah Overdorff of Duke University, North Carolina.*

a grizzled brown animal with a mainly black face. It has a rather strange, patchy distribution, occurring in at least three distinct areas: in the east, south of Lake Alaotra and around Andasibe; in the north only in a small area to the east of the Galoka mountains south of Beramanja; and in the north-west to the north and east of the Betsiboka river. The easiest place to see it is the forestry reserve of Ampijeroa south of Mahajanga, where it has been studied in detail. The group inhabiting the forest close to the reserve headquarters is used to people and will allow a close approach. In this area of low-canopied tropical dry forest, the animals have a home range of about 17 acres (7 ha) although this is not exclusive because there is some overlap with neighbouring groups.

Much the best studied of the subspecies is *Lemur fulvus rufus*, the red-fronted lemur, which is also the most widespread and abundant form. It inhabits a wide area of the eastern rainforests, as well as a considerable part of the dry forests of the west, such as around Morondava, although the precise limits of its large range are difficult to fix. Males and females are easier to tell apart than in *L. f. fulvus*, although they are still not as dramatically different as some of the subspecies mentioned below. In *L. f. rufus*, the female is a warm shade of light rufous brown, and has a grey head with orange cheeks. The male is pale grey, suffused on the upperside with a rufous tint. It has a distinctive black muzzle contrasting with whitish eye rings and topped-off by a reddish-orange crown.

Red-fronted lemurs live in groups of five to fifteen animals consisting of roughly equal numbers of males and females. The social arrangements are such that it can be difficult to decide exactly which individual is the leader. It seem certain, however, that in *L. fulvus* the females are not dominant over the males, although the group's travels are usually led by a female.

Where food is abundant, red-fronted lemur populations may be surprisingly dense with 2590 animals per square mile (1000 animals per sq km) having been recorded in a western forest. Here, plenty of large tamarind trees provide ample food in the form of leaves and fruit, although individual groups usually contained only about five animals ranging over a tiny territory of approximately 15 acres (6 ha). In the eastern rainforests, group size tends to be larger (10 to 12), but density much lower [78 per square mile (30 per sq km)], and the animals range widely throughout a huge range of 250 acres (100 ha) in search of food. They harvest a broad medley of foods,

although the bulk of their feeding time (up to 95 per cent in a given month) is devoted to taking fruits. Fresh young leaves from a wide variety of trees are also consumed, although their appearance is notably seasonal, with a small peak in November as spring arrives, and a larger peak in April at the end of the rainiest period.

The lemurs use their strong teeth to strip the tender young bark from twigs as well as to demolish the flowers of various trees. Although flowers do not normally constitute a significant proportion of the diet, they are eaten throughout the year. Only during December and January, at a time when they are most abundant, are flowers briefly crucial to the lemurs' diet. At this time, there is less available fruit and the bulk of the young leaf growth is still to come. Flowers often contain secondary defensive compounds which are apparently well tolerated by the lemurs. The red-fronted lemur is a destructive feeder on all flowers except one, a species of *Strongylodon* belonging to the pea family. These flowers are large and strongly constructed, and are carefully licked rather than swiftly

*Below left: **This female red-fronted lemur** Lemur fulvus rufus **in the rainforests of Ranomafana had just bitten off a segment of stem and was holding it in her hands while she chewed away on it. This is a common method of feeding in lemurs.***

*Below: **A male red-fronted lemur** Lemur fulvus rufus **in the rainforests at Ranomafana reaches upwards to pull a bunch of likely looking leaves towards his mouth. Most lemurs feed like this, relying on their dexterous hands to do most of the work.***

wrecked with the teeth. During its close contact with the flowers, the lemur's face becomes heavily dusted with pollen, possibly indicating that these primates may actually play a role in pollinating this species.

An interesting development has been the growing tendency to exploit the flowers of alien trees such as *Eucalyptus* and pines. These trees are being planted on an increasing scale to provide fuelwood and construction materials. Plantations are often established on degraded areas which have not seen any tree cover for many years. Groups of red-fronted lemurs have now established home ranges which extend into such plantations. Noisily feeding lemurs can be observed easily in the forest of tall *Eucalyptus* trees situated directly behind the railway station at Périnet. Although primary forest, with its plethora of native food plants, is available nearby, the red-fronted lemurs seem actually to prefer to loiter among the alien trees where, despite the virtual absence of native vegetation, there is obviously an adequate supply of food. The key to the lemurs' liking for this plantation seems to be the *Eucalyptus* trees themselves which

On most days, Deborah Overdorff's study group of red-fronted lemurs **Lemur fulvus rufus** *at Ranomafana descended to the ground in special places to feed on the earth itself. This activity is presumably designed to add certain essential minerals to the diet. Although well habituated to close human presence, this female was decidedly more nervous on the ground than in the trees.*

flower prolifically over quite an extended period.

The conspicuous white, sweetly scented flowers are apparently much to the lemurs' liking, and they will happily spend most of the day enthusiastically munching away on these floral delights. In fact, during their peak of production, these flowers make up nearly 40 per cent of the total daily intake of this lemur. The flowers seem to lack the unpleasant-tasting aromatic defensive compounds present in quantity in the leaves which are not eaten by the lemurs. *Eucalyptus* flowers are pollinated by insects and secrete abundant nectar which is probably one of the attractions for the lemurs. Pine flowers are wind pollinated, so they have no nectar, yet they still seem attractive and may contribute as much as to 10 per cent of the red-fronted lemur's daily intake at the peak of the flowering season.

The re-afforestation of some of Madagascar's degraded hillsides with alien trees, such as pine and *Eucalyptus*, has come in for severe criticism, mainly because of the supposed lack of food for native animals in such unnatural plantations. It seems that at certain periods, however, the trees may be capable of fulfilling the daily demands of the red-fronted lemur while, if the rows are not too close, a variety of native vegetation is able to develop beneath. This can diversify and extend the food supply as well as provide cover for animals living lower down. It is

interesting that grey bamboo lemurs *Hapalemur griseus* also forage regularly in the plantations at Périnet while, after dark, three species of nocturnal lemurs can regularly be found there.

There has long been speculation about whether or not *Lemur fulvus* regularly takes animal food in the wild although, in captivity, brown lemurs gladly accept meat. While carrying out her two-year study of red-fronted lemurs at Ranomafana, Deborah Overdorff of Duke University watched them crunching noisily on golf-ball-sized (when rolled up) *Sphaerotherium* giant pill millipedes which were simply treated like an extra kind of fruit. That these should provide an apparently welcome addition to the lemurs' diet is somewhat surprising, because many of these millipedes flaunt warning colours which would normally indicate a repellent taste or toxic properties, or both. Many millipedes are known to be chemically protected by their ability to secrete irritant substances, such as phenolic compounds, when severely molested. This seems to be the case with the large, 7-inch (17-cm) long, black-and-orange giant millipedes which are also common at Ramonafana. Deborah Overdorff also saw the lemurs preparing these unpleasant beasts for consumption by rubbing them between their hands and dribbling saliva over their shiny exteriors. This rough handling presumably stimulates the production of defensive secretions which the lemurs sometimes wipe off on their tail held between their hands; the drooled saliva may also play some vital part in the cleaning process. Once deprived of their protection, the millipedes are eaten. During the wet season, fungi are included on the menu, too. The lemurs also descend to the ground at certain regularly used spots to lick the earth, although they are noticeably more nervous when thus occupied, and soon scamper up the nearest tree if they feel even slightly threatened.

As in *L. catta*, scent plays an important role in marking territory, and *L. fulvus* also scent marks branches using handstands, although the chosen spot is normally at higher levels than it is for the ring-tailed lemur, as befits a highly arboreal animal which spends little time on the ground. Both sexes use urine as a marking agent, although the male also utilizes secretions from the naked anal region and glands on the underarm area. A male will often sniff with interest at a spot which a female has urine marked, following up by rubbing the area with his flanks and forehead.

It is becoming increasingly evident that brown lemurs are among several cathemeral species which space out their activities over the full 24-hour period. Anyone trying to sleep in the forest at night will be well aware of their nocturnal activity, as neighbouring groups bark loudly in territorial disputes and crash noisily from tree to tree, their fine sense of distance and direction apparently being undiminished in the dark. Brown lemurs are agile performers, and the sight and sound of a group moving quickly through the canopy is impressive. They are accomplished jumpers and can leap across gaps of 20 feet (6 m), landing and grasping with all four feet while the tail is held out as a counterbalance, perhaps only to make use of their

This male red-fronted lemur **Lemur fulvus rufus** *is sniffing with great interest at the horizontal bole of a fallen tree in gloomy, moss-festooned forest at Ranomafana. Most of the group gave the tree the same treatment but did not follow up by scent marking.*

momentum by launching themselves almost immediately across another yawning chasm. And so the nimble lemurs race through the canopy in this highly efficient way, while the poor earthbound observer flounders around on the steep slopes beneath.

Boldness and agility grow with age and experience, however, and the juvenile lemurs are noticeably less daring in their acrobatic endeavours, giving themselves time to calculate the distances carefully before taking the plunge. A female burdened with a well-grown infant is even more likely to be cautious. She will often pause for some time, carefully weighing up the situation before trusting herself to make the jump. Even then she may make it only to the very tip of the

target branch, which dips alarmingly as she lands, her baby clinging on tightly, unaware of the problems it is causing.

Brown lemurs are very sociable animals and spend a lot of time sitting as close as possible to one another. Mutual grooming is common and an intrinsic part of the resting periods. The participants are normally seated comfortably on a branch and gently lick and nibble away at one another's fur. The young are born from the end of August to October. The baby clings to its mother's belly fur for the first three weeks, after which it takes up a position on her back. The infants are centres of attraction, and the desire to touch and groom them is not restricted to their own mothers.

The white-fronted lemur *Lemur fulvus albifrons* is perhaps the most attractive member of the group. Although the female is a rather undistinguished dark brown, the male is far more decorative, with a light-brown back, white chest and beautiful snow-white fringe around the face, contrasting handsomely with the black muzzle and apricot eyes. This subspecies is restricted to the eastern rainforests, but the exact limits of its distribution are currently rather speculative. The southern limit seems to be near Tamatave on the coast while, inland, it occurs at least as far south as the Natural Reserve of Zahamena to the east of Andreba. Northwards its range extends as far west as the Marojejy massif while, along the coast, it reaches beyond the most northerly extent of the rainforest as far as the Fanambana river near Vohemar.

The only place to obtain good views of this attractive animal easily is on the island reserve of Nosy Mangabe. Here, one well-habituated group inhabits a small territory in the forest around the campsite. On two or three days during my visit in April, this group did not move more than 165 feet (50 m) from the buildings. Most of their time was devoted to gobbling down the berries of some small *Grewia* trees near the shore. Feeding would go on for an hour or more, broken by spells of rest in denser forest nearby, after which they would resume their meal. Although still green and apparently unripe, these pea-sized fruits were apparently greatly relished by the lemurs, which were loath to interrupt their feeding to avoid someone passing close by on the path beneath. When this happened, it was always the males that were the first to lose their nerve and retreat to a safer distance. Here they would sit on a branch, their tails waving back and forth like demented pendulums, their heads thrust forward in an intent stare as a succession of their characteristic 'guk-guk' alarm calls stuttered from their mouths. At one point, a female was so preoccupied

with her compulsive consumption of *Grewia* berries that her gradual advance down a branch eventually brought her dark snout almost to within touching distance of my upturned face. The sound of incessant chewing was clearly audible as she packed away berry after berry. It was now apparent that she was exercising a considerable degree of discrimination during the process. Although the berries all appeared to be uniformly green and unripe, she could obviously detect small differences in palatability, for each berry was briefly sniffed and graded before a decision was made to eat or not to eat. She sampled the berries by pulling the fruit-laden branches towards her with her hands, enabling her quickly and precisely to nibble off the chosen fruits.

Another powerful attraction for this group was a large cluster of ripe figs (*Ficus* species). The lemurs were evidently anxious to secure their share of these enticing fruits which had recently ripened. At least once a day, mostly in the afternoon, the group of

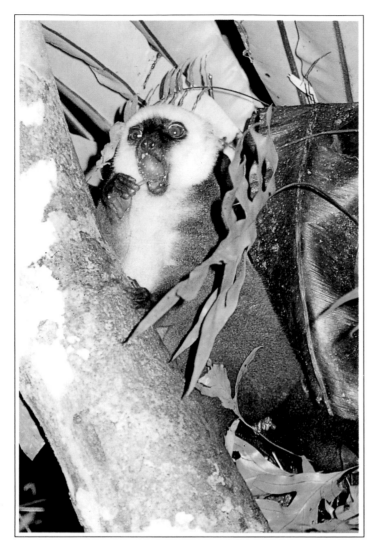

L. f. albifrons would make tracks for this tree. Usually, they were out of luck, for the ripeness of the figs had also been noticed by a ruffed lemur *Varecia variegata* which staked its claim by barking gruffly at the approaching white-fronts. The ruffed lemur is larger and heavier than the white-fronted lemur and it reinforced its barking by lunging and chasing if the intruders did not seem to retreat. On one occasion, three male white-fronts managed to sneak in unseen while the ruffed lemur was taking a break up in the forest. This trio was gobbling figs when a fusillade of barks from a neighbouring tree heralded the sudden arrival of the ruffed lemur. Only seconds were needed to establish which species was dominant as the white-fronts beat a hasty retreat, apparently with no thought that they outnumbered the lone *Varecia*. This submissiveness in giving up a prized food resource without a fight was in marked contrast to their treatment of their own females over the same figs. A male was inevitably the first to arrive; he would check that the *Varecia* was absent and establish a commanding position on top of the cluster of fruits. Figs are considerably larger then *Grewia* berries, perhaps twice the size of a large cherry. They cannot, therefore, be bolted down quickly because they need to be chewed and then swallowed, usually while the lemur sat protectively on top of the fruits. No sooner had a female edged rather timidly to within grabbing

Above left: **A male white-fronted lemur Lemur fulvus albifrons pops a large fig into his mouth. Access to this highly desirable fruit at this location on Nosy Managabe was usually prevented by a very possessive and bossy ruffed lemur Varecia variegata**

Above: **As a female white-fronted lemur gazes down longingly at the clump of ripe figs, a male munches away on one of the highly prized fruits. If the female dared to make the attempt to creep closer to the figs, the male would aggressively chase her away. He, in turn, would be routed by the protective ruffed lemur Varecia variegata arriving on the scene.**

distance of a fig than the resident male would round on her aggressively and chase her away, snapping at her and giving vent to a series of bare-toothed barks. While a male was in command, I did not once see a female feed on figs.

The subspecies most similar to *L. f. albifrons* is Sanford's lemur *Lemur fulvus sanfordi*, in which the male has a halo of fur sticking out around the head. Especially in the beard, the fur is much longer than it is in *L. f. albifrons*, but it is a rather greyish-white tinge. In addition, the forehead and crown in *L. f. sanfordi* are pale brown rather than white, and there are also two pale-brown V-shaped intrusions into the black of the muzzle on either side. The females are similar in both subspecies — basically dark brown and rather drab. Sanford's lemur inhabits a rather restricted area in north-west Madagascar, from around the Montagne d'Ambre, south to the limestone

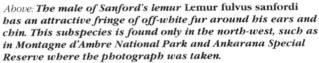

Above: **The male of Sanford's lemur Lemur fulvus sanfordi** *has an attractive fringe of off-white fur around his ears and chin. This subspecies is found only in the north-west, such as in Montagne d'Ambre National Park and Ankarana Special Reserve where the photograph was taken.*

Above right: **The female Sanford's lemur Lemur fulvus** **sanfordi** *is quite unlike the male; she is very similar to the female white-fronted lemur L. fulvus albifrons.*

massif of Ankarana which lies between Anivorano and Ambilobe, and on downwards to the south-west of Ambilobe. Some reports give the eastern range as extending widely down as far south as Sambava, but other authorities question this. Within this area, the natural forest is now increasingly fragmented, and Sanford's lemur is regarded as endangered, at least in the long term. It is hunted illegally and, even when present in reserves, these have been modified by the illegal exploitation of timber.

In the Montagne d'Ambre National Park, Sanford's lemur can be seen quite easily although it is always wary and difficult to approach, probably because it has been persistently hunted for meat and for the pet trade. Even in Ankarana Special Reserve, where this animal is common, it remains far more wary than the closely related but quite different crowned lemur *Lemur coronatus* even though, in this area, hunting lemurs for the pot is unknown because of a local taboo, or *fady*, which forbids it. In Ankarana, these

two species often feed together in the same trees, especially in a species of *Strychnos* which has large fruits attractive to them both. They do not appear to travel together, however, in the kind of mixed group which is often formed when different species of monkey co-exist in the same area of forest. Disputes over ownership of a particularly desirable fruit sometimes result in outbreaks of ill-tempered aggression between the two species, usually settled by females of the larger Sanford's lemur; they are able to throw their weight around and eject the smaller crowned lemurs. In Ankarana, the average group size for Sanford's lemur is nine although larger groups, containing as many as 15 individuals, occur. It seems to be quite at home in forest which has been disturbed or degraded by human activities although it is also able to thrive in mature canopy forest. There is a large, healthy population of this lemur in Ankarana, but the situation outside the reserve seems to be worsening steadily. The forests around Montagne d'Ambre have been extensively cleared over the last ten years, and there is now a gap of about 19 miles (30 km) separating the lemur populations in this reserve from those at Ankarana. Much of this gap is now totally lacking in woody vegetation so it represents an impassable barrier for genetic exchange between the two populations. The only other important areas of refuge for Sanford's lemur may be the 134 square miles (347 sq km) of forest in the Special Reserve of Analamera, and the very dry forests of Antsingy and Forêt des Sakalavas. Outside these reserves, Sanford's lemurs undoubtedly still exist, but in a steadily shrinking habitat dwindling into a desert of degraded savanna because of continuing forest clearance.

Lemur fulvus albocollaris, the white-collared lemur, is restricted to the eastern rainforests lying between the Mananara and Faraony rivers. Overall, they are a rich chestnut-brown colour but the male has a white beard. The collared lemur *Lemur fulvus collaris* is similar save for the orange beard of the male. This subspecies is found in south-western Madagascar, from the most southerly extensions of the rainforest north of Fort Dauphin, up as far as the Mananara river. Neither of these varieties has been well studied, nor are they likely to be seen by the average visitor to the island. Only *L. f. collaris* is found in a protected area, within the Natural Reserve of Andohahela, where entry is forbidden to all except accredited scientists with specific projects.

For many years, the brown lemur was regarded as a subspecies of the black lemur *Lemur macaco,* a species in which males and females differ markedly in colour. Only the males and young juveniles are a rich glossy black, while the mature females are a warm shade of brown with white beard and ear tufts. The black lemur is confined to humid forests in a small area in north-western Madagascar; it also occurs on the off-shore islands of Nosy Be and Nosy Komba. It is split into two subspecies: *Lemur macaco macaco,* found on Nosy Be and Nosy Komba and on the mainland almost as far north as Ambilobe, and south-westwards down to Moramandia; and *L. m. flavifrons,* Sclater's lemur, which is restricted to a small area between the latitudes of Moramandia and Befotaka.

Lemur macaco macaco lives in small groups of between seven and nine animals in which, very rarely among primates, the females are outnumbered by the males. Despite their greater numbers, however, it seems that the males are dominated by the females. Black lemurs are highly arboreal and prefer to travel through unbroken canopy whenever possible. They are mainly diurnal and subsist chiefly on fruit and leaves, much like brown lemurs. In the village of Ankazomborona on the island of Nosy Komba, some groups of black lemurs have become accustomed to a rather more exotic and easily obtained diet, consisting largely of bananas proffered by eager crowds of admiring tourists. The villagers have long regarded these lemurs as sacred, to the extent that killing, eating or just ill-treating one is forbidden. The tame black lemurs on this island have rapidly become a major tourist attraction, and large numbers of visitors go there just to feed the lemurs and take snapshots of them sitting on peoples' heads like furry topknots. Unlike monkeys, which may bite people who come into contact with them, black lemurs are placid and tourists obviously enjoy getting close to animals that are still, in effect, wild. Although they enjoy legal protection, however, black lemurs which consistently

raid crops elsewhere on the island may still be killed even though they are not hunted for the pot. On Nosy Be, several hundred *L. macaco* forage naturally in the 4¼ square miles (11 sq km) of forest in Lokobe Natural Reserve while, on the mainland, more groups inhabit the isolated 229-square mile (593-sq km) reserve of Tsaratanana. This species has apparently adapted well to living in the alien environment provided by plantations of exotic trees, however, and it may even attain densities higher than in natural native forest.

Sclater's lemur *Lemur macaco flavifrons* differs from the type in lacking the prominent ear tufts and in having blue eyes (in *L. m. macaco* the eyes are orange). For many years, the very existence of this subspecies was doubted, but its rediscovery in the Sambirano region in 1983 established beyond question its separate status, and several specimens have now been brought into captivity in the hope of breeding from them. Two expeditions to confirm the existence of this subspecies were organized, in November 1983 and July 1984. This entailed a painstaking piece of detective work designed to locate the lemurs, if there were any, in the forested regions lying on either side of the main road from Antsohihy to Ambanja. The investigators relied quite heavily on the traditional methods used by scientists to look for plants and animals. They questioned the people, the local villagers, most likely to know whether or not lemurs were present in their area. If an encouraging response resulted, the nearby forest was searched to discover which lemur species was present. The first Sclater's lemurs were found in November 1983 in a patch of forest 12½ miles (20 km) west of Andranosamonta. Following this, numerous groups were noted along the borders of the road about 6 miles (10 km) to the south of Maromandia. Subsequent explorations in 1984 to the north of Maromandia turned up only groups of *L. macaco macaco,* indicating that the northern limit for *L. m. flavifrons* is probably formed by the Andranomalaza river.

The capture of seven live specimens enabled these rare animals to be studied more closely. The males were of a less intense shade of black than in *L. m. macaco,* and their fur has a definite brown tinge. The female has a more prominent wash of orange across the fur than is typical in *L. m. macaco* females. The differences in the eyes and ears have already been noted above and, in addition, the male's crown in *L. m. flavifrons* is embellished with a stubby crest of hairs which *L. m. macaco* males do not have. At present, Sclater's lemur does not occur in any protected area, although it seems to exist at quite high densities within its limited range. The remaining forests in the Sambirano region are subject to heavy agricultural pressure, however, because the land is ideal for growing a variety of food crops, as well as for establishing plantations of cash crops such as cocoa and ylang-ylang.

While the tame and accessible black lemurs of Nosy Komba are seen by many visitors to Madagascar, the mongoose lemur *Lemur mongoz* is seen by few

The rare mongoose lemur Lemur mongoz *is not easy to see in the wild. The only place where a good sighting is likely is at the Ampijeroa Forest Reserve where this picture was taken.*

but the specialists willing to devote time and effort to observing this elusive animal. It resembles a rather diminutive brown lemur, but can be distinguished easily by its greyish-white muzzle, in contrast to the black muzzle characteristic of the brown lemur. The female has a grey head with white cheeks, a combination also seen in many males, although some males may differ in having the cap and cheeks orange instead of white. This is one of only two lemur species not confined to Madagascar, and is also found on the Comoro Islands, where it has most likely been introduced by people in the distant past. In both places it is severely threatened, mainly by destruction of its forest habitat, which continues apace. On the mainland, the mongoose lemur is confined to an area towards the north-west, although the exact limits of its distribution are imperfectly known because, in the past, it was often confused with the brown lemur. It certainly occurs near Lake Kinkony to the south of Mitsinjo, and extends to the west of the River Mahavavy but, unfortunately, its distribution in this region does not come within the protective enclave of the Tsingy de Namoroka reserve. It extends both to the east and west of the Betsiboka river and northwards as far as the Bay of Narinda.

The mongoose lemur inhabits the tropical dry forests, characterized by a marked dry period when many of the trees lose their leaves. The only place where it is reasonably easy to find is in the Ampijeroa forest reserve. Here it is quite abundant so that, in a single day in December 1988, I saw three separate groups within a short distance of the camp ground. By contrast, during eight days in June 1990 in the same area, I saw none. This is in line with the experiences of other observers, suggesting that this lemur is reasonably likely to be seen at Ampijeroa only between September and December. Perhaps this is connected with the suggestion that the mongoose lemur changes its pattern of activity, from mainly nocturnal to mainly diurnal, according to the time of year although, in December 1988, groups were seen feeding by day and at night.

In the peak of the dry season in July and August, their diet seems to be very restricted, confined to just five species of plants and, in four of these, it is only the flowers which seem to be acceptable. This is the flowering season for the giant kapok trees *Ceiba pentandra* which are such a prominent feature around the forestry station at Ampijeroa. Mongoose lemurs are most often seen perched high up in these giants, for they may spend up to 80 per cent of their feeding time licking nectar and pollen from the flowers or eating the nectaries.

The crowned lemur *Lemur coronatus* was once thought to be a subspecies of *L. mongoz*, but it is now accorded separate specific status. Like the mongoose lemur, it is rather a small animal, weighing only about 4½ pounds (2 kg). As in *L. macaco* and some varieties of *L. fulvus*, the sexes are noticeably different in appearance. The fur of the males is a rich reddish brown suffused with a fine haze of black; the eye ring and muzzle are a pale whitish colour, the cheeks and 'eyebrows' rufous; while the top of the head is surmounted by a solid black 'crown' which projects forwards in a triangle between the ears. The silky females are a very attractive, uniform steel grey, and this colour extends right across the head, save for a

Below left and below: **The crowned lemur** **Lemur coronatus** *is found only in a restricted area of the north-west. It is common enough in the Montagne d'Ambre National Park, and even more so in the Ankarana Special Reserve where this male was photographed.*

V-shaped rufous crown on the forehead. The underside in both sexes is off-white. Unlike brown lemurs, in which the males are usually the most handsome, female crowned lemurs are outstandingly beautiful little animals.

The crowned lemur inhabits a rather restricted area of northern Madagascar, extending from the Ankarana massif in the south, northwards to the arid countryside of the Cap d'Ambre, the most northerly part of the island. In the east, its range extends as far south as the Fanambana river. Within that area, this species is very tolerant of habitat change, and is able to survive even in small isolated patches of forest surrounded by savanna and cleared areas. It is found within a few miles of Diégo Suarez, in forest on the Montagne des Français, a popular tourist spot, and it also occurs in small pockets of forest near Windsor Castle to the north-west of the town, across the bay. Its habit of calling, loud and often sometimes rather like a bird and sometimes more like a dog yelping, makes it easy to record its presence, even when no animals are seen. It is also able to adapt to living in plantations of non-native trees and, in some areas, it is killed because of its raids on crops.

On the Montagne d'Ambre, crowned lemurs are

Below and below right: **With her soft grey fur and rufous crown, the female crowned lemur Lemur coronatus is particularly attractive.**

found, together with Sanford's lemur, in humid forest, well up on the flanks of the mountain but this is probably not a favoured habitat and its presence there may just emphasize its innate adaptability. It is fairly easy to locate although, because of recent hunting pressure, the resident groups are generally not very tame. In 1990 and 1991, a study was carried out within the park to determine the relationships between this species and Sanford's lemur, which is found within the same forest. This was designed to determine how two species of primates, both apparently with very similar foraging and dietary habits, can co-exist in quite large numbers without harmful competition. A similar situation also exists further south in Ankarana Special Reserve, which is actually by far the best place for getting close views of crowned and Sanford's lemurs. The forests here support perhaps the densest and least disturbed populations of crowned lemurs in Madagascar, and many of them are very tame. Some groups regularly cross the bare, sword-like pinnacles of the open tsingy, where the sharp edges are capable of tearing tough boots. The animals venture on to this hostile terrain to reach the fruits of some of the drought-adapted plants, such as certain figs, when these are in season.

Crowned lemurs seem quite at home travelling on the ground, and are second only to the ring-tailed lemur in this respect. They make use of a variety of

habitats, from high-canopied forest to disturbed areas where illegal logging has taken place and even, as just mentioned, the harsh open tsingy itself. During the extended dry season, when leaves are either absent or in an unpalatably shrivelled condition, and no tender young shoots are available, the main food seems to be fruit. In the logged areas, the extra light has stimulated the prolific growth of a species of *Strychnos* liana, and its fruits provide a vital reserve of food for each of the resident *Lemur* species at the end of the dry season. The seeds within these fruits are poisonous, but the lemurs deftly avoid eating them by biting off the peel neatly and chewing the flesh from the unwanted seed, which is then left to fall free.

Around its edges, the Ankarana forest grades into a kind of savanna which supports numerous trees of *Strychnos spinosa*, and its large, grapefruit-sized fruits are also eagerly sought by the lemurs (as well as by humans). During the dry season, it is only when fruits are scarce that the crowned lemurs seem to resort to eating leaves. This reluctance to eat leaves may be dictated by the shortage of available surface water at this season. Many trees try to protect their leaves by charging them with varying amounts of toxins or antidigestants. A considerable intake of water is necessary to render these innocuous. During the dry season, water is available only at a few sites in Ankarana, one of which lies in a cave entered by one 16-foot (5-m) deep vertical shaft, down which the lemurs scramble. At the beginning of the dry season, small pockets of water may still survive in miniature natural containers , such as rot-holes in trees. The lemurs are adept at finding these, and stick their heads inside to lap up the water, gradually craning their necks further and further as the water level drops. When pushing with the feet, craning the neck and stretching out the tongue are no longer enough, the thirsty animal repeatedly inserts its arm and licks the liquid from its hand. Identical behaviour has also been observed in some other species of *Lemur*.

Crowned lemurs seem to have an unusually loose group structure, and there is little evidence of a defined dominance hierarchy to regulate relationships within the group. Although the female animals generally seem to take the lead when travelling, the males are overwhelmingly dominant when it comes to soliciting bananas from campers, and will even deprive a successful female of her prize by snatching it out of her hands. Scent probably plays an important role in territorial marking, and both sexes indulge in ano-genital marking of particular trees or rocks.

The young are born at the very start of the wet season, when a flush of young growth and the maturing of more fruit provide extra resources for the lactating mothers. The babies are carried by their mothers, but soon begin to venture away and may even try hitching a ride on the back of a male. As in many primates, mothers with babies are endlessly fascinating to other members of the group, and the infants become the target for orgies of enthusiastic grooming.

Madagascar's largest predator, the fossa *Cryptoprocta ferox*, described in the previous chapter, is quite common and often seen in Ankarana; undoubtedly, it preys on the crowned lemur. The fossa is the most feared of the crowned lemur's enemies and, when one is detected, the group expresses its alarm by raucous grunting and shrieking and particularly by vigorously swinging tails. The crowned lemur is generally a very vocal animal, anyway, and has a wide repertoire of calls. The loudest and most frequently heard vocalization is a penetrating braying uttered by the male with upturned face, often in response to a similar call from a male in a neighbouring group. They also extend their activities into the night, so that the camper attempting to sleep

*Below: **Although widespread in the eastern rainforests, the red-bellied lemur** Lemur rubriventer **is seldom seen. This male is one of Deborah Overdorff's (Duke University) study animals at Ranomafana. His dark-brown coat blends into the sombre colours of the damp, mossy forest inhabited by his small family group.***

*Opposite top: **Another member of the same red-bellied lemur family at Ranomafana, the female. Note the dark overgrown nature of the habitat which makes it difficult to follow the lemur groups when they suddenly take it into their heads to move a long way in a hurry. Leaches abound in this part of the forest.***

*Opposite bottom: **The third member of the red-bellied lemur family, a juvenile female that was very inquisitive.***

in Ankarana is periodically disturbed by their cacophonous chorusing, accompanied by crashing sounds overhead as they leap confidently from tree to tree, and the intermittent pattering of bits of fruit and leaf on to the roof of the tent.

The last member of the genus, the red-bellied lemur *Lemur rubriventer*, is far more widely distributed than the mongoose lemur, but equally unlikely to be seen by the average person because it lives in inaccessible rainforest and because the population densities may often be low. It is an attractive animal, clad in rich, rusty brown fur with a black tail. The female has pale yellowish-white cheeks and a white chest, while the male is easily distinguished by his prominent white eye patches. It occurs at low densities throughout the eastern rainforests at mid-altitudes, from approximately the latitude of Ivohibe at the most southerly end of the Andringitra massif, northwards as far as the Tsaratanana massif. Within this large area destruction of the forests still goes on, especially for the shifting slash-and-burn farming or *tavy*, but also for logging. Although it is generally rather sparsely distributed, the red-bellied lemur is apparently abundant in certain areas, such as Ranomafana where densities of roughly 105 per square mile (40 per sq km) have been recorded. It is difficult to find an animal which lives in small groups, apparently spending much of the day dozing quietly in a tree, and seldom betraying its presence by uttering any sounds, so red-bellied lemurs may prove to be commoner than we think.

At Ranomafana studies have been carried out into its habits and ecology. Group size is rather small, varying from two to four animals, usually consisting of a family group of male, female and offspring, or bachelor groups of two or three individuals. The home territory usually covers 30-37 acres (12-15 ha) of forest which, at Ranomafana, is often situated on steep slippery slopes covered in dense stands of trees and liana tangles, all liberally draped with festoons of mosses. For much of the year, the red-bellied lemurs in this damp habitat maintain a cathemeral activity cycle, with bouts of feeding and resting alternating over a 24-hour period. Fruit provides the bulk of their diet but, at certain periods, the emphasis changes to flowers when these are seasonally available. When the Australian *Eucalyptus* trees — which have been introduced into the forest in the study area — are in flower, they are very attractive to the lemurs. Indeed, during July, *Eucalyptus* flowers may comprise 80 per cent of the diet, although they are consumed exclusively during the hours of darkness, possibly because of the risk posed by diurnal birds of prey to a lemur feeding on the exposed branches of an emergent *Eucalyptus* tree in broad daylight.

The red-bellied lemur seems to possess an innate recognition of the threat posed by large raptors and by the fossa *Cryptoprocta ferox*, for a sentinel is often posted, day or night, to oversee feeding activities by the other members of the group. This species is strongly territorial, and both sexes use scent glands in the ano-genital region to mark the boundary of the territory. The male can add its own extra set of marks using a gland on the top of its head. Despite such dedication to establishing ownership, boundary disputes with neighbouring groups are common and often erupt into noisy fights. One unique feature of this lemur is the male's habit of carrying its offspring. This seems to happen mainly when the infants are about three months old. Although they are still suckling, they are able to get around on their own to some extent but, when the exercise begins to wear them down, they might well hitch a ride on father rather than mother.

GENUS VARECIA

Anyone quietly watching a group of red-fronted lemurs is liable to be startled by a sudden burst of explosive barks shattering the peace of the forest. The sheer volume of these stentorian bellows, heard even through the dense tangle of vegetation, is hard to attribute to an animal no larger than a large domestic cat. Only the much larger indri makes louder calls than the ruffed lemur *Varecia variegata*. The ruffed lemur is also a resident of the eastern rainforests where it exists in two separate subspecies. One of these, *Varecia variegata variegata* the black-and-white ruffed lemur, seems to vary considerably from region to region and may be better split into three or four further subspecies. Taking this subspecies as a single unit, its distribution extends from somewhere to the north of Maroansetra, down as far as the region to the south of Farafangana.

The red ruffed lemur *V. v. rubra* is restricted to the wild Masoala peninsula east of the River Antainambalana. The boundary separating the two subspecies and preventing genetic interchange is probably the River Antainambalana north of Maroansetra. All the races are extremely beautiful animals noted for their luxuriant fur. Whatever the main colour pattern, the face is always black with a white chin and ear tufts. The red ruffed lemur is larger and heavier than any *Lemur* species, weighing in at about 9 pounds (4 kg). Although it is widespread and often heard at such places as Ranomafana, this is not an easy species to observe closely in the wild, except on the island of Nosy Mangabe where the black-and-white ruffed lemur is relatively approachable. Its status as a native on this island is doubtful, and it is thought to have been introduced deliberately during the 1930s.

Ruffed lemurs have unusual reproductive and parental habits. They usually give birth to twins and even triplets are quite frequent. Unlike most other lemur babies, they do not ride around clinging to the mother's fur. Instead, the female prepares a nursery nest in a hole in a tree, on a fork of a branch or perhaps among a conveniently shaped clump of epiphytic vegetation. During a study of this species in Nosy Mangabe, the preferred site was among dense tangles of lianas about 33-66 feet (10-20 m) above the ground on large trees. Here, the female constructs a well-concealed nest, firstly by chewing off slim, 16-19-inch (40-50-cm) long sections of branch. She then carries this material in her mouth back to the nest and

incorporates it securely into the structure, using her mouth and hands to consolidate it. She completes the nest by lining it carefully with soft fur plucked from her own flanks or thighs.

Her offspring enjoy the protection of her warm body for the first few days, before she leaves them to forage. She returns at regular intervals to enable them to suckle, and this also gives her a chance to clean their fur thoroughly with her tongue. Between one and two weeks after giving birth, she removes the young from the security of the nest and parks them high in the trees, usually selecting a relatively stable spot where a network of lianas or epiphytes provides a relatively level and safe surface. She carries each baby, one at a time, in her mouth, gripping it firmly but gently across its underside so that its head and rump stick out on either side, enabling it to grasp her neck securely with its arms and legs. The baby park is changed several times a day, especially within the second month when the youngsters may be moved as often as seven times a day.

During the first month, the female spends much of her time close to the parked infants but, as the days pass, she gradually spends more and more time away from them, foraging in the forest or indulging in social activities with other members of her group, often leaving her charges for several hours at a time. They are seldom completely alone during this period, however, for non-breeding females, as well as a male or two, will usually be nearby; they probably help to look after the infants in their mother's absence. This form of extra-parental guardianship may be an important factor in enabling the female to desert her offspring for long periods while she forages, freeing her from the burden of two heavy babies as she moves through the canopy.

The young develop far more rapidly than *Lemur* babies do, and they are completely mobile within three to four months. By about one month, they are usually able to hold on to small branches during their mother's excursions and are capable of clambering around unaided when she is sitting nearby, although she often extends a steadying hand. At two to three months, they are able to potter along behind their mother for distances of 100 yards (90 m) or so, although they still need assisted passage one at a time in her mouth to cross large gaps in the canopy. This mode of transport must cease when the infants become too big to be accommodated in the mother's jaws. At about two months, they may begin to test leaves and fruits for palatability by sniffing and tasting them without actually swallowing anything although, even at three to four months, they may still spend 10 per cent of their time at their mother's nipple. As in all lemur babies, play is a vital part of the growing-up process, and they indulge in frequent bouts of boisterous romping, with each other (in the case of twins) and with adults.

Although the ruffed lemur certainly eats leaves, it is likely that fruit is the preferred food. On Nosy Mangabe in late April 1990, I noted how an adult visited a cluster of ripe figs (*Ficus* sp) every afternoon

over a period of several days. It appears that these had ripened enough to become attractive only a day or two earlier yet, within eight days, the entire cluster, estimated at some 250 to 300 fruits, had been consumed by just this single animal, assisted only to a minor extent in its absence by the occasional brief sneak attack from the local white-fronted lemurs (*see* above). These particular figs were very solidly built, globular objects an inch (2.5 cm) across. It seems remarkable, therefore, that at a single sitting, lasting perhaps an hour-and-a-half, the ruffed lemur was able to tuck away some 30 to 40 of them. They were not taken at random, either, for each fruit was selected only after the piebald gourmet had sniffed at, and rejected, several. The chosen item was then firmly plucked with the teeth, and manoeuvred backwards into the correct position for chewing by an upward toss of the head. Mastication lasted 15 to 20 seconds, after which the lemur reached quickly forwards for another. On four afternoons, the fig feast finished when the ruffed lemur stopped for an hour's catnap on a nearby branch, close enough to the fruit to deter any would-be thieves. Then there followed another short feed on the rapidly diminishing stock before the satisfied animal slipped away quietly into the gathering gloom as night descended on the forest.

When not guzzling figs, this particular individual occasionally crossed to a large fruiting *Terminalia* tree towering above the nearby beach. To the ruffed lemur, these oval, green, rather flattened fruits were obviously much less tasty than the figs. Apart from any likely lack of flavour, *Terminalia* fruits are tough skinned so the lemur had a lot of chewing to do to peel the rind from the stones. The stones themselves are too hard to be cracked by the lemur's jaws, and are simply dropped once the outer coat has been removed and swallowed. It proved necessary to manipulate the fruit constantly in the mouth to accomplish this, turning it over and over with a head-tossing action as the flesh was gradually stripped

Above: **The black-and-white ruffed lemur Varecia variegata variegata is one of the most handsome of the lemurs. This individual spent a week plundering this clump of figs, vigorously defending its property against intruding white-fronted lemurs. Mastication of these large fruits involved tossing back the head to place the fig in the correct position between the teeth.**

Below: **The black-and-white ruffed lemur snoozes quietly above its clump of figs, keeping a watchful eye on its property.**

away. This laborious task took so much time and effort that the lemur usually tired rapidly and soon returned to the more easily won figs. As already mentioned, ruffed lemurs have powerful voices, and the 'roar-shriek' chorus which erupts so suddenly and startlingly through the forest can reach groups living up to 1000 yards (1 km) away. Although this is easily the most impressive of its calls, the vocal repertoire is very broad, consisting of at least 13 sounds. These have been defined as follows: roar-shriek; abrupt roar; pulsed squawk; wail; bray; quack; growl; growl-snort; chatter; whine; grunt; huff; and mew. Each of these has its own well-defined use, so that the mew sound is regularly exchanged between mother and infant while the chatter is a sign of submission, an unmistakable admission of the acceptance of subordinate status. Sound undoubtedly plays the major role in communication, and scent is of such minor significance, if any, that this species does not scent mark its territory, unlike most other lemurs.

GENUS *HAPALEMUR*

There are three species of lemurs known collectively as 'bamboo lemurs'. The grey bamboo lemur *Hapalemur griseus* (also known as the grey gentle lemur) is a relatively small, smoky grey animal weighing about 2 pounds (1 kg). There are four accepted subspecies: *H. g. griseus* which inhabits the rainforests in the east, from near Fort Dauphin northwards to the Tsaratanana massif; *H. g. occidentalis* which comes from two isolated regions in the west, one in the Sambirano region between Moramandia and Beramanja, the other between Maintirano and Belo-sur-Tsiribihina to the north of Morondava; the extensive reedbeds bordering Lake Alaotra provide the rather unusual home of *H. g. alaotrensis*; while *H. g. meridionalis* has only recently been described, and comes from a small area of forest approximately 6 miles (10 km) north of Fort Dauphin.

The grey bamboo lemur **Hapalemur griseus** *is by far the commonest of the three species of* Hapalemur. *This is* **H. g. griseus** *which is widespread and easily seen in the eastern rainforests.*

The only subspecies likely to be seen by the average visitor is *H. g. griseus* which can be found fairly easily in the reserve at Périnet and in the proposed national park at Ranomafana. Group size varies: four to six is usual but up to 40 animals have been recorded. The normal habitat is rainforest but secondary forest, dominated by bamboos, may support even higher numbers than primary forest, while open-canopied plantations of *Eucalyptus* are also used. The main diet consists of the tender new shoots, young leaf bases and inner stem pith of *Bambusa* species bamboos although leaves of other plants, as well as small fruits, are also included regularly in the diet in small quantities.

H. g. alaotrensis, on the other hand, eats the only palatable plants available in any quantity around its watery home, the leaves of *Phragmites* reeds and the buds and pith of *Cyperus* sedges. This subspecies is probably severely endangered by hunting for the pot, carried out by setting fire to the lemurs' reedbed home. As the flames surge forward, the lemurs flee, losing their home and, in many cases, their lives. By contrast, *H. griseus griseus* may actually benefit from human clearance of the forest, because it thrives in the secondary bamboo thickets which spring up once cultivation has ceased. This lemur is perfectly adapted for feeding on bamboo. A segment of the dentition is modified to form a clamp, designed to make a quick and neat job of stripping the tough outer sheath from the tender inner shoot of the plant. Once it has been prepared in this way, the shoot is repositioned in the side of the mouth and chewed thoroughly.

The long-term survival of the greater bamboo lemur *Hapalemur simus* (also known as the broad-nosed gentle lemur) is less certain for this is probably the rarest of the lemurs. It seems to have suffered a catastrophic decline over the last 1000 years or so because skeletal remains indicate that it was once widely distributed throughout most of Madagascar's forested areas. Even as late as the nineteenth century, it was still being recorded from localities scattered over a wide area, ranging from Mananara in the north down as far as Vondrozo near Farafangana. It then seemed to disappear for almost a century until its rediscovery in 1972. It is now known for certain from only restricted localities near Ranomafana, and to the east at Kianjavato near Mananjary. Not surprisingly, it is generally regarded as being critically endangered. Part of the reason for this dramatic decline was thought to be its specialized diet. This was said to consist almost entirely of the pith of the main stems, as well as the leaf stems, of the giant bamboo *Cephalostachyum viguieri*. This large, impressive bamboo grows in dense thickets in damp valley bottoms in forest and along the margins of forest rivers, habitats which have suffered considerably at human hands over the years. When the lemurs are busy feeding on the broad, woody stems of this bamboo, the cracking and snapping, as powerful teeth gouge into yielding wood, can be heard clearly from some distance away. Recent studies have established that this species is far more catholic in its diet than

had been thought, however. It has now been seen feeding regularly on such varied foods as the flower of the traveller's palm *Ravenala madagascariensis*, a member of the banana family Musaceae; fruits of the tree *Artocarpus integrifolius*, and figs *Ficus* species, both belonging to the family Moraceae; fruits of *Dypsis* palms; and leaves of an *Afromomum* species of wild ginger in the family Zingiberaceae. It also eats leaves of a grass, *Pennisetum clandestinum*, the sole member of this list which belongs to the same family as the bamboos.

The forests at Ranomafana also harbour a third species of *Hapalemur*, the golden bamboo lemur *H. aureus*. Its discovery and eventual recognition as a separate species took a somewhat convoluted course. In 1985 a French scientist, Corinne Dague, was looking at birds and mammals in the rainforest at Ranomafana when she noted that a second, unfamiliar species of bamboo lemur, was sharing the habitat with the familiar grey bamboo lemurs. This information reached the attention of the primatologist and lemur expert, Bernhard Meier in Germany, and Patricia Wright of the Duke University Primate Centre in North Carolina, United States. Both of these experienced primatologists made independent studies of this enigmatic lemur during 1986. Patricia Wright subsequently published her conclusions that this represented the rediscovery of the greater bamboo lemur *Hapalemur simus* which had vanished again after its initial rediscovery in 1972. Her paper pointed out, however, that the Ranomafana animals belonged to an undescribed subspecies differing in size, fur colour and voice from the subspecies already long recognized. Bernhard Meier, on the other hand, was sceptical about these conclusions, and was convinced that a completely new species of lemur had been discovered. Patricia Wright may originally have held this opinion, too, but kept it to herself on the grounds that it is sensible to be cautious before leaping into print with 'new species'. In the event, further

Above left: **The golden bamboo lemur Hapalemur aureus** *is probably the rarest of all lemurs, having been only recently discovered. This male is nibbling away in characteristic fashion at the leaf stem of the greater bamboo Cephalostacyum viguieri, its main foodplant.*

Above centre: **The same male golden bamboo lemur** *is now chewing away on a young stem of the greater bamboo. The ability of this lemur to cope with the high levels of hydrogen cyanide contained in the plant is quite staggering.*

Above right: **Fungi form a regular element of the diet of the golden bamboo lemur Hapalemur aureus.** *This male has just plucked a small bracket fungus from a fallen log in the gloomiest part of the rainforest (note the fungi still present on the log beneath the lemur's tail). His fur is looking wet and bedraggled, the regular consequence of moving through the dense tangle of bamboos and ferns after a night of continuous heavy rain. Pity the poor photographer having to move push through the same welter of dripping vegetation with high-powered electronic flash equipment draped around him!*

investigations proved Meier's assertion to be correct, and the golden bamboo lemur was described as new to science in a 1987 paper written jointly by Bernhard Meier, Roland Albignac, André Péyrieras, Yves Rumpler and Patricia Wright. I have explained this in full because, on several occasions, Patricia Wright has been wrongly credited with the initial discovery of this exciting new species. New kinds of insects are constantly being discovered, but a completely new primate is a rarity indeed. In view of the original confusion over identities, it is perhaps ironic that the true *Hapalemur simus* was subsequently discovered in the same area of forest — three different bamboo lemurs in one place! And happily, with a combination of luck and skilled guidance, it is quite possible for a visitor to see all three in a single day.

The new species, which lives in small groups of two to four individuals, has also been found in other areas of bamboo south of the Namorona river, and northwards at least as far as the village of Bevoahazo. The golden bamboo lemur is midway in size between the other two members of the genus, but it is a more attractive animal than either. The blackish-brown muzzle is bordered by biscuit-coloured cheeks and eyebrows, while the top of the head and the span of the back extending down on both sides are a light chocolate brown rather than gold which, strictly speaking, is confined to the chest fur. The male has a well-developed scent-producing gland on the inside of the upper arm, and there is a black patch with a hard, knobbly surface on the inner side of the lower arm. A viscous, smelly white fluid can be secreted from an orifice in the upper gland and brought into contact with the pad on the lower arm by raising the forearm. The male regularly applies this fluid to upright saplings within the group's territory, grasping the stem in all fours while looking upwards and swinging his body in a jerky action from side to side, at the same time rubbing the forearms firmly against the bark. He reinforces these territorial scent marks with penetrating calls several times a day, shortly before nightfall being the most favoured time. When calling, the male sits on all fours on a horizontal branch and points his snout skywards to give vent to a series of surprisingly loud, hooting notes. Both sexes regularly give a soft, rather cat-like contact call which is very useful for locating a group feeding quietly in a dense thicket of bamboo.

The presence of this lemur can easily be established from the characteristic pattern of indentations left by the teeth on the leaf stems of the giant bamboo, its main food plant. Dozens of leaves, bearing this instantly recognizable signature, often litter the ground beneath the bamboo. Sections of young growing stem are also bitten off and the juicy pith eaten, the lemur holding the severed portion to bite off large chunks as if dealing with a stick of celery. Although giant bamboo is the main food plant, the golden bamboo lemur also feeds on a species of slim-stemmed bamboo creeper, an unpopular plant with researchers because it contrives to entangle feet and equipment during helter-skelter dashes up and down the steep slopes in pursuit of rapidly moving lemurs. A species of bamboo grass is also included on the menu, but these animals do not depend entirely on members of the grass family. When the group's daily round leads it through the gloomier, damper reaches of the forest, the male in particular will often scamper along a fallen mossy log on the lookout for certain fungi which sprout from the soft, rotten wood. He neatly slices a piece off with his teeth and then holds it in his hands while he nibbles away. Several different kinds are eaten, one of which resembles a Eurasian species of *Stereum* in its broad sense; while another is very similar to the Eurasian *Hirneola* (= *Auricularia*) *auricula-judae*, a thin, rubbery fungus looking like a wrinkled, pinkish-brown human ear. The presence of familiar temperate-region fungi in a far-off tropical rainforest is not as unlikely as it seems, because some fungi have a near-cosmopolitan distribution. Red-bellied and red-fronted lemurs share a taste for this same, rather unusual food, which provides a small, yet consistent resource available throughout the rainy season and well into the dry period.

Because three species of bamboo lemur live in close proximity in the same small area of forest, and eat the same type of plant, there has been a lot of speculation about how they avoid wasteful competition with one another. In such situations, competition is usually avoided by utilizing different plants and/or different areas or layers of the forest. Detailed observations of the feeding behaviour of these three lemurs have brought to light their preferences for different parts of the bamboos. The golden bamboo lemur goes mainly for the tender growing tips, surprising in that these have been found to contain no less than 15 mg of cyanide per 100 g fresh weight of bamboo! Second in preference, particularly in the dry season when young shoots are in short supply, were leaf bases, which also contain cyanide, although at lower concentrations than in the young pith.

The greater bamboo lemur targets the mature woody culms of the same plant, a job for tougher jaws and teeth, and a practical proposition only for this heavyweight of the trio, for which its beaver-like enterprise is rewarded with a meal free from cyanide.

The grey bamboo lemur prefers the leaves of a different bamboo *Cephalostachyum perrieri* which are also free from cyanide. Thus, we are presented with the apparent conundrum of the golden bamboo lemur's daily intake of about 12 times the normal lethal dose of cyanide, contained in the pound or so (500 g) of bamboo it eats every day. It is not known how this small animal manages to deal with such a toxic load each day. Because of its rarity, and because of how recently it was discovered, one might think that the golden bamboo lemur would be among the most difficult of all lemurs for the visitor to reach and observe. Fortunately, this is not so, for one group at Ranomafana has been habituated to human presence by researchers from Duke University, and can normally be located reasonably easily by one of the expert local guides.

Genus *Lepilemur*

We now turn to the exclusively nocturnal lemurs. Of these the one most likely to make its presence obvious by its habit of squawking and chattering noisily at regular intervals from a vantage point on a tree is the sportive lemur *Lepilemur mustelinus* (also called the weasel lemur but, in Madagascar, everyone simply calls them 'lepilemur'). The precise assignment of names in this genus is currently the subject of some debate. According to which authority is being followed, there is either a single species with six subspecies (*mustelinus, ruficaudatus, dorsalis, leucopus, edwardsi, septentrionalis*) or seven distinct species using the above names at the specific level, but with the addition of *L. microdon* and the further splitting of *L. septentrionalis* into several subspecies. The latter view is based mainly on genetic differences backed up by small variations in anatomy. Here, mainly in the interests of taxonomic consistency, I shall treat the sportive lemur as a single species with six subspecies.

Lepilemur is a smallish grey-brown animal with rather large goggling, eyes which give it a somewhat vacant expression. It has a small, rounded head with a flattened face, projecting rounded ears and a long bushy tail. The various subspecies are distributed across the island in wet and dry forests. The territory of each animal is very small, consisting of an area which extends only for some 33 feet (10 m) around the sleeping hole, which is usually in a hollow tree trunk. *L. m. dorsalis* is an exception, however, because it spends the day among a tangle of vines in a tree.

During the day, it is not unusual to find a *Lepilemur* perched on the edge of its sleeping chamber or even sitting right out on the trunk, although it soon edges back inside if something makes it nervous. It leaves its hideaway soon after dark, and the males usually launch straight into one of the night's main activities, calling against one another from some suitable perch a good few feet up on a tree trunk. In the area near the campsite in the Grand Canyon in Ankarana Special Reserve, the nocturnal chattering of this lemur can often be heard coming from several directions at once, an indication of the very high densities of this species in such a favourable habitat, where individuals have been noted at 100-foot (30-m) intervals in the forest bordering the main track.

Although it occasionally takes fruit, its main diet consists of leaves, making it one of the most strictly folivorous of all lemurs. Leaves are difficult to digest, and the animal has symbiotic bacteria to help break down the cellulose which is potentially the most

Above left: **Weasel or sportive lemurs often sit right outside their sleeping quarters in a hollow tree during the afternoon. This is the dry-bush weasel (or sportive) lemur Lepilemur mustelinus leucopus** *from the arid south-west.*

Above right: **The northern weasel (or sportive) lemur Lepilemur mustelinus septentrionalis** *is restricted to the north. It is amazingly abundant in the Ankarana Special Reserve where this individual was perched outside its sleeping quarters in mid-afternoon.*

nutritious constituent of the leaf. Lacking the system of multichambered stomachs found in ruminants, or the expanded hind gut found in some other larger-bodied, leaf-eating primates (modifications to accommodate large numbers of bacteria), *Lepilemur* practises refection, eating its own droppings which have already been partly acted upon by the bacteria. This habit is also seen in rabbits and in some rodents, although it should be pointed out that its existence in *Lepilemur* has been disputed by at least one authority. Few studies have been carried out on the variety of leaves consumed by the *Lepilemur* subspecies in the eastern rainforests, but *L. mustelinus leucopus*, living in the 'spiny desert' relies heavily for part of the year on the small but numerous leaves of the octopus trees *Alluaudia procera* and *A. ascendens*, their slender, leafy, multistemmed spires being such a characteristic feature of the landscape in the south.

GENERA *CHEIROGALEUS* AND *MICROCEBUS*
Visitors staying at the Hotel Buffet de la Gare at Périnet often wander out after dark to look for

nocturnal lemurs in the forest bordering the road. As
well as *Lepilemur*, the two other nocturnal species
most likely to be seen are the greater dwarf lemur
Cheirogaleus major and the rufous mouse lemur
Microcebus rufus.

C. *major* is found throughout the eastern
rainforests, from Fort Dauphin in the south to
Montagne d'Ambre in the north. Westwards, it spreads
into the Tsaratanana massif and the Sambirano region.
In favoured areas it may be very abundant. It spends
the day either in a tree hole or in a specially built nest
of twigs, usually accompanied by a number of
sleeping companions. When these emerge at dusk
they go their own way to feed and, after dark, the
animals are invariably found to be alone. Unlike
Lepilemur, the greater dwarf lemur never eats leaves
but concentrates on fruit, the nectar and pollen from
flowers and, occasionally, the odd insect. Thus,
competition with *Lepilemur* is avoided where the two
occur together at high densities, as probably happens
in many areas.

In winter, the greater dwarf lemurs usually enter a
period of dormancy, lasting anything from just two to
three days to as much as several weeks. During this
period, the body temperature is reduced to near
ambient, and the animal subsists on reserves of fat laid
down under the skin and tail. This is remarkable
behaviour for a primate, and C. *major* is one of only
two primate species known to enter dormancy (the
other is the fat-tailed dwarf lemur *Cheirogaleus
medius*).

In C. *medius*, which occurs throughout the western
dry forests, the retreat into dormancy may extend right
through the long dry period, covering the six lean
months when fruit, flowers and insects are virtually
unavailable and many of the trees are leafless. Fat is
stored mainly in the legs and in the enlarged tail, and
several animals are usually closeted together deep
inside some hollow tree, all heaped up one on top of
the other. In some forests, the fat-tailed dwarf lemur is
obviously a highly successful animal, because densities
of 140 animals per 100 acres (350 animals per 100 ha)
have been recorded in the Marosalaza Forest. One
further trait sets both species of *Cheirogaleus* apart
from all other primates. They are the only ones known
to use feces for scent marking as a matter of course.
Regularly used pathways through the trees and the
edges of territories are clearly marked by dragging the
rear end along a branch, leaving behind an
umistakable trail of smelly droppings.

GENUS *PHANER*
In some of the dry western forests, *Cheirogaleus
medius* shares its habitat with the fork-marked lemur
Phaner furcifer. Although it is found mainly in the
west, the distribution of this lemur is very patchy, and
there are wide gaps between known habitats. There is
also one isolated region in the east on the Masoala
peninsula where this species can be found. It is an
attractive, golden-brown animal, notable for the
adornment on its back, consisting of a deep-brown
stripe which splits on the nape into a stripe above

each eye extending down to the nose. *Phaner* is
usually heard rather than seen, for its call is a loud,
piercing squawk. This is usually difficult to miss
because, commonly, several neighbouring animals
simultaneously strike up a discordant chorus shortly
after emerging from their daytime sleeping quarters.

Phaner has unusual feeding habits for it relies quite
heavily on resinous sap which oozes from the bark of
certain trees. Its adaptations to this specialized diet are
extensive, and involve the teeth, tongue, nails and
digestive system. It will also feed on fruit, nectar,
insects and the sweet secretions from certain kinds of
bugs which often gather on trees in dense clusters to
suck the sap from twigs and branches. Eating gum is
not unusual among mammals; it is a common feature
of certain South American marmosets and is found,
too, in the South African acacia rat *Thallomys
paedulcus*; but *Phaner* is the only lemur known to
feed in this way.

SPECIES *MICROCEBUS (MIRZA)* COQUERELI
Phaner's taste for homopteran honeydew is shared by
another lemur of the western dry forests, Coquerel's
mouse lemur *Microcebus (Mirza) coquereli*. This small
lemur, tipping the scales at $10\frac{1}{2}$ ounces (300 g),
devotes much of its foraging time to lapping up
honeydew, particularly during the long dry season
when little else is on offer. After the arrival of the
rains, the forest bursts into life, enabling the diet to be
expanded to include fruit, flowers, various insects and
possibly even the eggs or nestlings of birds. *M.
coquereli* is a rather rare, seldom-seen animal,
occurring only sparsely in the western forests in a
number of widely scattered localities. Its presence can
sometimes be established by locating its day nests
which are large, spherical constructions made from
twigs, often among a dense mass of lianas, so that
they are hard to spot from the ground.

OTHER SPECIES OF *MICROCEBUS*
The genus *Microcebus* also contains the world's
smallest primates The grey mouse-lemur *Microcebus
murinus* and the very similar rufous mouse-lemur
M. rufus are not much larger than an overweight
mouse, weighing in at a mere $1\frac{1}{2}$-3 ounces (45-90 g).
M. rufus was formerly treated as a subspecies of
M. murinus, but differs sufficiently on ecological and
morphological grounds to be regarded by most
authorities as a separate species. They are the most
abundant lemurs in Madagascar, and the only ones
which are not at the moment threatened with
extinction. They owe this success partly to their
tolerance of habitat modification, and partly to their
small size which enables them to find adequate board
and lodging even in relatively small pockets of forest
isolated by agricultural developments.

The grey mouse-lemur is typical of the western and
southern dry forests, while the rufous mouse-lemur is
found in the damper environment of the eastern
rainforests, where it enjoys a very wide distribution.
Both species feed mainly on fruit and flowers,
although insects are also taken regularly. The day is

The rufous mouse-lemur Microcebus rufus is common in the eastern rainforests, preferring to move around among slim-stemmed lianas and saplings, when its incredible agility and amazing prowess at leaping are very evident. It is strictly nocturnal, feeding mainly on fruit. The rufous mouse-lemur and its close relative, the grey mouse lemur M. murinus, are the world's smallest primates. The latter species inhabits the dry western and southern forests.

spent slumbering in groups in a nest built of leaves although, if a commodious tree hole is readily available, they will cram into that. During the prolonged dry season in its western home, *M. murinus* can enter a torpid state with a reduced body temperature, when it stays in the nest for several days at a time thereby minimizing daily energy requirements.

Mouse-lemurs have very sensitive noses and can detect a ripe fruit from a considerable distance. This acute sense of smell is also useful for keeping in touch with their neighbours, for both sexes mark twigs by urinating into their cupped hands, wiping them on to their feet, and then rubbing the whole lot on to a branch, broadcasting the message even more widely by leaving a trail of smelly footprints when they move off. The home range of a single, well-built male usually overlaps the rather smaller ranges inhabited by several females. A female usually gives birth to twins and, uniquely among lemurs, she may have two litters in a year. Mouse lemurs are extremely agile little animals, able to leap for distances of up to 10 feet (3 m) from one slim branch to another, as if their tiny

bodies are propelled by springs. The eyes glow brightly in the light of a torch, making them very easy to find at night.

GENUS *ALLOCEBUS*

Until 1989 any mention of the hairy eared dwarf lemur *Allocebus trichotis* would have been speculation about its continued existence, for no specimens had been found for many years, and only five skins in all were known in museum collections. Then, in 1989, Bernhard Meier and his co-workers rediscovered this lemur in a remote and inaccessible area of the eastern rainforests inland from Mananara. With a weight of under 3 ounces (80 g) it is, on average, larger only than the two mouse lemurs. Several specimens have now been captured, but nothing is known at present about the ecology of this small lemur.

Family Indriidae

This family contains the largest of living lemurs, the indri. All the indriids are very much at home in the trees, and are supremely accomplished jumpers. Leaps of 16 feet (5 m) or more are well within the abilities of all save the smallest member, the woolly lemur *Avahi laniger*, which is also the only nocturnal representative of the group.

THE AVAHI

Although most text-books refer to this animal as the 'woolly lemur', 'avahi' is such a short and easily

Left: The western avahi Avahi laniger occidentalis *is of a much more limited distribution, being restricted to quite a small area in the north-west of Madagascar. This pair was photographed in a typical daytime pose hidden away among a jumble of branches at the top of a tree in the Ampijeroa Forest Reserve.*

Above: A typical glimpse of a pair of eastern avahis Avahi laniger laniger *hidden away during the day in a dense thicket of vegetation at Périnet. This subspecies is wide-spread in the eastern rainforests.*

remembered name that most visitors to Madagascar use it as a matter of course, so I have used this name here. The avahi is a greyish-brown lemur weighing a little under 2¼ pounds (1 kg). It has a rather moon-faced, goggle-eyed appearance and spends the day clinging to a tree, usually deep among a tangle of twigs and lianas, often in a male-female pair. The eastern humid forests are home to *A. l. laniger*, the eastern avahi, which occurs almost throughout the region, although it is seldom abundant in any one place. The western avahi *A. l. occidentalis* is much rarer, and is restricted to the tropical dry forests of the north-west, from the forest of Ankarafantsika northwards as far as the Bay of Narinda. Within this area the only place where it is likely to be seen is the Ampijeroa Forest Reserve, where sleeping pairs can often be found near the campsite.

Avahis become active soon after dusk and feed mainly on the leaves of a wide variety of plants. At Périnet, leaves from 17 different species of plants have been seen disappearing down the eastern avahi's throat, together with occasional flowers and fruits.

Avahis are monogamous and a pair stays together for life, so there is none of the quarrelsome, rough-and-tumble in-fighting typical of some other lemurs during the brief mating season. The single baby, born in July or August, is rather slow in its development. It

clings to its mother's fur, at first on her belly, but later transferring to her back. Occasionally the father shares in the task of jockeying his offspring, which is slow to be weaned and continues suckling for about six months. Avahis are quite vociferous and often announce their nocturnal presence with twittering whistles exchanged between members of neighbouring groups. There is also a contact call, a soft, short 'tuif' which is often the first clue that an avahi has quietly arrived in a tree next to a forest campsite.

THE SIFAKAS

In contrast to the nocturnal avahi, the sifakas are strictly diurnal. Verreaux's sifaka *Propithecus verreauxi* is a strikingly beautiful animal, especially when the rising sun is shimmering on its dense white fur, enveloping the whole body in a radiant halo. It is split into four subspecies which differ in details of coloration and, to a certain extent, physiology and voice.

P. v. verreauxi, Verreaux's sifaka, is white, with a brown crown and white forehead above the black muzzle. It is found in the south and south-west, from a little to the west of Fort Dauphin, up as far as the Tsiribihina river in the north-west. Within this area, these attractive animals can most easily be seen in the

Above: **Juvenile lemurs are often delightfully inquisitive. This young Verreaux's sifaka** Propithecus verreauxi **came and stared intently at the photographer from arm's length. In this subspecies** P. v. verreauxi **the crown is dark chocolate.**

Right: **When the sifaka mother is feeding, anything goes, and her baby just has to hang on tight.**

private reserve at Berenty. They are also common in the Special Reserve of Beza-Mahafaly, where their fur seems to be particularly glossy and luxuriant. Coquerel's sifaka *P. v. coquereli* is an outstandingly lovely animal, the silky white of its fur continuing right across the top of the head, but replaced on the outer thighs and forearms by bands of rich deep russet, which comes alive and glows lustrously when struck directly by the sun's rays. This is one of the most beautiful of all the lemurs, perhaps surpassed only by *Propithecus diadema diadema* (*see* below). Coquerel's sifaka is confined to an area in the north-west, to the north and east of the Betsiboka river, where its range seems to have decreased alarmingly in recent years, so that it may now be virtually confined to the Ankarafantsika Special Reserve. This reserve is subject to continuing disturbance and destruction, including poaching of Coquerel's sifakas for the pot.

In the pure-white Decken's sifaka *P. v. deckeni* and black-headed *P. v. coronatus,* known as the crowned sifaka, studies of the structure of the skull indicate that these two are more closely related to one another than to the other subspecies. In certain aspects of their anatomy, they appear to be related to *Propithecus diadema* from the eastern rainforests. In fact, *P. v. deckeni* and *P. v. coronatus* may not be distinct subspecies, as their ranges seem to overlap, and one

may prove merely to be a form of the other. For the moment, however, the two subspecies are maintained, with *P. v. deckeni* being found along the west coast, from the region around Antsalova north to the Betsiboka river, while *P. v. coronatus* is found further north, more or less between the ranges of *P. v. deckeni* and *P. v. coquereli.*

The crowned sifaka has the most restricted distribution within the group, and its continued survival must be the cause for some concern although it does occur, together with Decken's sifaka, in the Tsingy de Namoroka Natural Reserve. Unfortunately, the degree of protection within this reserve is not high and, because there is no local *fady* forbidding hunting of lemurs, their future there is not as secure as it should be. The area is remote and human population density very low, however. *P. v. deckeni* also occurs in the vast Tsingy de Bemaraha Natural Reserve which likewise lacks adequate policing, although its sheer size and difficulty of access ensure a fair degree of protection.

P. v. verreauxi is one of the most intensively studied of all lemurs, partly because it is relatively easy to carry out research in Berenty Reserve. It lives in mixed, female-dominated groups of three to eleven animals, although four to six is the most common. There are usually a few bachelor groups composed

*Above left: **A female Verreaux's sifaka stuffs a spray of leaves into her mouth using her dexterous hands. Verreaux's sifakas can deal with chemically protected plants which would make other lemurs severely ill.***

*Above centre: **A Verreaux's sifaka strips the bark from a young sapling using its strong teeth.***

*Above right and right: **Verreaux's sifakas will go to considerable lengths to get their teeth around particularly favoured tender young buds.***

exclusively of males. In a favourable habitat with abundant food supplies, such as the gallery forest at Berenty, population densities may reach over 250 per square mile (100 per sq km) with home ranges of individual groups measuring only about 5.5 acres (2.2 ha). In drier country, where food supplies are scarcer and more scattered, such as in the 'spiny desert', densities are much lower and the territories needed to ensure an adequate living are twice as large as those in gallery forest. The boundaries of the territory are scent marked by females and by males. The males also possess a throat gland used for marking in addition to genital marking.

The diet consists mainly of leaves and fruit, with the regular addition of flowers and the bark of young saplings, which is carefully stripped off with the teeth. The tender buds of certain trees are particularly relished, and the sifakas will go to considerable lengths to get at them, hanging upside-down by their back legs from the swaying tips of slender twigs and looking like furry trapeze artists, as they crane forwards to get their teeth around the delicacy. Certain trees may be virtually defoliated by their daily depredations as they nibble off every bud before the leaf has a chance to break. Sifakas are well able to cope with chemically defended fruits or leaves, and have been seen browsing happily on shrubs of the Solanaceae, a family of plants renowned for their capacity to wage chemical warfare against attackers by booby trapping their leaves with powerful doses of

highly toxic alkaloids. Plants may also resort to this kind of chemical protection for their seeds. In Berenty, ring-tailed lemurs *L. catta* often eat *Nestina* seeds, a singularly profitless exercise because these seeds apparently contain a potent emetic. This rapidly provokes a violent reaction in the ring-tails which vomit up, not only the seeds, but also much of the palatable material eaten earlier. Yet, in the first three months of the year sifakas consume large quantities of the same seeds with apparent impunity, almost to the exclusion all other foods.

The sifaka is well equipped for its herbivorous lifestyle, because it boasts an elongated caecum or lower gut, a perfect mini-habitat for multitudes of symbiotic bacteria which break down the cellulose content of their host's tough, fibrous diet. As in many animals adapted to living in arid conditions, the sifakas' leafy diet provides all the water they need, and they never descend to the ground to drink although, when faced with dire extremes of prolonged drought, they may lick the early morning dew from their fur.

During the cooler winter months, the sifakas' day begins with a pleasurable session of sunbathing in the tops of the trees. They lie back and stretch out their gangly limbs to expose the greatest possible area to the warming rays, like furry washing spread out to

Above and left: **During the over heated period towards midday, Verreaux's sifakas adopt some entertainingly casual postures as they relax and wait for things to cool down a little. When conditions are more comfortable, they will resume feeding.**

Bottom left: **The prelude to resuming activities is usually a quick scratch followed by a session of playful wrestling and head nibbling with the nearest neighbour.**

dry. This habit has led them to be dubbed sun worshippers by the local people. Feeding occupies nearly half the day — typical for a mainly leaf-eating animal — and proceeds steadily until around midday, when a resting period begins which lasts until around 2.00 pm. Sifakas adopt some endearing postures as they relax, often using branches or each other as back rests. The prelude to a full resumption of activities may often be a quick wrestling bout with a neighbour, accompanied by generous amounts of mutual nose rubbing and neck biting. The latter is accomplished with the aid of the 'tooth-comb', the specially modified lower incisors which are found in many lemurs. The areas which receive the most attention are the head, face and back, all difficult-to-reach spots, which can be groomed only by courtesy of a second animal. During the uncomfortably hot, sultry weather which marks the beginning of the wet season, the midday rest period tends to become more and more drawn out. Now these highly arboreal animals seek solace on the ground, gently panting away the sweltering hours with legs and arms embracing the base of a tree. At such times they really appear to suffer in the heat, and it seems strange that an animal inhabiting such a torrid environment should be burdened with such a lavish coat of fur, but the cold nights in midwinter demand a reasonable level of insulation, and the coat thickens at the onset of autumn. At least their fur is white, and is highly reflective and a poor absorber of heat, useful attributes for an animal which spends much of its time feeding in the canopy at the full mercy of the sun.

For most of the year, sifaka groups are noted for

Top: **During the torrid conditions in mid-summer, the sifakas usually take refuge right down on the floor of the shadiest part of the gallery forest. When this mother and baby moved off, they did so by 'dancing' through the forest on the ground, along with the rest of their group, rather than ascending into the sun-baked canopy.**

Above: **On a stiflingly hot December day, this female Verreaux's sifaka and her baby are whiling away the hottest hours clinging comfortably to a tree trunk just a short distance above the ground in the shadiest part of the gallery forest.**

their harmonious relationships. This generally ensures an air of peace and tranquillity, interrupted only by the occasional brief squabble, usually a dispute over which member of the established feeding hierarchy is entitled to have first bite at a particularly favoured bunch of tender leaves. Generally, being assertive and 'pulling rank' pays off for high-ranking members of the hierarchy, and they exploit their status to take over a feeding position already occupied by a lower-ranking animal. Submissive gestures indicating that such aggressive tactics have worked consist of a grimace-like baring of the teeth, accompanied by hunching the back and rolling up the tail between the legs as the aggrieved animal yields its place.

The whole scene changes abruptly at the end of January when the females come into season. This brief event stimulates a short but belligerent outburst of rivalry among the males. They abandon their usual easy going, almost somnolent attitudes to such an extent that they may resort to physical aggression with rivals. This usually matches males suffering a lowly position in the feeding hierarchy against high-ranking animals. The contests are deadly serious affairs with everything to play for, not just the once-a-year access to a female, but also the position in the feeding hierarchy. With so much at stake, it is hardly surprising that the fighting can become so savage, when slashing teeth ensure that blood is often spilled.

After a long gestation period of 150 to 165 days, the female bears a single offspring. This appears in late July or early August although, in some years, it may be possible to spot a tiny, newly born baby cuddled beneath its mother's chest as early as the middle of June. After riding around in this position for about a month, the infant transfers to its mother's back, where it can enjoy a better view of the world and gain experience by watching her feeding activities. The babies are objects of constant attention from other group members, and they persist in attempting to groom them, although the degree of success is always governed by what their mothers will permit. The infant begins to sample its first solid food at about three months, but continues to suckle for a further three months. It seems noticeably reluctant to forsake its secure labour-saving position on its mother's back until, at six or seven months, its added weight makes it hard for the mother to leap safely across broad gaps in the canopy. The investment in time and energy devoted to rearing her single offspring is such that the female sifaka can afford to breed only once every two years. When annual procreation is attempted, the infant mortality during the first year is very high.

Sifakas are accomplished jumpers, catapulted into the air by their powerful back legs, which can propel them with ease across gaps of up to 33 feet (10 m). The landing is generally made in an upright position on all fours, gripping tightly with the large hands and feet. Quite how the sifakas which live in the 'spiny desert' avoid impaling their palms on the thorn-covered trunks as they jump between neighbouring *Alluaudia* trees is something of a mystery. If a gap is too wide to be crossed safely with a mighty leap,

Verreaux's sifaka **Propithecus verreauxi verreauxi** *is a powerful jumper, usually landing in a more-or-less upright position. This subspecies is easily seen in the private reserve at Berenty in the dry south.*

sifakas will not hesitate to descend to the ground and make the crossing on foot. This is accomplished by standing upright on the hind legs and using an awkward-looking gait best described as a dance-hop, when the arms are waved up and down between chest and head height, presumably to assist with balance. They will cover distances of more than 100 yards (100 m) in this fashion across bare open ground, and may not be as reluctant to travel on the ground as some statements have implied, for they move at remarkable speed despite their relatively small stature and unconventional style. During periods

On the ground, Verreaux's sifaka resorts to a peculiar dancing style of locomotion which, despite its apparent awkwardness, covers the ground at remarkable speed.

of exceptionally hot weather, they may prefer to travel in this way even in dense forest where the canopy is continuous. Several times, I have encountered groups of sifakas bouncing along for considerable distances across a carpet of dead leaves in shady gallery forest, presumably because they are reluctant to ascend towards the oppressive heat of the canopy. Any perceived threat on the ground triggers a series of the 'shefackh, shefackh, shefackh' alarm calls which have earned this animal its common name, coined by the local people. When the threat comes from the air, such as the unmistakable outline of a harrier-hawk drifting in easily over the tree tops, the reaction is completely different, and the whole group erupts into a torrent of raucous screams and roars.

Although it still occurs widely in the south and south-west, *P. v. verreauxi* is represented only in three government reserves (Lake Tsimanampetsotsa, Andohahela and Beza-Mahafaly) and two private

Above and right: **With its deep russet arms and thighs, Coquerel's sifaka** Propithecus verreauxi coquereli **is one of the most beautiful of all lemurs. This subspecies has a local distribution in the dry seasonal forests of the north-west; several groups can be easily observed in the Ampijeroa Forest Reserve.**

reserves (Berenty and Analabe). The protection previously afforded by a generalized *fady* forbidding hunting of sifakas is now likely to disappear in many areas as such taboos collapse in the face of modern pressures and improved education.

In the Ampijeroa Forest Reserve south of Mahajanga, several groups of the magnificent but rather rare Coquerel's sifaka are well habituated to human presence and can be observed at very close quarters. One group sleeps in a large mango tree directly over the camp ground, although a tall dead tree also serves the purpose occasionally. One of my abiding memories of *P. v. coquereli* is of a hunched figure seated high up in a crook of this bleached skeletal tree, its back supported against a branch, its hands resting on its knees, exposed and motionless in the beam of light, yet scarcely visible through the curtain of rain streaming down from a thunder-filled sky. The occasional fleeting glimpse of that solitary figure brilliantly illuminated for a split second by a flash of lightning served only to emphasize the degree of its exposure on that wild night. Yet, by morning, the group was feeding as normal, the heat of the day soon dried their saturated fur and, by noon, they were relaxing quietly on the ground as they escaped from the oppressive heat. This particular group seems to

suffer fairly frequent falls for, despite their prowess in jumping, accidents do happen, and a sifaka plummets from a considerable height. It hits the ground with a resounding thud, but seems to be remarkably resilient because, with a surprised expression on its face, it is usually able to shake itself briefly and then shin rapidly back up the nearest tree. This ability to survive a fall without serious injury has also been noted among other species of lemur.

The diadem sifaka *Propithecus diadema* prefers a different kind of habitat, for it inhabits the eastern rainforests. It is a bulkier, long-legged animal weighing 11-20 pounds (5-9 kg). Four subspecies are recognized including *P. diadema diadema*, a spectacularly beautiful lemur (some say the most beautiful of all) with a sooty black face surrounded by a contrasting white ruff, while the rest of the body is an attractive mixture of grey, rich dark brown and orange. The tail is much shorter than in the previous species, and looks quite out of character with the rest of the animal. This subspecies is distributed in the eastern forests from the Mangoro river in the south up as far as Maroansetra, although it is thought not to occur close to the town. It is a pity that this subspecies remains so little known, but a group does occur within a few miles of the reserve at Périnet, and it is hoped that it will eventually recolonize the reserve.

The silky diadem sifaka *P. d. candidus* is a pure white subspecies from the rainforests of the north-east, from somewhere north of Maroansetra up as far as the Marojejy massif, where it occurs within the Marojejy Natural Reserve. It is said to be fairly abundant here

Above: **In Milne-Edward's diadem sifaka** Propithecus **diadema edwardsi** *the overall blackish-brown colour is relieved by a broad pale 'saddle' across the back. This subspecies is fairly easy to observe in the eastern rainforests at Ranomafana.*

Above right: A Milne-Edward's diadem sifaka **Propithecus diadema edwardsi** *munches away on the fruit of a 'sebana' tree, a* **Micronychia** *species (Anacardiaceae) and a favourite food for sifakas as well as red-fronted and red-bellied lemurs.*

Right: **With all the other group members snoozing quietly in their midday siesta, a lone male juvenile is still so full of beans that he plays by himself, hanging like a furry trapeze artist beneath a branch which is providing a seat for one of his elders.**

and not difficult to approach quite closely, although little is yet known of its ecology and behaviour.

P. d. edwardsi, Milne-Edward's diadem sifaka, is mostly blackish brown save for a broad 'saddle' of creamy white across the base of the back and flanks. In some localities the darker shade replaces most of this pale colour. Its exact range today is difficult to assess, but lies to the south of *P. d. diadema* down as far as the Mananara river. This range is now known to overlap that of the subspecies formerly known as *P. diadema holomelas*. This is a dark blackish variant which the British lemur expert, Ian Tattersall, has now concluded, after a considerable amount of detective work involving delving into historic records, is merely part of the natural variation within *P. d. edwardsi*.

The subspecies with the most restricted distribution is the all-black Perrier's diadem sifaka *P. d. perrieri*. A population containing perhaps only 500 animals is restricted to a tiny area in the north-west of the island, almost exclusively in the dry forests of the Analamera Natural Reserve. At present this remote area is visited by few people, although WWF's plans for this reserve may in the future increase the number of visitors able to see this rare animal.

The only subspecies that has been studied at any length is *P. d. edwardsi*. It has been the subject of a long-running research project by teams from Duke University based in the forest at Ranomafana. The group size is four to eight, ranging over a territory of $^1/_3$-$^3/_4$ square mile (1-2 sq km), an area perhaps 15 times larger than that required to support an equivalent-sized group of *P. verreauxi*. Extrapolating from these figures gives us an approximate density of only 10 *P. d. edwardsi* per square mile (4 per sq km), the lowest figure so far recorded for any lemur.

More than half the food consumed consists of leaves, the rest split almost equally between flowers and fruits. A broad selection of leaves seems to be acceptable, not only from trees but also from vines, herbs growing at ground level and epiphytes perched up on branches. In fact, the variety of palatable species is so wide that it aroused the curiosity of the Duke researchers, who queried why certain species of leaves should consistently escape the lemurs' attacks. In an admirable display of endeavour, great efforts were made to collect as many of these as possible, to be dried and sent to laboratories in the United States for chemical analysis. It is hoped to discover whether chemical defences are present in the leaves which could render them toxic, inhibit digestion or just make them plain nasty to taste. In the absence of such substances, it could be that tough texture or irritant hairs might keep the hungry sifakas at bay. As in many other species of lemur, soil is also on the menu and, at special well-known places, the sifakas regularly come down to lick the earth, presumably to obtain salts present only in certain localities.

Even the adults are very playful and regularly descend to the ground for bouts of extremely energetic high jinks, usually in some favourite playground. During these sessions, the participants turn somersaults, leap over one another, play tag and grapple playfully in mock wrestling matches, rolling over and over on the ground and generally behaving like a bunch of carefree youngsters. They will also rush up to a human observer standing close by and look up as if inviting participation in the fun. This frantic activity subsides after a few minutes while the animals take a short breather, relaxing on the ground until the most high-spirited member of the band decides that the time has come time to resume the fun and dives on top of one of its playmates.

Juveniles sometimes make their own amusement when the adults are not in a playful mood, and then a piece of dead grass snatched from the forest floor becomes a toy to be manipulated in the mouth, as the infant rolls over and over among the ferns, or swings beneath a branch, trying to touch an adult's head with its feet. I have felt very privileged to watch these antics at close range, and credit is due to the original researchers who so painstakingly and exhaustingly habituated the animals to trust human observers. The sheer hard work involved soon becomes obvious if you try to follow a rapidly moving group of sifakas as they career effortlessly through the canopy, rapidly swarming up one of the steep slopes typical of Ranomafana. Often, only the amazing fleetness of foot of the local Malagasy guides, as they slip with little apparent effort through the forest's viny tangles, is the only way the researchers can stay in touch with the sifakas, when the group decides to move far and fast. To arrive, leech-bitten, caked in dirt, totally exhausted and desperately short of breath at the top of an appalling slope cruelly littered with snag-ridden tree falls, only to discover that the sifakas have changed their minds and headed straight back down again, does tend to make you question the parentage of the lemurs and the wisdom of studying them.

If this account of sifakas had been written before 1974, this would be the end of the description of the different species. In that year, however, Dr Ian Tattersall reported the discovery of a lemur which he tentatively assigned to *P. diadema candidus*, but which he also acknowledged could be distinct, because of its very noticeable ears which project prominently from the head. The two species of sifakas recognized at that time had much smaller ears. An orange patch on the crown also set the new discovery apart from all other known varieties of *P. verreauxi* and *P. diadema*.

These puzzling animals lived in an area of forest near Daraina, about 19 miles (30 km) to the north-west of Vohemar, well north in Madagascar and lying outside the previously known range of *P. d. candidus*. In 1986, the news that this area of forest was scheduled for clear-cutting for the manufacture of charcoal came as something of a bombshell. Duke University quickly obtained permission to capture a few of these enigmatic creatures to form a breeding nucleus at their Primate Center in the United States, noted for its success in keeping and breeding lemurs in captivity. The subsequent capture of several animals led immediately to the realization that here was something noticeably different from *P. diadema candidus*.

The captured specimens were much smaller, even smaller than the average for *P. verreauxi* which itself is considerably smaller than *P. d. diadema*. The white fur was short and rather sparse, in marked contrast to the luxuriant silky pelage sported by *P. d. candidus*. The large, projecting, pixie-like ears were furnished with a complete covering of fur which extended well beyond the tips in long wispy tufts. This was quite different from the rather sparse covering on the ears of the other sifakas. Even after only a brief on-the-spot study, it seemed likely that here was a momentous discovery, nothing less than a completely new species of lemur, a conclusion which was confirmed by subsequent analysis of voice and genes. The new species was eventually named *Propithecus tattersalli* in honour of its discoverer.

It is one of the rarest of the lemurs, inhabiting an

area only about 15 miles (25 km) in diameter. Within this area, the forests are fragmented into patches surrounded by agriculture and degraded vegetation, thus isolating one population from another and preventing genetic interchange. Luckily, a local *fady* inhibits hunting of sifakas and, during 1990, researchers from Duke University newly arrived to study this striking and beautiful new species, found the task of habituating the animals fairly straightforward, because of the lack of persecution. Yet the forests of this region continue their retreat before the human onslaught, and there is a desperate need for some kind of conservation plan which will ensure the continued survival of this species in the wild. It would be tragic, indeed, if such an attractive and interesting animal were to become extinct within as little as a mere decade or two of its discovery.

THE INDRI

We must hope that such a fate will not eventually befall the largest of the Indriidae, the indri itself *Indri indri*, which exists at very low population densities over a wide but threatened area of the eastern rainforests. The common comparison of the indri to a black-and-white teddybear is apt, although the white is heavily tinged with grey. Fortunately, large numbers of visitors to Madagascar are able to enjoy close views of these magnificent animals in the reserve at Périnet which, in recent years, has enjoyed a boom in

popularity such that it is now included on the itineraries of most tours to the island. A visitor is now virtually guaranteed to see an indri within a few minutes of arriving in the forest. Such predictability and convenience are far cries from the days in the early 1950s when David (now Sir David) Attenborough had to roam the forest for several tiring days merely to catch a glimpse of an indri, before the creature (which in those days was considered to be almost mythical and treated with awe and reverence) was eventually filmed successfully. Now, as then at Périnet, indris are often heard before they are seen, when their eerie morning chorus trumpets through the forest, surely one of the most exciting and neck-tingling sounds in nature, perhaps rivalled only by the resounding roar of a male howler monkey or the howling of gibbons.

The purpose of this loud calling is to space out the groups within well-defined territories in the forest. This long-distance way of signalling territorial ownership is well suited to an animal which has a rather slow metabolism, and often does not move very far in a day, thus reducing the opportunities for regular scent marking throughout the territory. Anyone standing directly beneath four or five indris intent on 'giving it all they've got' will be almost painfully aware of why the calls are able to carry across the deadening canopy of the forest for a distance of close to 2 miles (3 km). This explains why faint, yet distinct, replies can be heard from groups far off in the forest, not just from the immediate neighbours. The call is amplified by the membranous throat sac and is started suddenly by one member of the group. It is then taken up quickly by the rest, so that each animal has its own part in the weird descending cadence of the song. It is amusing to watch the local Malagasy children playing at being indris, fluently mimicking this unearthly song,

Left: **Even indri babies are playful. This boisterous infant scrambles around over his parents while they are doing their best to have a short siesta.**

Below: **Indris do not have a prolonged rest period during the middle of the day but instead take several shorter breaks.**

Above and right: **The indri** Indri indri *is the largest of the lemurs and the most lethargic. This mother and baby are part of the habituated group admired by thousands of tourists every year in the reserve at Périnet.*

which is obviously the most enjoyable part of the game.

The indri lives in family groups of two to five individuals and is perhaps the most strictly diurnal and arboreal of all lemurs. It stirs into activity later than any other day-active species and, even then, the prelude to getting under way on the day's foraging is an extended session of sunbathing, a necessity rather than a luxury, designed to recharge the indri's slightly sluggish metabolism. When they do finally get going, they show that they are no sluggards when it comes to jumping, easily managing several consecutive leaps of 16 feet (5 m) or more in a burst of trunk-thudding action. Indris always land on all fours, usually hugging the trunk rather than landing among flexible branch tips which might not bear their weight.

They feed mainly on leaves, often spending a considerable time on a single branch, carefully picking over a bunch of foliage and selecting the most tender morsels. The group is led by a female, and she normally has first right of access to all the most favoured food sources; these include flowers and fruits in addition to leaves. Indris are not fussy feeders and utilize at least 70 different species of plants. A male eating peacefully may be displaced by the female group leader if she notices that he is obviously enjoying his meal and has found a particularly rewarding tree. She rarely needs to assert her authority in an aggressive way to supplant him, for he normally accepts his place in life and gives way gracefully, although the stylized submissive gestures characteristic of *P. verreauxi* seem to be absent in the indri. Feeding is a slow and methodical process, and an indri family may cover only 550 yards (500 m) or so in a day's wanderings. There is no prolonged midday rest period; instead, several brief breaks are taken at regular intervals throughout the short active day. This tranquil existence is disturbed briefly during January

and February when mating takes place although, even then, the drama which occurs among other lemurs is wanting.

The single offspring is born in May or June, at first clinging tightly beneath its mother's belly, but taking up a position on her back after four or five months. Even indri babies are playful and, while the rest of the group is trying to enjoy a short siesta, a frisky youngster may clamber boisterously over the glassy eyed adults in an effort to get them involved in a game of acrobatics or tag. Such an effervescent desire for physical contact seems to wither as the babies mature, and mutual grooming between the adults seems to rate low in their priorities. When it does occur, it is in short bouts and only areas which cannot be reached, such as the head, are groomed. Scent seems also to be unimportant to an indri so that marking, although regular, is much less intense than it is among other lemurs.

Whether the indris' dramatic duets will continue to resound through the canopy for much longer is in doubt because their rainforest home continues to be destroyed. In some areas, hunting is still prohibited by local *fady* because of the indri's traditional role in human ancestry but, as traditions collapse under the influence of western ideas, such protection may not have long to last. A much larger rainforest reserve, capable of housing a much larger genetically viable population of these impressive animals, must be established.

Family Daubentoniidae

The aye-aye *Daubentonia madagascariensis* is the sole member of this family, established on the basis of characteristics which are so unusual that, for 100 years, scientists could not agree whether the aye-aye was even a lemur. This is no longer in doubt, but no-one would dispute that it is very unusual. About the size of a domestic cat, the aye-aye is densely covered in a coat of black fur, through which projects a fuzz of much longer, curved, white-tipped guard hairs that gives the aye-aye a shaggy, grizzled appearance. The tail is thick and bushy similar to that of a squirrel. The hands and face of the aye-aye are quite characteristic inspiring curiosity among scientists and fear in the local people. The head looks too big for the body, much larger relatively than in any other lemur. The huge, highly mobile ears are like those of a bat, their inner surfaces shiny black as if lacquered. The eyes are set wide apart above an almost dog-like muzzle, and the front teeth, which continue to grow throughout life as a rodent's do, are prominent and set in powerful jaws capable of cracking hard nuts and ripping chunks of bark from trees. The fingers are thin and bony but the long third finger is almost skeletal and plays a key role in the aye-aye's lifestyle.

The swivel-mounted, bat-like ears are highly sensitive, capable of picking up the faint sounds of beetle larvae chewing away in their galleries inside a woody liana or rotten log. To assist in its quest for wood-boring insects, the aye-aye beats a rapid tattoo against the bark with its third finger as it moves slowly up a trunk. No one knows for sure the purpose of this. It may stimulate hidden insect larvae to move around thereby making sounds which would betray their presence. Or perhaps the aye-aye's finger-tapping performance detects the hollow sound of insect galleries within the tree. When the aye-aye hears something interesting, it sets to work with its chisel-like teeth, vigorously tearing away the bark and upper layers of wood, which rain down to the ground in a hail of debris. One of the best ways of locating aye-ayes in a forest is to listen for the patter of falling detritus. With its quarry finally exposed, the aye-aye carefully inserts its skeletal third finger into the hole and skewers the prey on its pointed tip. Withdrawing the impaled prey with a delicate precision, it offers up the prize, kebab-style, to its waiting mouth. An aye-aye will gradually work its way methodically up a promising stem, particularly the thick woody trunks of certain lianas, biting out holes at regular intervals. It will also descend to the ground to chew open rotten logs inhabited by the huge, fat, juicy grubs of wood-boring scarab (Scarabaeidae) or longhorn (Cerambycidae) beetles.

Exposing and spearing wood-boring insect larvae are not the only specialized applications for the aye-aye's strong teeth and peculiar finger. It is also partial to coconuts, ramy nuts and *Terminalia* nuts. When it feeds on ramy nuts, the aye-aye is faced with the problem of extracting the contents from within a very hard shell which lacks an easily separable joint. The ramy presents additional problems because it is divided internally into three separate chambers so that the kernel can not be extracted easily through a single hole chewed through the outer casing. The aye-aye's solution is to use its chisel-like teeth to pare away an entrance hole large enough to allow the slender third finger to probe inside and winkle out pieces of the kernel with a rapid flicking action. At certain times of the year, aye-ayes seem to devote much of their time to eating these nuts, and heaps of discarded shells showing the characteristic signs of aye-aye damage can be found beneath the trees. The depth of these piles has been used as evidence for suggesting that nuts form the bulk of the diet, making the aye-aye the Madagascan equivalent of the absent squirrels. This theory contradicts the more usual idea that the aye-aye fills the role of a woodpecker. Woodpeckers are also absent from Madagascar although two birds, the sickle-bill vanga *Falculea palliata* and the coral-billed nuthatch vanga *Hypositta corallirostris*, are both specialized feeders on wood-boring larvae so that, effectively, they occupy the woodpeckers' niche in Madagascar. The aye-aye probably fails to fit either of these two role models neatly, however, and why should it? It is a complex animal able to take advantage of a variety of difficult-to-get-at food resources. In other countries, each of these can be exploited only by one type of animal which has been forced to become a specialist by the kind of extreme competition that does not exist in Madagascar. Indeed, yet another type of resource is regularly exploited by the aye-aye which, at certain seasons, devotes much of its time to some woody excrescences which often erupt prolifically from the bark of *Eugenia* trees. These large, gall-like pustules take two forms: either star-shaped and flattened; or more radish-like and knobbly. While many of these are left untouched, others, which are superficially identical, seem to be extremely attractive to the aye-ayes, and they may spend many hours each night busily gnawing away at them. Over many months, the original swollen tissues are often completely erased leaving shallow indentations in the trunk bearing the score marks made by frequent gouging of aye-aye teeth. These indentations are filled with a yellowish, slightly smelly, spongy tissue which appears to be wood modified by the action of a fungus or bacterium. Superficially, these galls are like those of the American blight aphid *Eriosoma lanigerum* on apple. But repeated searches have failed to turn up any similar kind of aphids, or indeed any other insects. It seems probable, therefore, that fungi or bacteria are the cause. Even when gleaning such unlikely sustenance, the aye-aye's unusual anatomical accessories come into play, for the third finger is used to scoop out a quantity of the

Strange gall-like formations on the trunks of many **Eugenia** *trees provide a great attraction for aye-ayes. By dipping her almost skeletal third finger into the odorous spongy substance uncovered by her gnawings, this female can extract enough to be worth sucking off, like a child with a sherbet-dip.*

spongy tissue which is then sucked from the finger tip.

Generally, an aye-aye leads a solitary life, spending the night alone in a large twig nest wedged high up in a tree, usually one of the tallest in the forest. Several nests are scattered around within each territory and utilized in an irregular rotation, so that one nest may be used for several nights running and then not visited again for a few days. The occupant emerges shortly after dark and devotes the first few minutes to a thorough wash and brush-up, suspended by its feet as it completes a meticulous toilet, before it is ready to set off through the canopy in its search for food. Chance meetings between neighbours are not noted for their amicability, and a male stumbling across a female outside the breeding season will probably react by chasing her out of his favourite feeding tree. But, at certain seasons, relations become much more sociable, the barriers break down and several animals may share amiably the comfort of a single nest.

For many years, especially during the 1960s and 1970s, it was believed that the aye-aye was the rarest of all the lemurs and in imminent danger of extinction. Fortunately, it is becoming increasingly obvious that this is not the case. With their very restricted distributions and small populations, *Hapalemur simus* and *Hapalemur aureus* are undoubtedly far rarer and more endangered than the aye-aye. It has been discovered in so many new localities in recent years that it now appears that it may be one of the most widespread lemurs of all. Unlike many of the others, it occurs not only in the eastern rainforests but also in the western deciduous forests, such as in Ankarana Special Reserve. Its existence over such a wide area does not imply that it must be common for it is probably absent from many areas which look suitable. And, when it is present, population densities may be very low although aye-ayes are notoriously difficult to locate at night even when they are known to be in the area. It is certainly able to increase its populations quite well when living in undisturbed forest, such as on the island reserve of Nosy Mangabe, where nine individuals were released in 1966 in a last-ditch effort (as thought at the time) to provide a secure home and stave off extinction on the mainland. These nine seem to have prospered to the extent that aye-ayes now appear to be relatively abundant on Nosy Mangabe.

Near Mananara, the aye-aye is considered a nuisance because it enters gardens and plantations to feed on coconuts, apparently regarding their flesh as a delicacy. As animals caught in the act of poaching coconuts are usually killed by the irate owner of the trees, urgent measures are needed to solve this problem. The unfortunate aye-aye is also killed by villagers who regard this bizarre and outlandish-looking animal as a harbinger of evil. Even so, the future for the species looks brighter than it did a few years ago, and only the final destruction of the last stands of natural forest will bring it to extinction. But such an unhappy event would, of course, also destroy all the other lemurs as well, save for any breeding colonies established in captivity. Let us hope that it never happens.

Chapter 8

The National Parks and Nature Reserves

Although nature conservation has a long history in Madagascar, it is only recently that sufficient funds have started to become available to enable at least some of the thirty or so reserves (1.8 per cent of the island) to enjoy protection in practice, rather than just on paper. The World Wide Fund for Nature (WWF) has now had an office in Antananarivo for several years, and has plans for increasing the degree of on-the-ground protection in several reserves, for opening up specified reserves to controlled tourism, and for establishing new ones. WWF also runs a major programme of education designed to inform the Malagasy people about the wealth of plant and animal life which can be found only in their land. Other conservation and academic organizations are involved in similar projects, allied to rural development schemes, bringing renewed hope for the long-term conservation of many of the island's most important habitats and their wildlife.

National Parks

There are only two reserves in this category; they were established to protect areas of outstanding biological and scenic interest which can be visited and enjoyed by the general public.

ISALO NATIONAL PARK

Location This mountain park lies astride the main road RN7 from Fianarantsoa to Tulear, between Ihosy and Sakaraha. The small town of Ranohira lies just to the north-east of the escarpment. The altitude varies between 1686 feet (514 m) and 4160 feet (1268 m) and winter nights can be cold but not frosty.

Topography The park covers an area of 201,403 acres (81,540 ha) comprising the entire stretch of the Isalo massif. The sandstone rocks have been subjected to eons of erosion, giving rise to a spectacular landscape reminiscent of parts of the south-western United States. The area is dissected by numerous, rather narrow canyons, many with crystal-clear, fast-flowing streams so that, even in the height of the dry season, there is fresh water in the park, although some watercourses are only seasonal. For much of the year the climate is dry, and from June to August the sky is usually cloudless. The rains arrive in October and last until March, with November and December the wettest months. The total average annual rainfall is 33 inches (850 mm). Winter days are pleasantly warm; summer can be hot, although the absolute maximum (in February) is not more than 94.5 °F (34.7 °C).

Vegetation Fire and grazing have severely degraded the natural plant cover which is given little chance to recover because, despite official protection, illegally set bush fires still ravage parts of the park every year. A low-canopied, deciduous woodland covers about one-fifth of the area although, in many places, an open woodland of the small, fire-resistant tree *Uapaca bojeri* is the only relief from bare rock and sparse grassland. The rivers are marked by lines of brilliant green, generally made up of numerous *Pandanus pulcher* and the delicate, slim-stemmed, feathery leaved palm *Chrysalidocarpus isaloensis*. The shady banks of these rivers are thick with dense, pale-green stands of *Pteris* and *Sticheris* ferns. An attractive pool surrounded by such vegetation can be seen at la piscine naturelle. Succulent enthusiasts come to see the endemic elephant's foot *Pachypodium rosulatum* var. *gracilius*, its bulbous grey stems adorning cliffs and rocky outcrops in large numbers throughout the massif, the main stronghold. Fortunately, the flames cannot reach most of these fascinating plants in their rock-girt habitat. The large yellow flowers start to appear in early July. The local guides call them 'petits baobabs' but the genuine baobabs are much larger and in a different family. The beautiful *Aloe contigua*, with its striking terracotta rosettes often grows near the pachypodiums. *Aloe isaloensis* is endemic to this massif but, with its narrow leaves, is far less attractive. *Euphorbia duvani* is another interesting small succulent.

Fauna Animal life is not prominent. Most of the 55 species of birds are found along the watercourses, although the rocky outcrops spattered with colourful mosaics of orange and lime-green lichens are the favourite haunt of Benson's rockthrush *Monticola bensoni*, a rare endemic of this massif. It is very tame and will usually allow a close approach. Mammals include three species of lemur, of which the ring-tailed *Lemur catta* is the most likely to be seen. There are also sifakas *Propithecus v. verreauxi* and brown lemurs *Lemur fulvus*. Lizards and snakes are surprisingly rare. Poaching is a constant problem. Young men from nearby Ranohira scour the park daily for small birds which are killed with catapults. Lemurs and fruit bats are also taken for the pot.

Visiting Visitors should first obtain a permit in Antananarivo. This should be handed in at the local office of *Eaux et Fôrets* in Ranohira, the base for visiting the park. The *chef* will offer you a guide who

Even in the dry rock-scape of the Isalo mountains, there are permanent water courses where the damp margins provide the habitat for plants such as the pandan palm **Pandanus pulcher.**

will speak little or no English or French. You may prefer to enlist freelance guides who can be contacted (if they don't contact you first) at the small hotel in town. The freelancers not only speak good French, they also know the park and its wildlife better than the 'official' people.

A typical day-long outing starts by crossing the cultivated area between the town and the escarpment (about 1 hour). You then climb up a defile on to a rocky plateau with scattered trees, ending up at a beautiful natural pool (*la piscine naturelle*) in one of the canyons. Other trips may yield lemurs in denser woodland, while a three-day camping expedition can be made to the *grotte des Portugais*. Porters and cooks can be hired for this via the freelance guides, if required. This trip is possible in a day with a four-wheel drive vehicle in the dry season (the time to visit).

The number of visitors seems to be increasing rapidly. In 1985 the total was 82, dropping to 67 in 1986. During just four days in late June 1990, I noted more than 30 people visiting the park, a dozen of whom made the three-day camping trip to the caves. The small hotel was full for several days and a local

sparse and you may have to wait 24 hours for a ride out in a truck or pickup (forget taxi-brousses). Isalo is not, therefore, for those on a tight schedule using public transport, nor for lemur enthusiasts.

MONTAGNE D'AMBRE NATIONAL PARK

Location Approximately 15 miles (24 km) from Diégo Suarez in the far north. The road is tarred and in generally good condition as far as Joffreville, just over 4 miles (7 km) from the park entrance. The altitude is 2789-4836 feet (850-1474 m).

Topography The park has a surface area of 44,954 acres (18,200 ha) covering a volcanic massif composed mainly of basaltic rocks. Numerous rivers arise here and flow out in different directions, so the park is a vital water catchment area for the nearby town of Diégo Suarez. There are several attractive crater lakes and some spectacular waterfalls. The area directly around Diégo Suarez is warm and tropical, but distinctly dry, with only sparse forests and numerous succulent plants adapted to withstand the hot dry months from May to September. The total annual rainfall here is only 39 inches (1000 mm) yet, in the nearby park, this leaps to 141 inches (3585 mm) giving a humid climate similar to that of the eastern

restaurant had to take the overflow. The hotel itself provides excellent meals, although cheap food can also be obtained in a nearby restaurant, which is the main truck stop for many vehicles on the RN7 route. This is important, because arriving in Ranohira is a lot easier than leaving, unless you have your own vehicle or are part of an organized tour. North-south traffic is

The eroded sandstones of the Isalo mountains in the Isalo National Park provide some of the most breathtaking scenery in Madagascar. Mammals are relatively scarce but the endemic bird, Benson's rockthrush Monticola bensoni, is confined to this desolate area, which is also the home of several rare succulents, such as Pachypodium rosulatum gracilius, Aloe contigua and the endemic A. isaloensis. The picture was taken in the dry season in mid-June.

rainforests. Rainfall in the park is more or less spread throughout the year, although the period from June to September is noticeably drier. A strong, gusty wind, the *Varatraza*, often batters the forest during the winter months, when the nights can be unpleasantly cold.

Vegetation Much of the park is covered with upland tropical moist forest, with numerous giant trees up to 130 feet (40 m) high festooned with lianas and large clumps of the bird's-nest fern *Asplenium nidus*, as well as other smaller ferns and several species of orchid. Tree-ferns (*Cyathea* spp) are abundant in some areas, together with many small kinds of palms (*Neodypsis* spp and *Chrysalidocarpus* spp). As in most rainforests, the ground flora is scarce and unspectacular. In a number of places, there are plantations of alien conifers and *Eucalyptus*, while around the Station Forestière des Rousettes there are large stands of alien trees including pines, *Eucalyptus* and huge stately *Araucaria*. The broad, vehicle-width tracks are bordered in many places by dense, pungent-smelling stands of the very invasive alien bush *Lantana camara*.

Fauna The park has a notably rich and varied fauna, much of which is also found in the eastern rainforests, but with the addition of many local endemics found only in the north-west. These include the two animals which most visitors come to see, the crowned lemur *Lemur coronatus* and Sanford's lemur *L. fulvus sanfordi* both of which are quite abundant in the park. There is also a degree of local endemism at the subspecific level; for example, the ring-tailed mongoose *Galidia elegans dambrensis* and the forest rockthrush *Monticola sharpei erythronotus*, a confiding grey and russet bird easily seen along the forest paths. With a total of 73 species, this is a good area for birdwatching. The large, impressive crested wood ibis *Lophotibis cristata*, though common and easy to find, is rather wary.

The reptile fauna is impressive, and the endemics include the bark-living gecko *Homopholis boivini*, the dead-leaf gecko *Uroplatus alluaudi* and the small *Brookesia tuberculata*, stump-tailed chameleon. Larger chameleons are not abundant in the park (but *Chamaeleo pardalis* is common on the roadsides in nearby Joffreville, preferring disturbed habitats) although the small *Chamaeleo boettgeri* is relatively common and worth finding just for the male's protruding blue 'nose'. The snakes *Sanzinia madagascariensis* and *Leioheterodon madagascariensis* are often seen basking beside the trails.

Insect life is particularly rich, with many gaudy beetles and bugs; this is also one of the best places in Madagascar to see butterflies.

Visiting The reserve is within easy reach of a day trip from Diégo Suarez. Renault 4 taxis can be hired either directly from the driver (just negotiate the rate) or from the Madagascar Airtours office in town,

Alternatively, take one of the regular (but unpredictably timed) taxi-brousses which ply to and from Joffreville. These are incredibly crowded and overloaded, so be prepared for a cramped but very cheap trip. You will be dropped in Joffreville whence a dirt road runs 3¾ miles (6 km) to the park entrance, slightly uphill all the way but pleasant-enough walking. Look out for chameleons on the roadsides. There are plenty of endemic Madagascar wagtails *Motacilla flaviventris* as well. Joffreville has a very basic but bearable hotel (under improvement in 1990) which also serves adequate meals upon request. There are also two stores in town selling canned meat and fish as well as chocolate, biscuits, toilet rolls and candles etc. Bread must be ordered in advance. There are plenty of rivers in the park, so no problems with water, but play safe and use purifying tablets.

Permits must be obtained from *Eaux et Fôrets* in Tana or in the local office in Diégo Suarez. In 1990 only scientists with specific research projects were allowed to use the brick-built cabin within the park. The local WWF office has plans to open up the area to controlled tourism, however, and intends to establish camp grounds within the park. Improvements to the trail system are also under way, making good extensive damage done by the 1982 cyclone. Additional guides are also being trained, although there are already one or two local guides who can be hired in Diégo Suarez. If you are in need of extra information, contact the WWF office just up the road from Air Madagascar.

Montagne d'Ambre is not one of the better parks in which to see lemurs. Both the crowned and Sanford's lemurs have been poached for the pot and the pet trade, and are rather wary as a result. WWF's increasing involvement in managing the park should eventually improve matters. Some unlucky visitors spend a day wandering the trails without seeing a single lemur. On other days you might see six different groups within an hour, and get within 15 feet or so (4-5 m) of certain animals. Most people follow the broad trail to *la grande cascade*, a superb waterfall poised at the head of a gorge in primary forest. It is worth the walk just to see the falls, but this is also a good spot to see crowned lemurs and lots of butterflies, including several kinds of large swallowtails and the superb Madagascar diadem *Hypolimnas dexithea*. A smaller trail signposted '*jardin botanique*' goes up through lush forest and comes out on the main trail near the park headquarters. Past the buildings, there is a signpost to *la petite cascade*, a smaller, but breathtakingly beautiful waterfall spilling into a dark brooding pool surrounded by fern-covered cliffs — a superb spot and utterly tropical in its atmosphere. Beware when it rains — leeches are a problem — smear ankles and calves with insect repellent.

Special Reserves

There are 23 special reserves, created to conserve specific ecosystems or particular endangered species of plants and animals. Entry to the majority of these is

The large white flowers of **Pachypodium decaryi** *appear in June. This strange plant grows mainly on the open 'tsingy' limestones of the north-west, as here in the Ankarana Special Reserve.*

possible only by obtaining a special research permit. Several reserves are open to the public, however, upon obtaining the necessary permit from *Eaux et Fôrets*. These reserves are as follows:

ANALAMERA SPECIAL RESERVE
Location To the east of the Diégo Suarez-Ambilobe road, west of Anivorano, off the Sadjoavato-Irodo road.

Topography A limestone plateau bordered on several sides by steep cliffs and containing a number of small northward-flowing rivers. The annual rainfall is 49 inches (1250 mm), with April the wettest month.

Vegetation A mixture of western dry forest and humid eastern-type rainforest.

Fauna The focus of interest is the black sifaka *Propithecus diadema perrieri* which occurs only on this plateau, where it probably numbers fewer than 2000 individuals. Most of the other mammals and birds are much the same as in nearby Ankarana, although there are exciting additions, such as the discovery in 1987 of the rare Van Dam's vanga *Xenopirostris damii*, formerly known only from Ankarafantsika. Analamera is little known, however, and other treasures could well be awaiting discovery.

Visiting Access is difficult and almost impossible during the wet season (November-May) when the road from Sadjoavato to Irodo is impassable. Guides are available in the villages of Menagisy and Irodo. Anyone contemplating a visit should obtain their permits in Diégo Suarez, after first discussing their proposed visit at the WWF office. WWF has plans to improve access to the reserve and provide marked campsites and trails, so that people can more easily visit this remote area. These improvements should have been completed by the end of 1992.

ANKARANA SPECIAL RESERVE

Location The reserve lies 40 miles (65 km) south of Diégo Suarez to the south-west of Anivorano.

Topography The area consists of 45,016 acres (18,225 ha) covering a massif of Jurassic limestone rising abruptly from a surrounding savanna-like plain. The massif is spectacularly eroded into a chaos of karst pinnacles known locally as *tsingy* (said to resemble the sound made by striking the rocks). The limestone plateau is pierced in several places by forest-filled canyons. Below the ground run extensive cave systems with accompanying fast-flowing rivers. The grotte d'Andrafiabe is nearly 7 miles (11 km) long and, to date, more than 62 miles (100 km) of passages have been explored. The climate is markedly seasonal, with November-April wet and May-October dry. The mean annual temperature is 80 °F (26.7° C); even in June the nights are pleasantly warm — far warmer than in nearby Montagne d'Ambre.

Vegetation. Typical western dry deciduous forest occurs on the perimeter of the massif and penetrates up the canyons, especially well developed in the Grand Canyon. Although illegal logging has depleted many of the larger trees, there is still a canopy at 65-80 feet (20-25 m). Dominant canopy trees include *Dalbergia* spp and *Cassia* spp (both Leguminosae), various figs *Ficus* spp (Moraceae), and superb specimens of the baobab *Adansonia madagascariensis* (Bombacaceae). The shrub layer includes numerous palms. Epiphytes are few but include many specimens of a vanilla orchid with its leafless, rope-like, green stems clinging to the tree trunks; most puzzling until they produce their typical orchid flowers.

The tsingy harbours a fascinating assemblage of drought-adapted succulent plants. These include *Pachypodium decaryi*, which produces its large white flowers in June; the obese, grey, rock-like *Adenia neohumbertii*; four highly succulent species of

Euphorbia including *E. ankarensis* (flowering in June) and *E. pachypodioides*. Visitors should note that even seedlings of these plants are **not** to be dug up, and they are liable to be searched if suspected of illegal collecting activities — with dire results if caught.

Fauna Ankarana is renowned for its riches, with many endemic species finding their sole known refuge within the reserve. This is the best place to see the rare crowned lemur *Lemur coronatus* and Sanford's lemur *Lemur fulvus sanfordi*. Both species are abundant, particularly in the forests of the Grand Canyon, and are much more approachable than in Montagne d'Ambre. After dark the forest resounds to the calls of *Lepilemur mustelinus* which is present at high densities. There are also avahis *Avahi laniger*, mouse-lemurs *Microcebus murinus*, fork-marked lemurs *Phaner furcifer*, fat-tailed dwarf lemurs *Cheirogaleus medius* and the aye-aye *Daubentonia madagascariensis*. The beautiful form, *G. e. dambrensis*, of the ring-tailed mongoose *Galidia elegans* is common and very tame. One family group calls regularly on campers·staying at the *campement des Anglais* in the Grand Canyon. They are so fearless that they make a nuisance of themselves, raiding the camp for unattended food. Their tameness also tempts people to feed them by hand, something which should not be done because they may carry rabies. Ankarana is also one of the best places in Madagascar for seeing a fossa *Cryptoprocta ferox*. The tenrecs *Tenrec ecaudatus* and *Setifer setosus* are often seen after nightfall.

Bird life is rich and varied, with 85 species recorded, including the local banded kestrel *Falco zoniventris*, the nationally rare white-breasted mesite *Mesitornis variegata* (described as 'common' in some areas of the reserve), and the Madagascar fish-eagle *Haliaeetus vociferoides*. The crested wood ibis *Lophotibis cristata* is common and often occurs in flocks of ten or more. The Madagascar paradise flycatcher *Terpsiphone mutata* is constantly seen or heard, while the crested coua *Coua cristata* utters its raucous call from the tree tops. The beautiful orange-and-white forest kingfisher *Ipsidina madagascariensis* is tame and often visits the campsites.

The reptiles are also of great interest, with more than 36 species recorded so far. These include two geckoes: *Paroedura rarus*, a rare species confined to the north-east and seldom encountered, although it is common enough at Ankarana; and *P. bastardi* which has its sole northern locality at Ankarana. The local form of the widespread day-gecko *Phelsuma madagascariensis* is particularly large and beautiful. These brilliant emerald-and-orange lizards can often be seen sitting conspicuously on the tree trunks in the Grand Canyon. Two widely distributed chameleons *Chamaeleo oustaleti* and *C. pardalis* are present, but a

Although widespread throughout the island, the large day-gecko Phelsuma madagascariensis *presents a far more gaudy spectacle in some areas than in others. This is the most spectacular form of all, from the dry forests in Ankarana Special Reserve.*

The subspecies G. e. dambrensis *of the ring-tailed mongoose* Galidia elegans *is restricted to an area around Diégo Suarez in the north of the island. This beautiful animal, with its light russet fur, is particularly easy to see in the Ankarana Special Reserve.*

third species *C. petteri* is endemic to the massif. The stump-tailed chameleon *Brookesia stumpffi* occurs in the shadier spots. The caves are home to a fascinating fauna including the Nile crocodile and several rare freshwater shrimps, as well as nine species of bats.

Visiting Ankarana is not easy to reach but is such an extraordinary place that it is worth making the effort. It is administered from the WWF office in Diégo Suarez, and anyone contemplating a visit should first go there to discuss their plans. A guide is absolutely essential. Ankarana is a dangerous place in which to get lost because surface water is extremely scarce. The best time to visit is during the dry season from June until October. These are more or less the only months when even a four-wheel drive vehicle can negotiate the poor dirt road from Anivorano to Matsaborimanga. During the wet season, zebu carts are the only available method of transport. The reserve can still be reached during the rainy season, but only by hiking up one of the canyons for 7½ miles (12 km) from the Anivorana-Ambilobe road. Take all the food you will need, plus a tent. When camping, beware of scorpions

which creep under the groundsheets during the day; they sting when you kneel on them. Buy a raffia mat from the market in Diégo Suarez to prevent this.

If wildlife is your main interest the best campsite is the *campement des Anglais*. This is in the Grand Canyon, so handy for lots of wildlife, including very tame crowned lemurs which hang around hoping for banana handouts; also present are the ring-tailed mongooses mentioned earlier.

The only water supply is deep in a cave, so you will need a large jerrycan and a guide to show you the place. He will also take you to the most spectacular spot on the massif, the serene jade-green Lac Vert, superbly set among forest and a spectacular area of razor-edged tsingy. It is a long walk, but there is a stream half way where you can bathe and drink (take water-purifying tablets!). You can also climb on to the tsingy nearer the camp, but it is a difficult scramble. Caving enthusiasts should enter the park from further south at Andrafiabe.

In 1990, the WWF made plans to improve access and facilities at Ankarana. Local guides are being trained and proper campsites established, eventually with some kind of toilets and hopefully with improved access to water. They also plan to produce a map showing the trail system, which will be improved and marked. The road from Anivorano will also receive attention.

BEZA-MAHAFALY SPECIAL RESERVE

Location About 22 miles (35 km) north-east of Betioky-Sud, just west of the Sakamena river.

Topography The reserve is currently divided into two parcels. The first [250 acres (100 ha)] lies alongside the Sakamena river which contains water only during the rainy season, usually from November until March. For the rest of the year, it is just sun-baked sand. Water for drinking and washing has to be collected laboriously from deep pits dug in the river bed. The second parcel of 1186 acres (480 ha) lies 3 miles (5 km) from the first; it contains a rocky ridge among flat areas of 'spiny desert'. Rainfall is 22 inches (550 mm) per year. Summer days are hot, winter days pleasantly warm, but the nights are cool from June until September.

Vegetation The first parcel is dense gallery forest dominated by huge tamarind trees *Tamarindus indica*. The second parcel is typical 'spiny desert' with many large *Alluaudia procera* mixed with small spiny trees (*Acacia* spp) and large specimens of *Pachypodium geayi* and *P. rutenbergianum*. The rocky ridge also supports coralliform euphorbias, such as *E. alluaudii*, and species of *Aloe*. The succulent *Xerosicyos danguyi*, with its thick coin-like leaves, is very much a feature of this area, climbing up over the other plants.

Fauna There are five species of lemurs. Sifakas *Propithecus v. verreauxi* are common and particularly beautiful here, although not as tame as in Berenty. The same applies to the large population of ring-tailed lemurs *Lemur catta*, most of which are collared for research purposes. *Lepilemur mustelinus leucopus* is common and approachable, and there are plenty of mouse-lemurs *Microcebus murinus* and fat-tailed dwarf lemurs *Cheirogaleus medius*. There are five species of tenrecs, including the large-eared tenrec *Geogale aurita* which is generally rare, yet common at Beza-Mahafaly.

Among the 61 species of birds are several local ones characteristic of the southern 'spiny desert'. These include the running coua *Coua cursor* and Lefresnaye's vanga *Xenopirostris xenopirostris*. Flocks of black-and-white sicklebill vangas *Falculea palliata* dash noisily through the forest, and the crested coua *Coua cristata* hunts for insects in the trees on the campsite. The hoopoe *Upupa epops marginata* can often be seen probing the ground for insects in the *Alluaudia* forest.

There are 25 species of reptiles, including a large population of the handsome radiated tortoise *Geochelone radiata*.

In the wet season there are some spectacular insects, including big jewel-like buprestid beetles.

Visiting Beza-Mahafaly is primarily a research reserve, and there are long-term studies on the sifakas, ring-tailed lemurs and radiated tortoises. Large numbers of lemurs have been collared and the shells of most of the tortoises have been marked with a large blue

number, so opportunities for photography are limited. Nevertheless, its very remoteness makes this a worthwhile reserve to visit, but access is difficult. The road is sometimes passable (with difficulty) in the wet season by four-wheel drive vehicles; and in the June-October dry season by a sturdy car although, even then, a four-wheel drive would be safer.

A guide is essential, as a confusing maze of tracks leads from Betioky towards the reserve. Visitors should take all their own food, plus cooking equipment and tents. There is covered accommodation on the reserve, but it is frequently full of visiting scientists, so a tent is a must. There are toilets, but washing facilities are limited by the shortage of water during the long dry season. During the rains much of the campsite becomes a sea of mud and it may even be flooded for weeks at a time, so a visit between June and October is really the only practical proposition. Madagascar Airtours in Tulear can arrange vehicles and a guide. As the access road is basically flat, keen (and fit) backpackers capable of carrying all their own food could walk in (with a guide) from Betioky in a day.

NOSY MANGABE SPECIAL RESERVE

Location In the Bay of Antongil 3 miles (5 km) from Maroansetra.

Topography This 1285-acre (520-ha) island is composed of granite rocks rising quite steeply out of the sea. It is clothed in dense rainforest beneath which are frequent jumbles of huge boulders and numerous small permanent clear-water streams. The centre of the island rises steeply to 1086 feet (331 m) above sea level. Rainfall occurs more or less throughout the year, with the risk of cyclones in February and March. Peak rainfall occurs from December to February; September to November are the driest months. The annual total is over 118 inches (3000 mm). Thunderstorms are frequent.

Vegetation The whole island has a dense mantle of low-altitude rainforest, much of which is secondary; a large quantity of timber was felled 200 years ago. Even so there are good numbers of giant trees, often with buttressed trunks, and the canopy may reach to 115 feet (35 m). The trees are typical eastern species such as *Canarium, Ocotea, Ravensara* and *Tambourissa*. Ferns and epiphytic orchids (such as *Angraecium* spp) are abundant and there are dense stands of the wild ginger *Afromomum angustifolium* in the flat deeper soils along the bay.

Fauna Small islands generally have a limited fauna, and such is the case with Nosy Mangabe. Nevertheless, the animals which do occur are of interest and are often exceptionally abundant. The best example of an abnormally high population density occurs in the leaf-tailed gecko *Uroplatus fimbriatus*. This incredibly cryptic lizard is always well scattered and difficult to find on the mainland, but easily spotted on tree trunks throughout the island. In

one instance, 13 were located within a small area, while 29 were found along a single coastal path in the space of a week. This abundance may be due to the absence of the fossa, and the scarcity of predatory birds such as certain vangas, couas and falcons. *Chamaeleo pardalis* is common around the campsite and the small *Brookesia peyrieresi* occurs throughout. The island has yielded three specimens of the snake *Pseudoxyrhopus heterurus* which has so far never been found anywhere else. Two kinds of day-gecko, *Phelsuma lineata* and *P. guttata*, perch on the tree trunks, together with the cryptic gecko *Homopholis antongilensis* which is endemic to the area around Antongil Bay.

Birds are scarce; only 39 species and mostly at markedly low densities.

Of the mammals, there are two species of tenrec, *Oryzorictes talpoides* and the greater hedgehog tenrec *Setifer setosus*. The latter is easily seen, because one or two individuals visit the campsite most nights to scavenge in the rubbish pit. There are five species of lemurs. The aye-aye *Daubentonia madagascariensis* was introduced in 1966 and now seems common. Several day nests are situated near the campsite, and aye-ayes often come right into the camp to feed. The black-and-white ruffed lemur *Varecia variegata* is also present, although it is thought to have been introduced in the 1930s. The white-fronted lemur *Lemur fulvus albifrons* is common, and the group living near the campsite is well used to people. The rufous mouse-lemur *Microcebus rufus* frequently feeds in trees within the campsite; but the greater dwarf lemur *Cheirogaleus major* is less often seen.

Frogs are abundant but insects, especially butterflies, rather scarce. Large hermit-crabs scuttle along the beach after dark and smaller crabs with crimson claws climb the trees.

Visiting Permits should be obtained in Antananarivo and presented for inspection at the *Eaux et Fôrets* office in Maroansetra. Only one boatman seems to be available and, in 1990, his boat (or at least the outboard motor) was in poor condition. For details ask at the Hotel Coco Beach on the edge of town. The cost is quite high. Visitors must take all their own food, enough to last for their entire stay. There are often researchers resident on the island and they have quite enough to do without coming to the rescue of poorly prepared visitors by supplying food from their own scarce resources. There are also examples of people arriving on the island not only with inadequate rations, but without even having pre-arranged to be picked up again! The researchers then find themselves being called upon to provide not only provisions but also a boat.

There is a brick-built laboratory in which it is possible to sleep if you bring a bedroll, mosquito net and can get permission from any researchers to move

In the lowland tropical rainforest on the island nature reserve of Nosy Mangabe, the trees and other plants grow even on the steep, shear cliffs which plunge straight down into the sea.

The bases of the trees in lowland tropical rainforest are often covered in a dense growth of ferns, clubmosses and the leaves of various flowering plants. This is on Nosy Mangabe.

their things and give you enough room. But remember, they have priority. It is far better to be independent; take your own tent and do your own cooking. You will need charcoal, as there is no dry wood on the island, or a camping stove, plus a jerrycan or bucket for collecting water. There is a toilet, and a good supply of fresh water from a nearby waterfall; this is pure enough not to need treatment. Clothes and sweaty bodies are washed in a pool below the waterfall. Don't swim in the sea — the threat from sharks should not be underestimated. There is an excellent network of paths in the forest.

PÉRINET-ANALAMAZOATRA
Location 19 miles (30 km) east of Moramanga, near the Antananarivo-Tamatave railway line.

Topography The reserve is situated within a crystalline massif consisting of numerous steep hills. The soils are of the red laterite so typical of much of the island. The annual rainfall is 67 inches (1700 mm), reaching a peak in January. A drier season extends from June to October when the forest seems rather lifeless. Winter nights are cool, and the weather is never unpleasantly hot.

Vegetation The reserve is covered in medium-altitude tropical rainforest. Trees forming the canopy are mainly species of *Weinmannia, Tambourissa, Symphonia, Dalbergia, Ravensara* and *Vernonia.* Tree ferns (*Cyathea*) are abundant and form part of a particularly dense and varied understorey. Epiphytes are common.

Fauna The reserve is famous for its mammals, with nine species of lemurs (plus two more, *Varecia variegata* and *Propithecus diadema diadema*, in forest nearby), ten tenrecs, three carnivores and five rodents. The bird count has reached 109 species. There are such rarities as the brown mesite *Mesitornis unicolor*, slender-billed flufftail *Sarothrurus watersi* and Madagascar red owl *Tyto soumagnii*. The presence of at least three species of ground-rollers is of particular interest.

The reptile life is especially rich, with 28 species so far recorded. Of special note is the occurrence of two species of stump-tailed chameleons *Brookesia thieli* and *B. therezieni*, both of which are restricted to this area. Six species of *Chamaeleo* are found within the reserve, including the large and impressive *C. parsonii*, as well as *C. nasutus*, the smallest member of the genus.

These forests are among the richest in Madagascar for amphibians, with 24 species recorded, many of which breed in the small streams which permeate the forest. The most noteworthy frog is the tiny golden mantella *Mantella aurantiaca* which is found only in and around Périnet. Unfortunately, it has been collected in large numbers for export for the pet trade, together with numerous specimens of chameleons and day geckoes. Spiders and insects are quite abundant and include such bizarre creatures as the dead-leaf mantis *Phyllocrania illudens* and the rare and colourful skipper butterfly *Malaza empyreus*.

Visiting After years of comparative obscurity, Périnet has suddenly enjoyed such a boom in popularity that it is now essential to pre-book a room in the nearby Hotel Buffet de la Gare (on the station platform beside the railway). Chance arrivals can, however, usually be found some kind of accommodation in the village. It is advisable to obtain a permit in advance in Antananarivo, although they are also available at the entrance to the reserve. Even if you have a vehicle, it is better to walk to the reserve because there is plenty to see in the mile or so of plantations and secondary forest between the hotel and the reserve entrance. These roadsides are often good for chameleons and excellent for insects and spiders. Most visitors come to see the indri *Indri indri*, largest of the lemurs and noted for its spectacular whooping calls. Plenty of guides are available to take you straight to them and you will be very unlucky not to see one — but be warned, it does happen. Negotiate your guide's fee in advance but remember that guides here are more expensive than in other reserves, despite the generally easier nature of the work at Périnet.

Although you should be able to see indris as close

as 10-20 feet (3-6 m), Périnet is not a good place for close-up views of other lemurs because no effort has been made to habituate any other groups. Some of the guides are very adept at locating avahis *Avahi laniger*. You may also see red-fronted lemurs *Lemur fulvus rufus* or grey bamboo lemurs *Hapalemur griseus*. Nocturnal lemurs are abundant and easily seen along the roadsides, where tenrecs can also be found snuffling around in the dead leaves.

Lemurs: *Avahi laniger laniger; Cheirogaleus major; Daubentonia madagascariensis; Hapalemur griseus; Indri indri; Lemur fulvus rufus; L. rubriventer; Lepilemur mustelinus; Microcebus rufus.*

Tenrecs: *Hemicentetes semispinosus; Microgale cowani; M. gracilis; M. melanorrhachis; M. pusilla; M. taiva; M. thomasi; M. talazaci; Oryzorictes hova; Setifer setosus; Tenrec ecaudatus.*

Forestry Stations
AMPIJEROA FORESTRY STATION
Location 71 miles (115 km) south of Mahajanga beside RN4.

Topography The station covers 49,500 acres (20,000 ha) of deciduous forest on mainly sandy soils at altitudes of 245-1280 feet (75-390 m). Rainfall is 39-59 inches (1000-1500 mm) per year, almost all between December and April (peaking in January). From May until November there is a marked dry season when most of the trees lose their leaves; a strong wind also blows for much of this time. Temperatures in summer are quite high, up to 95 °F (35 °C), and the annual mean is 79 °F (26 °C). The reserve is important for the conservation of a rich example of western forest which, in this case, also protects a vital water-catchment area. When the forest is felled on these sandy, easily eroded soils, productive rice-growing areas downstream are ruined and the people of Madagascar are the all-round losers.

Next to the Ampijeroa Forestry Station lies the Strict Nature Reserve of Ankarafantsika, covering 149,484 acres (60,520 ha) of a similar kind of habitat, but with the inclusion of rocky cliffs and their associated vegetation.

Vegetation Much of the area is still covered with the original forest, which is dense but low canopied compared with the eastern rainforests. The forest is of the typical western deciduous *Dalbergia-Commiphora-Hidegardia* association. The ground flora is sparse but contains some interesting orchids. Epiphytes are virtually absent. Within the closed forest there are outcrops of almost bare, steeply sloping white sand. These form an isolated habitat for succulent plants such as *Pachypodium rosulatum rosulatum* and a species of *Aloe*. Around the station headquarters, there are plantations of alien trees such as teak, mango and kapok.

Fauna The fauna is rich and interesting. Thirty-two species of reptiles have been recorded and new species are added to the list every year, mainly due to

the efforts of Don Read (see below). One of his major discoveries in recent years was a specimen of the extremely rare *Uroplatus guentheri* leaf-tailed gecko, until recently known only from a single specimen from an unknown locality. *Chamaeleo rhinoceratus* and *C. oustaleti* are common and easily found, while the iguanid *Oplurus cuvieri* abounds throughout the reserve. The cordylid *Zonosaurus laticaudatus* is commonly found basking on logs. Snakes are seen every day, especially the large *Leioheterodon madagascariensis*.

The bird life is rich and varied, with 101 species recorded. Van Dam's vanga *Xenopirostris damii* is almost restricted to these forests. Other rare species include the white-breasted mesite *Mesitornis variegata* and Madagascar fish-eagle *Haliaeetus vociferoides*. The sicklebill vanga *Falculea palliata* is a noisy and conspicuous element of the fauna.

There are fifteen species of mammals. The small grey long-tailed mouse *Macrotarsomys ingens* is only found on the Ankarafantsika plateau. Here it occurs with *M. bastardi* which is widespread in the western forests. There are two tenrecs, *Tenrec ecaudatus* and

*Left: **The large* Oplurus cuvieri *is the typical iguanid lizard of the dry western forests. It is common in the Kirindy forest near Morondava and at the Ampijeroa Forest Reserve further north. Note the spiky tail which is used to close off the entrance to the lizard's lair, usually in a crevice in a tree trunk.***

*Below: **Chamaeleo rhinoceratus *is found in scattered localities in the forests of the west; it is common in Ampijeroa Forest Reserve. The male has a single nasal appendage and is quite unlike the female.***

Opposite left: **Pachypodium rosulatum** *var.* rosulatum *growing on an open 'sand reef' among the dry forests in the Ampijeroa Forest Reserve. The large yellow flowers start to appear in May just as the leaves have finished dropping at the onset of the dry season.*

Opposite bottom: **With its all-black face, the L. f. fulvus** *race of the brown lemur* Lemur fulvus *is the least attractive of the subspecies around the island. In addition, it is only in this subspecies that the sexes are virtually identical. This group is relaxing in the dry forest of the Ampijeroa Forest Reserve, by far the best place to see this form in Madagascar.*

Opposite right: **With its deep-russet arms and thighs, Coquerel's sifaka** Propithecus verreauxi coquereli *is one of the most beautiful of all lemurs. This subspecies has a local distribution in the dry seasonal forests of the north-west; several groups can be easily observed in the Ampijeroa Forest Reserve.*

Right: **The spectacular** Atrophaneura antenor (Papilionidae) *is the largest butterfly in Madagascar. It flaunts a typical warning pattern resulting from the caterpillar's diet of poisonous plants in the Aristolochia family. A strong flier, it is common and widespread over much of the island; this mating pair is perched on planted teak in Ampijeroa Forest Reserve.*

the greater hedgehog tenrec *Setifer setosus* which is often encountered at night scuttling along the paths near the campsite. There are seven species of lemur. The easiest to see is Coquerel's sifaka *Propithecus verreauxi coquereli*, one of the most beautiful of all the lemurs. A visit to Ampijeroa is worthwhile just to see it. Three groups occur near the campsite, and can be approached to within about 6-13 feet (2-4 m). One group sleeps in a mango tree directly above the campsite. The brown lemur *Lemur fulvus fulvus* is also common, and one group is well habituated because it has been studied, as has the much rarer mongoose lemur *L. mongoz*. Ampijeroa is the only place in Madagascar where you have a good chance of seeing this elusive animal. During December it is mainly diurnal and often seen near the campsite. There are four nocturnal lemurs: the grey mouse lemur *Microcebus murinus*; sportive lemur *Lepilemur mustelinus edwardsi*; fat-tailed dwarf lemur *Cheirogaleus medius*; and the western avahi *Avahi laniger occidentalis* which has its centre of distribution in these forests.

Insects are not abundant but are very varied, with a few interesting species such as a giant green and red *Achrioptera* walking stick (Phasmida). After dark on a damp night large hissing cockroaches rummage among the leaf litter.

Visiting First get a permit at *Eaux et Forêts* in the capital or Mahajanga. During 1990 extensive facilities for scientific visitors were completed. It is hoped to follow these up with tourist facilities at a later date. For now, prospective visitors must bring a tent. It is also advisable to bring as much food as possible, although basic foodstuffs are usually available in the village of Andranofasika 2½ miles (4 km) away. The only water supply is a lake, so if you don't want to have to boil all your water, take purification tablets, plus a jerrycan for fetching water, and a cooking-pot. The lake is also the only available place to bathe. Wood is freely available for cooking fires, but a gas or kerosene camping stove would be better.

Ampijeroa is easily reached by public transport. A taxi-brousse from Antananarivo will drop you at the gate, usually at around 3 am. (Note: The worst stretch of road was being rebuilt in 1990, so this time will probably change.) Or you can fly to Mahajanga and take a taxi from there, a trip of two or three hours. Leaving to go directly back to the capital is more difficult. You will need to go (or send someone) to Mahajanga to buy your taxi-brousse ticket in advance. Ask one of the forestry staff how to arrange this.

There is a good series of trails and resident guides to help you find the wildlife. Ampijeroa was the place selected by the Jersey Wildlife Preservation Trust-WWF joint project for the captive breeding of two rare species of tortoises, the angonoka *Geochelone yniphora* and flat-tailed tortoise *Pyxis planicauda*. In 1990 the project was being run by a British herpetologist, Don Read, with a Madagascan assistant. It is of considerable interest to visitors, but try not to take up too much of their time.

MANJAKATOMPO FORESTRY STATION

Location East of the RN7 between Antananarivo and Antsirabe, 10½ miles (17 km) east of Ambatolampy.

Topography The area comprises part of the rocky Ankaratra massif; the altitude is 5085-8530 feet (1550-2600 m). There are numerous cold clear streams. The

Above: **The River Mandrare in Berenty Nature Reserve. The reserve contains an area of gallery forest with large populations of ring-tailed lemurs** Lemur catta

Below: **The giant coua** Coua gigas **is the largest of the couas. This impressive endemic is found mainly in the dry south-west but extends eastwards as far as the Berenty Private Nature Reserve and the Andohahela Strict Nature Reserve. It spends most of its time picking around on the forest floor for insects.**

Opposite: **The quintessential view of ring-tailed lemurs at Berenty — strutting down a path with tails on high.**

annual rainfall is 79 inches (2012 mm), mainly occurring from October to April. The climate is cool, with winter night temperatures falling as low as 41 °F (5 °C).

Vegetation There are 5680 acres (2300 ha) of plantations of alien trees, mainly pines, and 1600 acres (650 ha) of natural forest split up into a number of small parcels, mainly clinging to the steepest slopes.

Fauna Thirty-eight species of birds occur, of which the most important are the Madagascar cuckoo-falcon *Aviceda madagascariensis*, the grey emu-tail *Dromaeocercus seebohmii* and a local subspecies of the forest rockthrush *Monticola sharpei salomonsenii*.
   There are at least 14 species of reptiles and amphibians, including three species of chameleons and the attractive cordylid lizard *Zonosaurus ornatus*.
   The only mammals are two species of tenrecs.

Visiting With its close proximity to the capital, Manjakatompo is an ideal spot for a day visit using transport hired in Tana.

Private Reserves
Berenty Private Reserve
Location Near Amboasary about 50 miles (80 km) from Fort Dauphin.

Topography The reserve is split into five parcels surrounded by extensive sisal plantations. The total

area of about 655 acres (265 ha) is situated along the Mandrare river. The reserve lies within the dry zone, with an annual rainfall of only 24 inches (600 mm) and a dry season from May to October.

Vegetation Parcel 1 [494 acres (200 ha)] is a narrow band of 'spiny desert' dominated by *Alluaudia procera*, adjacent to an area of gallery forest beside the River Mandrare. The gallery forest is dominated by huge tamarind trees *Tamarindus indica* and is suffering from a severe invasion by the alien rubber vine *Cissus quadrangularis*. The other parcels contain small areas of 'spiny desert' with an interesting succulent flora including *Alluaudia procera, A. dumosa, Decarya madagascariensis* and *Didierea trollii*.

Fauna Twenty-six species of reptiles have been recorded, including the rare Madagascar spider tortoise *Pyxis arachnoides*. The lizard *Chalaradon madagascariensis* abounds everywhere and is the most commonly seen reptile. Only two chameleons are present, *Chamaeleo verrucosus* and *C. lateralis*.

Berenty is a good place to watch birds, and 83 species have been listed. Birds of prey are particularly prominent and nine species are recorded. The most abundant is the Madagascar buzzard *Buteo brachypterus*. The giant coua *Coua gigas* is easily seen and very tame. Four other couas occur, including the rather local running coua *Coua cursor*. There are six species of vangas, the rarest being Lefresnaye's vanga *Xenopirostris xenopirostris*.

There are large populations of ring-tailed lemurs *Lemur catta* and Verreaux's sifakas *Propithecus v. verreauxi*. Grey mouse lemurs *Microcebus murinus* and fat-tailed dwarf lemurs *Cheirogaleus medius* can be seen at night, especially in the 'spiny desert'. *Lepilemur mustelinus leucopus* is also common; the reserve's staff can usually point one out as it peers out from a hollow tree during the day. Red-fronted lemurs *L. fulvus rufus* have been introduced. All the lemurs are very tame.

During the rainy season, insect life is abundant and includes a number of brilliantly coloured beetles, as well as large colonies of the fascinating bug *Phromnia rosea*. The white nymphs are adorned with fluffy white 'tails' which look like cotton wool. They cluster on branches and, when they moult into the pink adult form, the resulting groups resemble spikes of pink flowers.

Visiting The reserve is accessible throughout the year. Most visitors book through a travel agent as part of a guided tour. You can also reserve a tour at one of the hotels (Miramar, Galion, Dauphin) in Fort Dauphin owned by M. de Heaulme, who also owns the reserve. There is good accommodation and a restaurant serving excellent food. Most visitors pay only a brief visit, just long enough to thrust a few bananas into the eager hands of the ring-tailed lemurs. This is a pity because Berenty is a fascinating place and warrants a stay of at least two or three days.

Proposed Reserves
RANOMAFANA

Proposed status National Park

Location North-east of Fianarantsoa on the road to the east-coast town of Mananjary.

Topography The proposed park of 98,800 acres (40,000 ha) consists of a series of steep hills from which numerous small streams run into the River Namorona, which tumbles down the valley in a series of waterfalls and rapids. The area is wet, and the annual rainfall of 102 inches (2600 mm) is spread over about 200 days a year. There is no true dry season, although October sees a slight lull in precipitation. When it rains, the days can be remarkably cool, even in summer, bearing in mind that the altitude is 2625-3937 feet (800-1200 m).

Vegetation The area is covered with forest. Only the eastern section still retains its primary forest cover; the rest has been selectively logged over many years. Much of this secondary forest is dominated by the introduced tree *Psidium cattleyarum*. In the higher areas, the trees are festooned with mosses and lichens; tree ferns are abundant throughout and there are large clumps of the giant bamboo *Cephalostacyum viguieri*. The humid zones along the streams are rich in epiphytes, particularly various orchids such as *Bulbophyllum* and *Eulophiella*. The open rocky banks above the Namorona support a special flora, including large *Crinum* lilies and the insectivorous sundew *Drosera madagascariensis*.

Fauna The fauna is of outstanding interest, with no fewer than 29 species of mammals. Several of the lemurs have been extensively studied by researchers from Duke University, North Carolina, in the United States, and by the German primatologist Bernhard Meier. Ranomafana is probably the most important site in Madagascar for lemurs, with 12 species recorded. It is the only confirmed site for the two rarest species, the greater bamboo lemur *Hapalemur simus* and the

Opposite top: **Tropical rainforest above Ranomafana clothes the steep slopes above the gorge of the Namorona river as it tumbles off the central plateau in a series of waterfalls and rapids. This forest is home to 12 different kinds of lemurs, including the two rarest, the golden bamboo lemur Hapalemur aureus and greater bamboo lemur H. simus. The river itself provides one of the few known habitats for the rare aquatic tenrec Limnogale mergulus.**

Opposite: **Tropical rainforest under pressure at Ranomafana. Here, close to the town, the forest is retreating under increasingly ferequent cycles of shifting agriculture or 'tavy'. A plot of bananas in the foreground has been planted on a level shelf above the river Namorona, just visible centre-right.**

Opposite right: **Studying an animal's behaviour and ecology can lead to an understanding of its needs which provides a basis for practical conservation measures. Here two volunteers from Duke University, accompanied by a skilled local guide, study the daily behaviour of Milne Edward's diademed sifaka Propithecus diadema edwardsi in the rainforests of Ranomafana.**

Opposite top left: **Giant millipedes up to 6 inches (15 cm) or more in length are a common sight in the eastern rainforests. Despite its bright warning coloration, this large species, which is an everyday sight in the rainforests at Ranomafana, is eaten by red-fronted lemurs. Every one of the numerous kinds of giant millipede is endemic to the island.**

Opposite centre left: **Huge** Sphaerotherium **pill millipedes the size of golf balls (when rolled up defensively) abound in the west and in the dry forests. This individual is grazing on rotten wood in rainforest at Ranomafana.**

Opposite bottom left: **The endemic genus of 'browns',** Strabena **(Nymphalidae : Satyrinae), has speciated vigorously in Madagascar. This species,** S. batesii, **is found in the rainforests of Ranomafana.**

Opposite top right: **Many of Madagascar's huge number of orchids grow on damp rocks and cliffs. This** Cynorkis **species was growing on a saturated mossy cliff in the eastern rainforests at Ranomafana.**

Opposite bottom right: **Large stands of the giant bamboo** Cephalostachyum viguieri **occupy the damp valley bottoms in the rainforest at Ranomafana. The leaf stalks are eaten by the rare golden bamboo lemur** Hapalemur aureus.

Above: **Phelsuma quadriocellata** *is a day-gecko from the forests of the central and south-east regions; it is common at Ranomafana.*

Above right: **Chamaeleo balteatus** *has a very restricted distribution in the south-central region of the eastern rainforests such as. at Ranomafana. This is a female; the male has a prominent bifid appendage on his nose.*

Right: **A male** Lemur fulvus rufus **(note his ginger cap and paler fur) in dense moss-festooned forest at Ranomafana. This subspecies has been well studied at this site by Deborah Overdorff of Duke University, North Carolina.**

golden bamboo lemur *H. aureus*. The red-bellied lemur Lemur rubriventer is probably more abundant here than in any other area. The other species are the red-fronted lemur *L. fulvus rufus*, ruffed lemur *Varecia variegata*, grey bamboo lemur *Hapalemur griseus*, avahi *Avahi laniger*, rufous mouse-lemur *Microcebus rufus*, sportive lemur *Lepilemur mustelinus*, Milne-Edward's diadem sifaka *Propithecus diadema edwardsi*, greater dwarf lemur *Cheirogaleus major* and aye-aye *Daubentonia madagascariensis*.

There are five species of viverrids, of which the ring-tailed mongoose *Galidia elegans* is tame and often seen in daytime; the striped civet *Fossa fossana* is equally tame but strictly nocturnal. The area is full of extremely confiding red forest rats *Nesomys rufus* which, being diurnal, are regularly seen; the interesting white-tailed tree rat *Brachytarsomys albicauda* is fairly common but nocturnal. Seven species of tenrecs have been recorded, several of which are often seen walking along the paths at night. The very rare aquatic tenrec *Limnogale mergulus* occurs on the nearby river.

The bird list has reached 98 species and includes a number of rarities which are locally common within the reserve. Of note is the occurrence of four species of ground-rollers including the rare short-legged ground-roller *Brachypteracias leptosomus* and rufous-headed ground-roller *Atelornis crossleyi*. Pollen's vanga *Xenopirostris polleni* and the brown mesite *Mesitornis unicolor* are also present.

The reptiles are currently under-recorded but include at least five species of chameleons, one of

The Hotel Thermal at Ranomafana is a lovely building and is convenient for those tourists visiting the adjacent National Park. It boasts a restaurant serving excellent meals.

which, *Brookesia superciliaris*, mimics dead leaves on the forest floor. The smallest of the *Chamaeleo* species, *C. nasutus*, is also present along with the slightly larger *C. fallax*. The attractive cordylid lizard *Zonosaurus ornatus* is common on rocks above the river, and bright green day-geckoes *Phelsuma quadriocellata* sit around on trees. The area is thick with amphibians, but little work has yet been done on listing them thoroughly.

The insect life is of exceptional interest and includes several species of localized *Charaxes* butterflies and a huge variety of moths. The bizarre giraffe-weevil *Trachelophorus giraffa* is common near the river and there are several species of large, bizarre-looking, hairy *Lithinus* spp and *Lixus* spp weevils. Brightly coloured $6^{1}/_{2}$-inch (16-cm) long millipedes saunter through the forest, and there are *Sphaerotherium* pill millipedes the size of golf balls.

Visiting Once the area becomes a park, a permit will be needed. The small village of Ambotalehy a few miles towards Ranomafana is the place to pick up guides. They are very familiar with the forest and have been trained expertly over many years by Bernhard Meier and the Duke University scientists. All the guides are outstandingly adept at finding and staying with groups of lemurs (several species are completely habituated to human presence) but have less knowledge of the other wildlife. Visitors should ask about guides at the Hotel Thermal in the nearby town. This is a lovely old building with a restaurant serving excellent meals. There are also thermal baths close by where one can wash off the day's grime and sweat. Taxi-brousses from Fianarantsoa will drop you near the hotel. Nearby shops sell all the basic foodstuffs etc. One problem if you have no transport of your own is the lack (at least up to 1990) of any means of getting up to the reserve itself. There is a choice between a 4¹/₂-mile (7-km) walk up the road or attempting to hitch a ride. Remember, however, that this is one of the most rewarding walks in Madagascar, with magnificent views over the river gorge, with the forested hills rising beyond. Walking back is all downhill, so less strenuous, but it is often easier in the afternoon to stop a passing truck or car. The boa *Sanzinia madagascariensis* can often be seen basking on top of the roadside walls.

The Strict Nature Reserves

There are 11 reserves in this category. In principle, they can be visited only by accredited scientists after obtaining a special research permit. The rules do not always seem to be strictly applied, however, and tour operators actually include visits to some of these reserves on their itineraries. The most important areas are listed below.

ANDOHAHELA
Location 25 miles (40 km) north of Fort Dauphin

Topography The area is split into three parcels. Parcel 1 [155,857 acres (63,100 ha)] has a wide altitudinal range, from 330 feet (100 m) to the 6417-foot (1956-m) Pic d'Andohahela; parcel 2 [30,677 acres (12,420 ha)] varies from 330 feet (100 m) to the 3297-foot (1005-m) summit of Pic de Vohidagoro. It is an important watershed containing the source of more than ten rivers. Parcel 3 [1235 acres (500 ha)] is mostly situated at 410 feet (125 m). Parcel 1 has a rainy climate [59-79 inches (1500-2000 mm) a year] with precipitation occurring throughout the year. Parcel 2 receives only 20 inches (500 mm) of rainfall annually and has a five- to six-month dry season.

Vegetation Parcel 1 includes the most southerly example of tropical moist forest in the island, with large buttressed trees and a dense growth of epiphytes. Parcel 2 is a superb example of 'spiny desert' with several representatives of the Didiereaceae as well as *Pachypodium, Aloe* and *Euphorbia.* The local baobab *Adansonia za* is also present. Parcel 3 was established mainly to protect the rare three-cornered palm *Neodypsis decaryi.* The vegetation in the reserve is of unique interest because it represents the only meeting place between the tropical moist forests and southern dry forests.

Fauna The meeting of the fauna from the two climatic zones is of equal interest. There are 22 species of mammals which include 13 species of lemurs, making this the richest place for lemurs in Madagascar and putting it among the world's top primate habitats. The most interesting of these is the very localized collared lemur *Lemur fulvus collaris.*

Sixty-five species of birds have been reported and the reptile fauna is rich. A great deal more recording requires to be carried out before the full vast potential of the site is realized.

ANDRINGITRA
Location 22 miles (35 km) south of Ambalavao

Topography The reserve covers 76,965 acres (31,160 ha.) Its altitude is 2297-8720 feet (700-2658 m), covering the major part of the granitic Andringitra mountains. Several rivers rise in the reserve. The highest altitudes have recorded the lowest temperatures known in Madagascar of 18 °F (-8 °C), and snowfalls occur in some years.

Vegetation The vegetation varies with altitude. From 2300-2600 feet (700-800 m) patches of eastern lowland rainforest occur in which the leguminous tree *Dalbergia baroni* predominates. From 2600-5000 feet (800-1500 m) there is medium-altitude rainforest, supplanted above this by dwarfed montane evergreen

One of the 14 species of **Mantidactylus** *found in the nature reserve of Andringitra,* **Mantidactylus aglavei** *(Ranidae) spends the day on a mossy branch. Note the moss-like fringes on the hind legs.*

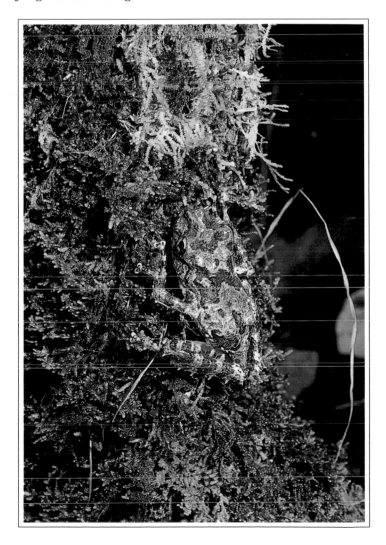

The bright-blue fruits of a species of Dianella frequently add a splash of colour to the drab understorey in the medium-altitude eastern rainforest.

woodland and lichen forest with a great deal of heath scrub. The rock outcrops host a drought-tolerant flora of *Aloe, Kalanchoe* and *Helichrysum.* Damp, peat-filled depressions are home to a specialized selection of plants, most of which are endemic, as are the majority of the drought-tolerant plants.

Fauna The area is famed for its amphibians with 22 species recorded, 14 of them species of *Mantidactylus.*

The total of 70 bird species includes a number of localized types.

There are seven kinds of tenrecs and three of rodents, including the very localized *Brachyuromys betsiloensis* and *B. ramirohitra.* There are seven species of lemurs.

BETAMPONA
Location 25 miles (40 km) north-west of Tamatave.

Topography The reserve of 5500 acres (2228 ha) constitutes a series of ridges jutting up above the flat coastal plain; it is the source of several rivers. The rainfall of 79 inches (2000 mm) occurs throughout the year, with no marked dry season.
Vegetation The plant-rich low-altitude forest in Betampona comprises an island of trees lying in a sea

of devastation. Such is its importance that the reserve is the type locality for many species of plants.

Fauna Little recording work has been carried out but there are 10 (probably 11) species of lemurs.

LOKOBE
Location On the eastern side of the island of Nosy Be.

Topography The 1828-acre (740-ha) reserve lies atop rocky hills and is an important source of water for local streams. Climatically, it falls within the mainland 'Sambirano' regime, wet for much of the time but with a three- or four-month dry season.

Vegetation Nosy Be has been largely deforested and Lokobe represents virtually all that remains. It is a dense rainforest similar to those of the east, but with numerous local endemics.

Fauna Forty-two species of birds have been recorded. The four species of lemurs include good populations of the local black lemur *Lemur macaco*. Approximately 35 species of reptiles have been seen, seven of which are chameleons.

MAROJEJY
Location North-west of Andapa in the province of Diégo Suarez.

Topography The reserve of 148,570 acres (60,150 ha) encompasses a wide variety of microclimates within the rugged Marojejy massif, which reaches an altitude of 7011 feet (2137 m). The area is probably the wettest in Madagascar, with parts of the eastern slopes having more than 118 inches (3000 mm) of rainfall annually.

Vegetation Several regional endemics are counted among the more than 2000 plant species so far recorded. The lower zone [165-2600 feet (50-800 m)] consists of lowland rainforest with a very high species diversity. At 2600-3000 feet (800-900 m), this gradually changes into mid-altitude rainforest with a lower canopy and an abundance of tree ferns. Between 4750 and 6000 feet (1450 and 1850 m) a lichen or moss forest occurs characterized by small [up to 40 feet (12 m)] trees and a rich ground layer. Above 6000 feet (1850 m) is a heathy vegetation composed of low shrubs.

Fauna The fauna is rich with numerous endemics. There are 17 species of amphibians, several of which are endemic to the area, and 22 reptiles. These include 12 species of chameleons, five *Brookesia*, among them *B. karchei*, endemic to this massif, and seven *Chamaeleo* of which *C. peyrieresi* is also endemic to the area.

One-hundred-and-three species of birds occur, including the Madagascar serpent eagle *Eutriorchis astur* in its sole confirmed locality.

The 23 species of mammals probably do not represent the real total. Most notable of these is the rare silky diadem sifaka *Propithecus diadema candidus* which is fairly common and approachable in the reserve.

TSARATANANA
Location South-east of Ambanja in the province of Diégo Suarez.

Topography The reserve of 120,100 acres (48,622 ha) takes in a group of massive crystalline rocks which includes Madagascar's highest mountain Mont Maromokotra at 9436 feet (2876 m). The area is extremely wet and, during the summer, the slopes are drenched by almost daily downpours.

Vegetation The flora is noted for its high rate of endemism. The lower levels are covered with rainforest which is noticeably rich in epiphytes. This is replaced at higher levels by a more dwarfed moss forest, but what should have been the heath bush of the highest levels has been severely degraded by fire.

Fauna. Fifty-four species of birds are found, among them the grey-crowned greenbul *Phyllastrephus cinereiceps*, known only from a handful of scattered localities.

The reptile list is short — only four species — yet three of these are endemic to the area, the chameleons *Chamaeleo guibei* and *C. tsaratananensis* and the skink *Amphiglossus tsaratananensis*.

Among the eight frogs are the endemic *Platypelis tsaratananensis*, *Mantipus guentherpetersi* and *Platyhyla alticola*.

There are seven species of lemurs including the black lemur *Lemur macaco* and red-bellied lemur *L. rubriventer*.

TSINGY DE BEMARAHA
Location To the east of Antsalova south-east of Maintirano.

Topography This vast 1375,440-acre (52,000-ha) reserve (the biggest in Madagascar) includes a spectacular area of limestone pinnacles or tsingy. The climate is rather dry, with a seven- or eight-month rainless period and generally high temperatures, which never drop below 68 °F (20 °C).

Vegetation The flora consists of a dry western deciduous forest alongside plants typical of these dry limestone areas, such as species of *Aloe* and baobab *Adansonia*, as well as the red-flowered flamboyant tree *Delonix regia* which is so widely planted in the tropics but so seldom seen in its original habitat. Madagascar's sole native banana *Musa perrieri* also occurs.

Fauna Difficulty of access to this amazing reserve is probably the reason for the relative paucity of animal records. For example, only eight species of reptiles have been recorded to date. These include, however, the stump-tailed chameleon *Brookesia perarmata* known from only a handful of specimens.

The bird list currently contains 53 species.

The seven species of lemurs include Decken's sifaka *Propithecus verreauxi deckeni.*

TSINGY DE NAMOROKA

Location South of Soalala in the province of Mahajanga.

Topography Much as in the previous reserve. The area is 53,702 acres (21,742 ha).

Vegetation Similar to that of the previous reserve, but more open with extensive areas of a savanna-like formation. The baobab *Adansonia fony rubrostipa* is particularly common, and this is the sole locality for the rather enigmatic *Pachypodium ambongense.* The tsingy is rich in drought-tolerant plants, such as species of *Kalanchoe.*

Fauna The reptiles are probably greatly under-recorded because only six species are listed, although this includes the endemic *Brookesia bonsi.*

There are 56 species of birds and 12 of mammals. The numerous caves are rich in bats.

TSIMANAMPETSOTSA

Location 62 miles (100 km) south of Tulear and 4¹/₂ miles (7 km) from the west coast. Access is via a sandy road (four-wheel drive vehicles only, but negotiable year-round) of 81 miles (130 km) from Betioky.

Topography The total area is 106,704 acres (43,200 ha). The western-most section comprises the shallow brackish Lake Tsimanampetsotsa. The eastern part is a superb example of 'spiny desert' on calcareous soils. Annual rainfall is less than 16 inches (400 mm) with drought prevailing for 9-11 months. Summers are very hot. The minimum winter temperature averages 59-68 °F (15-20 °C).

Vegetation The chief vegetation consists of a low spiny forest of *Didierea madagascariensis, Alluaudia procera, A. dumosa* and the rare *A. montagnacii,* accompanied by various coral-shaped species of *Euphorbia. Pachypodium geayi* and the baobabs *Adansonia fony* and *Adansonia za* occur frequently. In one area various small [33-39-foot (10-12-m)] trees such as *Cassia meridionalis, Delonix adansonioides* and *Acacia bellula* form a dense thicket which is difficult to penetrate.

Fauna There are four viverrids in the reserve, one of which, *Galidictis grandidiensis,* was described only in 1986 and is known from nowhere else so far.

Three species of lemurs occur, including a thriving population of ring-tails *Lemur catta.*

The radiated tortoise *Geochelone radiata* is common and the rare Madagascar spider tortoise *Pyxis arachnoides* is present.

Seventy-two species of birds have been recorded,

among them several with a local southerly distribution, such as the Madagascar plover *Charadrius thoracicus,* Verreaux's coua *Coua verreauxi,* the running coua *Coua cursor* and littoral rockthrush *Monticola imerina.* The lake provides a habitat for large numbers of waterbirds, including the greater flamingo *Phoenicopterus ruber.*

ZAHAMENA

Location To the east of Ambatondrazaka in Tamatave province.

Topography The reserve of 180,705 acres (73,160 ha) is split into two zones covering steep-sided valleys. The climate varies with altitude, which varies in the range 1650-5000 feet (500-1500 m).

Vegetation Low-altitude primary and secondary eastern rainforest in the lower areas, grading into high-altitude forest at increasing elevations.

Fauna The fauna is relatively poorly known but, with the increasing fragmentation of the eastern rainforests, it is clear that Zahamena will gain in importance as a forested refuge. Of the 71 species of birds, the most notable are the scaly ground-roller *Brachypteracias leptosomus,* the red-breasted coua *Coua serriana* and Bernier's vanga *Oriola bernieri.*

Mammals include the ruffed lemur *Varecia variegata* and diadem sifaka *Propithecus diadema diadema.*

By midwinter the octopus tree **Didierea madagascariensis** *has shed its leaves, clearly revealing the dense armament of long spines which cover the stems.*

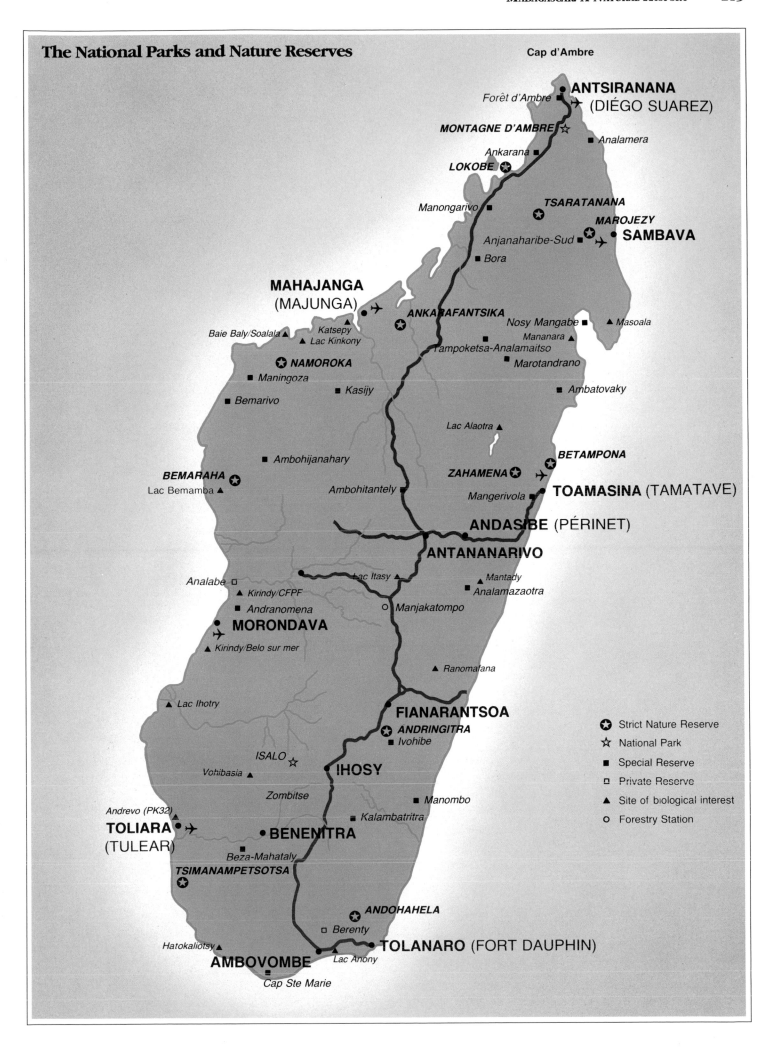

The National Parks and Nature Reserves

Cap d'Ambre

Forêt d'Ambre ■ **ANTSIRANANA**
(DIÉGO SUAREZ)

MONTAGNE D'AMBRE ☆
■ *Analamera*

Ankarana ■

LOKOBE ✪

TSARATANANA ✪

MAROJEZY ✪
Anjanaharibe-Sud ■ ✪ ● **SAMBAVA**

■ *Bora*

MAHAJANGA
(MAJUNGA)

Nosy Mangabe ■   ▲ *Masoala*

Katsepy ▲   ✪ ***ANKARAFANTSIKA***   *Mananara* ▲
Baie Baly/Soalala ▲   ▲ *Lac Kinkony*
Tampoketsa-Analamaitso ■

✪ ***NAMOROKA***   ■ *Marotandrano*
■ *Maningoza*

■ *Kasijy*   *Ambatovaky* ■

■ *Bemarivo*

Lac Alaotra ▲

■ *Ambohijanahary*   ***BETAMPONA*** ●
BEMARAHA ✪   ***ZAHAMENA*** ✪
Lac Bemamba ▲   *Ambohitantely*   **TOAMASINA** (TAMATAVE)
Mangerivola ●

ANDASIBE (PÉRINET)

ANTANANARIVO

Analabe □   *Lac Itasy* ▲   ▲ *Mantady*
▲ *Kirindy/CFPF*   ■ *Analamazaotra*
■ *Andranomena*   ○ *Manjakatompo*
● **MORONDAVA**

▲ *Kirindy/Belo sur mer*

▲ *Ranomafana*

▲ *Lac Ihotry*

FIANARANTSOA
✪ ***ANDRINGITRA***
Vohibasia ▲   ■ *Ivohibe*
ISALO ☆
IHOSY
Zombitse   ■ *Manombo*
■ *Kalambatritra*
Andrevo (PK32) ▲
TOLIARA ●
(TULEAR)   ● **BENENITRA**
Beza-Mahataly ■
TSIMANAMPETSOTSA ✪
ANDOHAHELA ✪
□ *Berenty*
Hatokaliotsy ▲   **TOLANARO** (FORT DAUPHIN)
AMBOVOMBE   *Lac Anony*
Cap Ste Marie

✪ Strict Nature Reserve
☆ National Park
■ Special Reserve
□ Private Reserve
▲ Site of biological interest
○ Forestry Station

Climax Vegetation Types

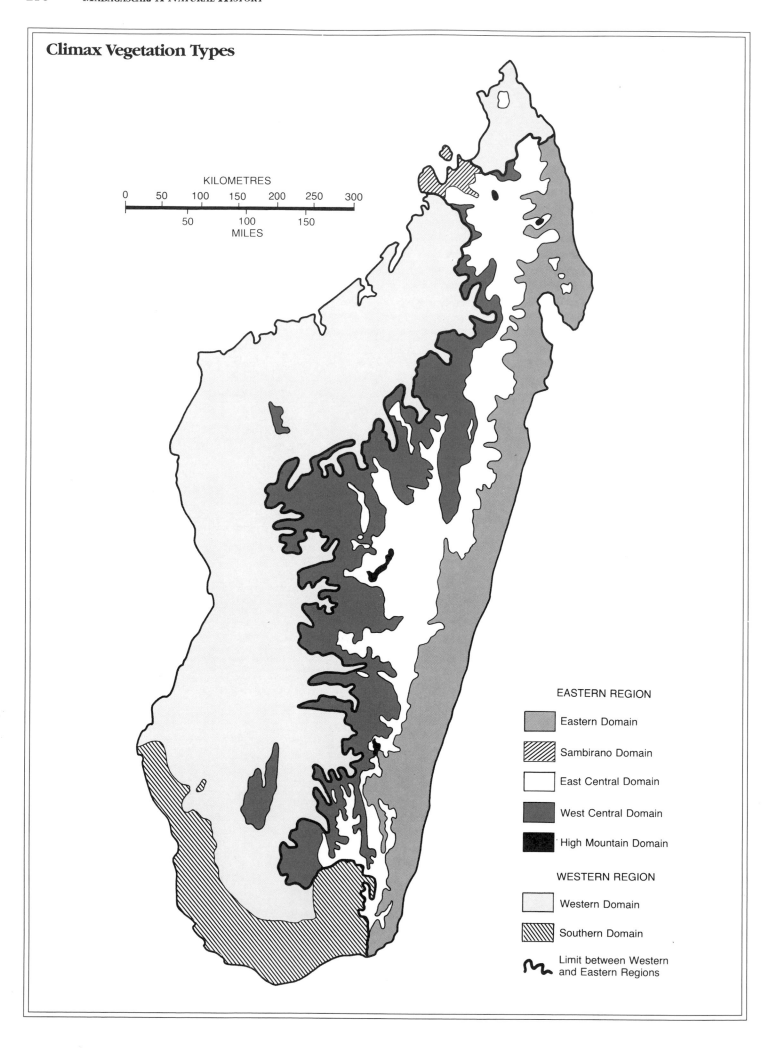

KILOMETRES

0   50   100   150   200   250   300

50   100   150

MILES

EASTERN REGION

Eastern Domain

Sambirano Domain

East Central Domain

West Central Domain

High Mountain Domain

WESTERN REGION

Western Domain

Southern Domain

Limit between Western
and Eastern Regions

The Vegetation of Madagascar

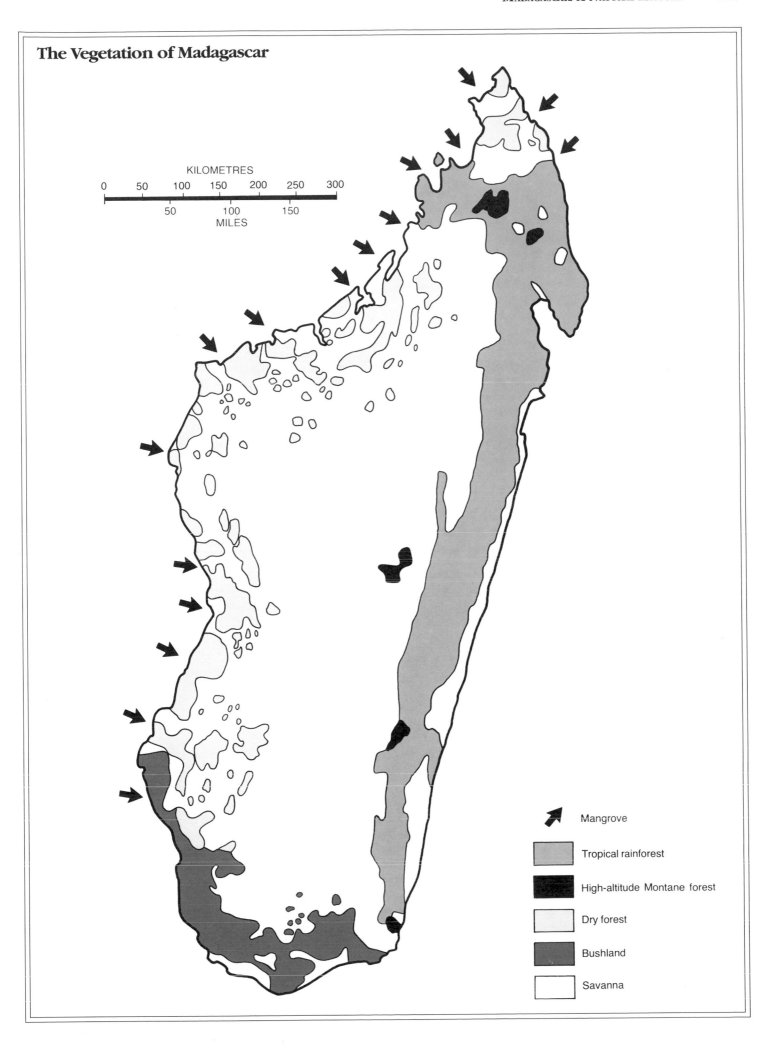

KILOMETRES

0   50   100   150   200   250   300

50   100   150
MILES

Mangrove

Tropical rainforest

High-altitude Montane forest

Dry forest

Bushland

Savanna

The Climates of Madagascar

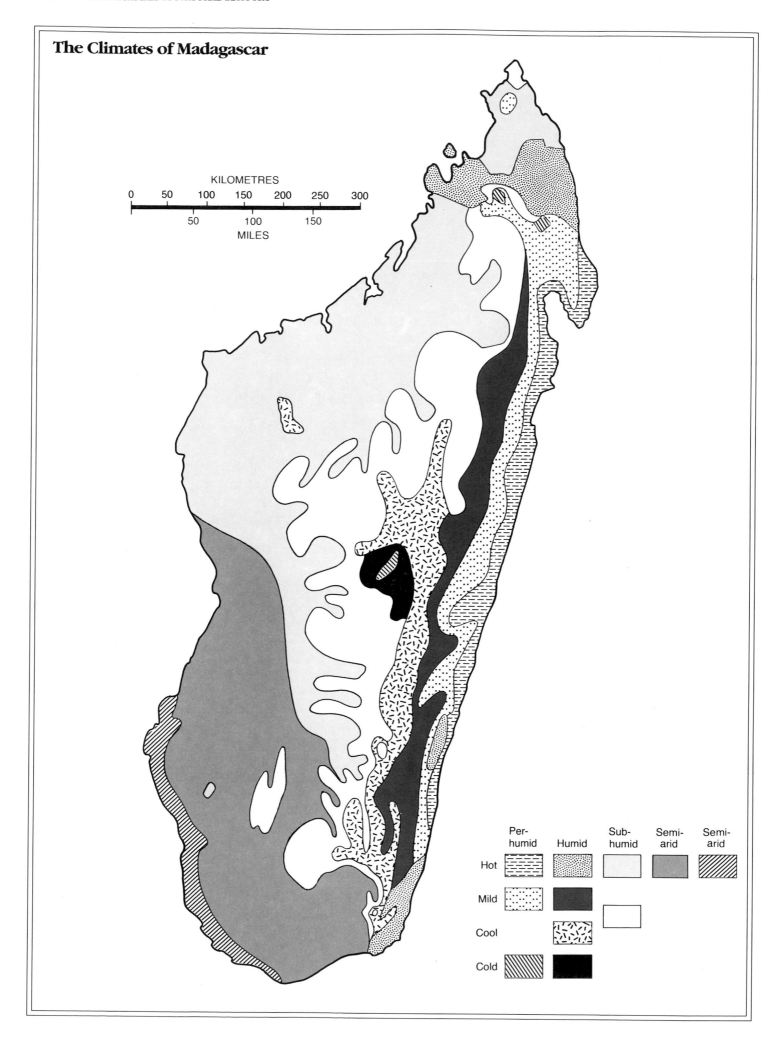

KILOMETRES

0   50   100   150   200   250   300

50   100   150

MILES

	Per-humid	Humid	Sub-humid	Semi-arid	Semi-arid
Hot					
Mild					
Cool					
Cold					

The Threatened Rainforests of Madagascar

*The four maps (A, B, C, and D)
show the change in the distribution
of rainforest in eastern
Madagascar from its original
extent through 1950, 1973, to 1985.
Before people first arrived on
Madagascar, it is believed that
most of the east, including the coast
was swathed in forest.*

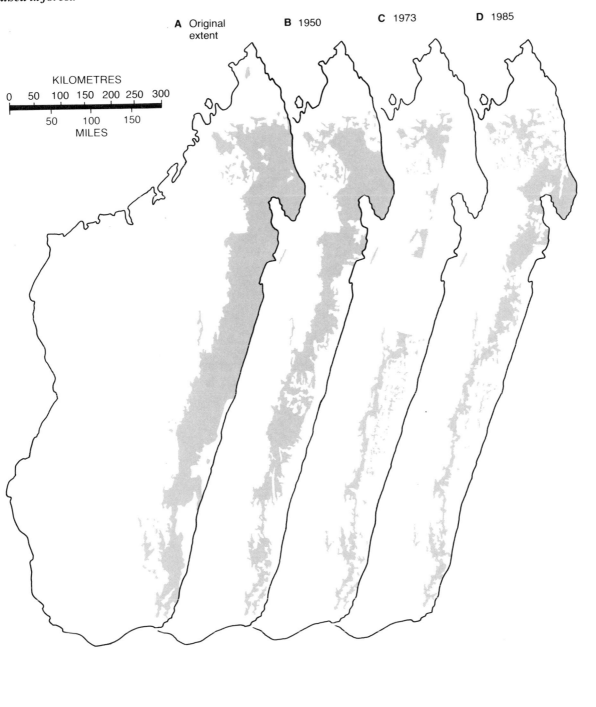

A Original
extent

B 1950

C 1973

D 1985

KILOMETRES

0   50   100 150 200 250 300

50   100   150

MILES

Glossary and Bibliography

Glossary

biotype a naturally occurring, true-breeding group of individual plants or animals within a larger group.

caudex a thickened, water-storing stem base of a plant.

cephalothorax the fused head and thorax of a spider.

chelicerae the jaws of a spider.

cipolin a type of marble with a laminated structure alternating white and green in colour.

coralliform shaped like a coral.

cyme a broad, flattened type of flower cluster.

decaploid having ten sets of chromosomes.

depauperate impoverished.

endemic restricted to only one place or country.

epiphyte a plant which grows on another plant but not as a parasite; epiphytes are mostly plants, such as orchids, bromeliads and ferns, which grow on the branches and trunks of trees.

fady taboo.

geophytic describing plants which have underground storage tubers which tide them through dry or cold weather when the above-ground leaves die back.

holotype the specimen from which the original species description was made; the holotype is usually deposited in a museum or herbarium.

inselberg an isolated, rounded rock outcrop looking like an 'island mountain' (*lit.*) from a flat plain.

karst a special type of highly eroded and dissected limestone outcrop.

lateritic describing a type of impoverished tropical soil with a high iron content, hence the red colour.

leaf axil the upper angle formed by the union of a plant's stem with the leaf.

mutualistic describing the relationship in which mutual dependence between two unrelated species is necessary for the well-being of both.

non-dehiscent not opening to shed seeds.

papilla tiny, elongated protuberance.

pleurocarpous bearing reproductive organs on the side of stems.

pronotal (noun: pronotum) describing the dorsal skeletal plate lying immediately behind the head and covering the front part of the thorax.

pteridophyte a flowerless, vascular plant which shows a distinct alternation of generations, ie clubmosses, horsetails and ferns.

relict an animal or plant which has survived in an unaltered form since previous ages, often now with a very restricted distribution, such as a single mountain top.

ruderal a weed of waste places, often introduced.

rupicolous growing on rocks.

serology the study of blood proteins etc.

stolon a creeping stem which roots at intervals.

stridulation sound production, such as the 'singing' of grasshoppers, by means of rubbing one structure against another.

taxi-brousse bush taxi.

tomentum a dense pubescence with woolly, entangled hairs.

vascular furnished with vessels. This term is usually used to distinguish flowering plants, ferns, horsetails etc from algae, mosses and liverworts.

viviparous bearing live young as opposed to laying eggs.

xerophytic describing a plant which is tolerant of drought.

Bibliography

Albignac, R, Jolly, A and Oberlé P. *Key Environments — Madagascar.* (Pergamon Press, Oxford, 1984).

Angel, F. 'Les Lezards de Madagascar'. (*Mem. Acad. Malg.*, 36, 194 pp, 1942).

Blanc, C P. 'Reptiles Suariens Iguanidae'. (*Faune de Madagascar* 45, 197 pp, 1977).

Bradt, H. *Guide to Madagascar,* (Bradt Publications, Buckinghamshire, 1988).

Brygoo, E R. 'Reptiles Sauriens Chamaeleonidae, genre *Brookesia*, et complement pour le genre *Chamaeleo*'. (*Faune de Madagascar*, 47, 173 pp, 1978).

Glander, K E, Wright, P C, Seigler, D S, Randrianasolo, V and Randrianasolo, B. 'Consumption of Cyanogenic Bamboo by a newly discovered Species of Bamboo Lemur'. (*Am. Journ. of Primatology*, 19, 119-124, 1989).

Jenkins, M D (Ed.). *Madagascar — an Environmental Profile.* (IUCN, Cambridge, 1987).

Koenders, L, Rumpler, Y, Ratsirarson, J, Péyrieras, A. '*Lemur macaco flavifrons* (Gray, 1867): a Rediscovered Subspecies of Primates'. (*Folia Primatol.*, 44, 210-215, 1985).

Meier, B, Albignac, R, Péyrieras, A, Rumpler, Y and Wright P. 'A New Species of *Hapalemur* (Primates) from South East Madagascar'. (*Folia Primatol.*, 48, 211-215, 1987).

Morland, H S. 'Parental Behaviour and Infant Development in Ruffed Lemurs (*Varecia variegata*) in a Northeast Madagascan Rain Forest'. (*Am. Journ. of Primatology*, 20, 253-265, 1990).

Overdorff, D. 'Preliminary Report of the Activity Cycle of the Red-bellied Lemur (*Lemur rubriventer*) in Madagascar. (*Am. Journ. of Primatology*, 16, 143-153, 1988).

Pereira, M E, Kaufman, R, Kappeler, P M, and Overdorff, D. 'Female Dominance Does Nor Characterize all of the Lemuridae'. (*Folia Primatol.*, 55, 96-103, 1990).

Symons, E L. 'A new Species of *Propithecus* (Primates) from Northeast Madagascar'. (*Folia Primatol.*, 50, 143-151, 1988).

Tattersall, I. 'Notes on the Distribution and Taxonomic Status of Some Subspecies of *Propithecus* in Madagascar'. (*Folia Primatol.*, 46, 51-63, 1986).

Wilson, J M, Stewart P D, Ramangason, G, Denning, A M, and Hutchings, M S. 'Ecology and Conservation of the Crowned Lemur, *Lemur coronatus*, at Ankarana, N. Madagascar'. (*Folia Primatol.*, 52, 1-26, 1989).

Index